TWAYNE'S WORLD AUTHORS SERIES
A Survey of the World's Literature

GERMANY

Ulrich Weisstein, Indiana University, Bloomington

EDITOR

Ernst Toller

TWAS 509

Sonderblatt.

№ 53.

München, 15 Mai 1919.

Bayerisches Polizeiblatt.

Herausgegeben von der Polizeidirektion München.

3040

10000 Mark Belohnung.

Wegen Hochverrats

nach § 81 Ziff. 2 des RStGB ist Haftbefehl erlassen gegen den hier abgebildeten Studenten der Rechte und der Philosophie

Ernst Toller.

Er ist geboren am 1 Dezember 1893 in Samotschin in Posen Reg.-Bez Bromberg, Kreis Kolmar, Amtsger. Margonin, als Sohn der Kaufmannseheleute Max u. Ida Toller, geb. Kohn

Toller ist von schmächtiger Statur und lungenkrank, er ist etwa 1,65 — 1,68 m groß, hat mageres blasses Gesicht, trägt keinen Bart, hat große braune Augen, scharfen Blick, schließt beim Nachdenken die Augen, hat dunkle, beinahe schwarze wellige Haare spricht schriftdeutsch

Für seine Ergreifung und für Mitteilungen, die zu seiner Ergreifung führen, ist eine Belohnung von

zehntausend Mark

ausgesetzt.

Solche Mitteilungen können an die Staatsanwaltschaft, die Polizeidirektion München oder an die Stadtkommandantur München — Fahndungsabteilung gerichtet werden.

Um eifrigste Fahndung, Drahtnachricht bei Festnahme und weitmöglichste Verbreitung dieses Ausschreibens wird ersucht.

Bei Aufgreifung im Auslande wird Auslieferungsantrag gestellt.

München, den 13 Mai 1919.

Der Staatsanwalt bei dem standrechtlichen Gerichte für München

Police poster offering a reward for Toller's arrest in 1919.

ERNST TOLLER

By MALCOLM PITTOCK

Bolton Institute of Technology

TWAYNE PUBLISHERS
A DIVISION OF G. K. HALL & CO., BOSTON

Copyright © 1979 by G. K. Hall & Co.

Published in 1979 by Twayne Publishers,
A Division of G. K. Hall & Co.
All Rights Reserved

Printed on permanent/durable acid-free paper and bound
in the United States of America

First Printing

Library of Congress Cataloging in Publication Data

Pittock, Malcolm.
Ernst Toller.

(Twayne's world authors series ; TWAS 509 : Germany)
Bibliography: p. 205–12
Includes index.
1. Toller, Ernst, 1893–1939
Criticism and interpretation.
PT2642.065Z8   838'.9'1209   78-27129
ISBN 0-8057-6350-3

To the memory of Erich Mühsam

"In Mühsam lebte der Geist"

Ernst Toller

Contents

About the Author

Malcolm Pittock graduated B.A. with Honours in English Language and Literature from the University of Manchester, U.K. in 1950. In 1951 he received the degree of M.A. for a thesis on Charles Reade and Wilkie Collins, and in 1956 that of Ph.D. for one on certain aspects of the Chester and Towneley cycles of miracle plays, both from the same university. Since 1956 he has published articles, reviews, and short pieces on various aspects of English Literature from Chaucer to William Golding in such journals as *Essays in Criticism, English Studies, The Use of English, Études Anglaises, Criticism, The Durham University Journal*, etc. and is the author of *Chaucer: "The Prioress's Tale' and 'The Wife of Bath's Tale'* (Basil Blackwell).

Dr. Pittock is currently a Lecturer in Literature (including some German Literature) at the Bolton Institute of Technology, where he helps to prepare students for the degree of B.A. with Hons. in the Humanities. For eleven years he was a Lecturer in English at the University of Aberdeen, a post which he vacated for personal reasons. In his spare time Dr. Pittock is a keen road runner over distances ranging from 5 to 55 miles and has taken part in several races.

Preface

After many years of neglect, there has been a revival of interest in the work of Ernst Toller. This study is an attempt to bring his work to the notice of a wider public. It was a neglect that was beginning to overtake him even before his suicide on May 22, 1939, in the Mayflower Hotel, New York. His services as a public speaker were no longer required, and the plays he had written were no longer performed. Indeed, a fashionable hostess in New York even asked him what his occupation was.[1]

And yet, in the 1920s and early 1930s, how well he was known even in the English-speaking world. Richard Hughes, in his novel, *The Fox in the Attic* (London 1961), in which he tries to recapture the atmosphere in Britain of the interwar years, makes his hero refer to Toller in the early twenties as "surely one of the greatest German dramatists of all time" (page 153), not because he had arrived at this judgment by an independent study of his works, but because it was the fashionable view of his Oxford set. Hughes may, of course, have been exaggerating, but it is certainly true that in Britain and the United States Toller was *the* German Expressionist. Not only were most of his plays translated and collected but the bulk of his non-dramatic works—his poems, letters, and autobiography—as well. His lyrical sequence, *Das Schwalbenbuch*, (The Swallowbook), was even translated twice, once by Ashley Dukes and once by Ellis Roberts. Indeed, of one play of his, *Nie wieder Friede* (No More Peace), which was written and performed in England during his exile, only the English text has been published in its entirety, while *Seven Plays* enshrines English versions of *Wunder in Amerika* (Miracle in America) and *Die blinde Göttin* (the Blind Goddess), which are not easy to obtain in Germany; so much so that Kurt Hiller, the editor of the most recent selection of his work, seems to have been unaware that the original versions of these plays are still extant.

Toller's work had indeed a worldwide reputation; his plays were performed from New York to Tokyo and translated into twenty-seven languages. And he himself, particularly after his exile in 1933, was an internationally famous figure. His friend and collaborator Hermann Kesten relates how universally he was recognized, whether it was by an Arab taxi-driver in Tripoli or a bar-tender in a London pub. And Kesten sums up:

> He was as popular with the ordinary man the world over as a baseball star is in America. In Zagreb, students carried him shoulder high; in Taormina, Mussolini's secret police, ordered to keep a watch on his movements, quoted his Swallowbook to him.[2]

When Toller visited Russia in 1926 his threat that he would leave the country if he was not allowed to answer a political attack on him which had appeared in *Pravda* was sufficient to ensure that his reply was printed.[3]

It is, of course, difficult to separate Toller's political from his literary reputation. His legendary exploits in the Munich Räterepublik of 1919, in which he played a leading role, his subsequent five-year imprisonment for high treason; his courageous opposition to Hitler, and his tireless work to relieve suffering in Spain—these activities as much as his plays made him famous. Indeed, in the Germany of the Weimar Republic, where both praise and blame of his dramatic work were often politically motivated, it was sometimes suggested—a taunt to which Toller was particularly sensitive—that his plays were performed only because he was in prison. And even now interest in his work in Germany is clouded by political controversy.[4] An East German like Martin Reso attacks him not only in general terms as a bourgeois utopian socialist but repeats the old *Pravda* charge of 1926 that he betrayed the revolution in Munich. And this Marxist attack on his political activities has gone hand in hand (in Reso and Ernst Schumacher) with an attack on his plays as examples of the rhetorical *O Mensch* (O Man) drama, where sentimental feeling took the place of dispassionate analysis.[5] For the Marxists look on Expressionist drama as a bourgeois form, Schumacher even going so far as to see it as peculiarly connected with the Independent Social Democrats, a party of which Toller was a member until 1924.

But the Marxists are right after all: Toller's life and work cannot be separated; for what is remarkable about him is the extent to which he lived, often with unbearable immediacy, some of the more representative experiences of our time, and in so doing obtained an unusual awareness of some of its central tensions—tensions so unsupportable that, honest as he was, he could not face all their implications so that in the end they broke him. At its best, Toller's work is an embodiment and exploration of those tensions; whatever its imperfections it still offers an undoubted sense of a living voice with the right to speak urgently to us about our common condition. Pondering Toller's life and work we return to ourselves and our own situation. In this book I intend to examine Toller's plays in detail in relation to their characteristic themes and to the persistent criticism of his work.

A Note on Citations

The sources of page reference to Toller's works cited in the text are indicated in the footnotes except in the case of the following: *Eine Jugend in Deutschland, Die Wandlung, Masse-Mensch, Hinkemann* (cited from E. Toller *Prosa Briefe Dramen Gedichte* with a preface by Kurt Hiller, Reinbek bei Hamburg, 1961).

Feuer aus den Kesseln! Vormorgen cited from E. Toller *Ausgewählte Schriften*, prefaced by Bode Uhse and Bruno Kaiser, edited by the Deutschen Akademie der Künste zu Berlin, 2nd ed., Berlin 1961).

All the translations of passages from those works of Toller of which the German text is extant are by the present author.

Acknowledgments

I should like to express my thanks to Professor Arrigo Subiotto for vital help; to the General Editor of the Twayne German Authors series, Professor Ulrich Weisstein, for the improvements he suggested to the original manuscript; to my colleague, David Cutler, for further help; to Edward Carankshaw and The Bodley Head for generously answering my queries, and to Carl Hanser Verlag, Munich for permission to quote from Toller's works.

Chronology

1893   Born December 1 in Samotschin, East Prussia (now part of Poland). Father a Jewish shopkeeper.

1893– Attends Jewish grade school, Knabenschule, and the Real-
1910   gymnasium in Bromberg. Begins to contribute to *Ost-deutsche Rundschau* (East German Examiner) and to write poetry and plays. Frequently ill.

1910   Father dies.

1913   Abitur (high school diploma); attends University of Grenoble until the outbreak of war. Writes first poem (*Der Ringende*) (The Striver) to be preserved.

1914   Volunteers in Munich for service in a Bavarian artillery regiment.

1915– Posted to front, first to an artillery batallion at Metz; later to a
1916   machine gun unit at Bois le Prêtre; and later to an artillery unit near Verdun. Becomes an N.C.O. May, 1916: breaks down with psychosomatic symptoms in heart and stomach. Recovers in a monastery at Strasbourg. Later transferred to a convalescent unit in Munich.

1916– Attends Munich University: comes to know Rainer Maria
1917   Rilke and Thomas Mann, who gives him helpful criticisms of the poems he has written. Discharged (January, 1917) from active duty as *"kriegsuntauglich"* (unfit for warfare). Begins writing *Die Wandlung*. Meets Max Weber and Richard Dehmel at a gathering at Castle Lauenstein. Goes to University of Heidelberg, where he is the guest of Max Weber. Founds Kulturpolitischer Bund der Jugend in Deutschland (cultural and political union of German youth) to oppose war. Military authorities arrest German members of the Bund, but Toller escapes to Berlin. Meets Kurt Eisner.

1918   Helps Eisner organize antiwar strike in Munich, later becomes his secretary; uses extracts from *Die Wandlung* (Transformation) as political leaflets. Arrested and incarcerated in the military prison in the Leonidstrasse, Munich, for attempted treason. Reads Marx, Lenin, Rosa Luxemburg. Becomes a socialist. Finishes *Die Wandlung*. Later posted to a reserve batallion at Neu Ulm. Gets to know Gustav Landauer. At the instigation of Mrs. Toller is confined in mental hospital. Later released and discharged from Army. Becomes a member of Eisner's discussion group at the Goldene Anker in Munich. In November becomes member of the new Bavarian Nationalrat after the revolution in Bavaria led by Eisner. Becomes Deputy Chairman of the Zentralrat of Workers', Peasants' and Soldiers' Councils, and attends National Congress of Councils in Berlin.

1919   Defeated in January elections to the Landtag (Regional Parliament). Accompanies Eisner to a conference of the Second International in Switzerland. Becomes Chairman of the Munich branch of the U.S.P.D. (Independent Social Democrats) in March. Becomes President (April 7) of the Bavarian Räterepublik (Soviet Republic). Decrees issued in his name, notably for the establishing of a Red Army, the disarming of the bourgeoisie, and the establishment of a revolutionary tribunal. April 13: uprising in Munich by soldiers loyal to the Prime Minister Hoffmann, whose government had moved to Bamberg, suppressed. Toller in the fighting. Establishment of a second Räterepublik with the Communist Leviné at its head. April 14: Toller Field Commander of the Red Army; takes Dachau. April 26–27: resigns his command because of disagreements with Leviné, particularly over the question of negotiation with the Hoffmann government. Thirty-five thousand soldiers marching on Munich. Toller, Männer, and Klingelhofer form new government in Munich. The Red Army still controlled by the Communists. April 30: shooting of ten hostages without Toller's knowledge in the Luitpold-Gymnasium, Munich. May 1: White troops enter Munich. Toller escapes. May 1–June 4: Toller in hiding. Reward of 10,000 marks is offered for his capture. June 4: arrested and taken to Stadelheim prison. July 6: tried for High Treason. Condemned to five years of fortress imprisonment. Begins to write *Masse-Mensch*, (Masses and Man) poems. *Die Wandlung* (Transformation) published and performed.

1920   Writes *Die Rache des verhöhnten Liebhabers* (The Scorned Lover's Revenge). Finishes *Masse-Mensch*. Is offered a pardon by the Bavarian Government because of success of *Die Wandlung*, but refuses it. Writes *Tag des Proletariat* (Day of the Proletariat). *Requiem den erschossenen* (later *ermordeten*) *Brüdern* (Requiem for the Brothers who were Shot). Studies economics, politics, sociology. Begins *Die Maschinenstürmer* (The Machine Wreckers) (early title: *Die Ludditen*), finished in 1921.

1921 Publication of *Gedichte der Gefangenen* (prison poems). Begins *Hinkemann*. Supports Russland-Komitee zur Organisierung der Arbeiterhilfe, recently formed to help feed the hungry in Russia, with donations.

1922 Finishes *Hinkemann*; provides the script for the Massenfestspiel in Leipzig (*Bilder aus der grossen Französischen Revolution*) (Pictures from the Great French Revolution). Attempts by outside sympathizers to petition for Toller's release unsuccessful, as are other petitions to allow him to attend the rehearsals and the production of *Die Maschinenstürmer*. Appointed in absentia to the Bavarian Landtag, and almost elected to the Reichstag, which would have ensured his release. Becomes an honorary member of the Auslandskomitee der internationalen Arbeiterhilfe for the relief of famine in Russia and donates 5000 marks.

1923 Provides another script for Leipzig Massenfestspiel (*Krieg und Frieden*) (War and Peace). Writes *Das Schwalbenbuch* (The Swallowbook). Writes *Der entfesselte Wotan* (Wotan Unchained).

1924 Writes script for Leipzig Massenfestspiel (*Erwachen!*) (Awake!). Released from Niederschönenfeld (July) but banished from Bavaria. Guest of honor at the Arbeiter-Kulturwoche, Leipzig (August), and speaks to an antiwar meeting. Testifies to a Reichstag Committee about injustices in Bavaria and begins his campaign for the release of political prisoners from Bavarian prisons. Gives public readings from his works in Germany and Czechoslovakia. Travels in Switzerland.

1925 Continues his lecture tour of Germany, which is interrupted by an operation in January. Goes to Near East and Palestine on a tour planned to last eight months, but cut short by illness. At end of year goes to England.

1926 Begins writing first version of *Hoppla, wir leben!* (Hoppla! Such is Life!) Meeting of Schutzverband der deutschen

Schriftsteller (Protective Union of German Writers) at which Toller proposes that writers should side with the proletariat ends in uproar. Tours Russia March–May.

1927   Refuses to appear before a Bavarian court so long as the decree expelling him is not annulled. Attends an anti-colonial congress in Brussels; visits Vienna; goes to Copenhagen to give a series of six lectures and continues with lectures and public readings from his work. *Justiz,* compiled from articles which have been appearing over the previous eighteen months, published. Campaigns for the release of Max Hölz. Finishes *Hoppla! Such is Life!*

1928   Joins agitation to get blasphemy proceedings dropped against Johannes R. Becher. Travels in Italy, Denmark, and England. Begins to consider *Feuer aus den Kesseln!* (Draw the Fires!).

1929   *Bourgeois bleibt Bourgeois* (Once a Bourgeois always a Bourgeois) a failure in February. Writes radio play *Berlin Letzte Ausqabe* (Berlin: Last Edition). Joins group of radical pacifists founded by Kurt Hiller. Goes on speaking tour of U.S. September–December, and visits Mexico.

1930   *Feuer aus den Kesseln!* (Draw the Fires!) completed and produced. *Quer durch* (Right across) published. Radio discussion with Alfred Mühr, a leading Nazi. Attends International Congress of the P.E.N. club in Poland (July) and the Congress of the World League for Sexual Reform in Vienna (September).

1931   *Wunder in Amerika* (Miracle in America) completed and staged. Article leads to discontinuation of certain methods of punishment in Swiss prisons; goes to Switzerland and Spain.

1932   *Die blinde Göttin* (The Blind Goddess) completed and produced. Tour through Spain (spring). Attends International P.E.N. Congress in Budapest (May).

1933   In Switzerland (February) when Nazis try to arrest him; his books among those publicly burned (May 10). Gives main address at the International P.E.N. Club Congress in Dubrovnik; makes a lecture tour of Yugoslavia. Completes *Eine Jugend in Deutschland* (Growing up in Germany). Deprived of German citizenship (August 23). Goes to England.

1934   Founds anti-Nazi German P.E.N. Club. Gives lectures in England. Testifies to Parliamentary committee about

Reichstag fire; attends International Congress of P.E.N. Club in Edinburgh (June). Meets Christiane Grautoff. Is a delegate to First Congress of the Union of Soviet Writers held in Leningrad (August); remains in Russia until October. Goes to Switzerland. Publishes *Weltliche Passion* (Secular Passion). Begins *Nie Wieder Friede* (No More Peace). Begins to compile *Briefe aus dem Gefängnis* (Letters from Prison).

1935   Produces *Draw the Fires!* at the Opera House, Manchester, England (February). Marries Christiane Grautoff (March). Goes to Ireland. Campaigns in France and England to improve the lot of his fellow refugees. Speaks to Youth Section of English P.E.N. Club.

1936   Goes to Spain and Portugal (March–April). *No More Peace (Nie wieder Friede)* finished and produced. Gives opening speech at International P.E.N. Club Congress in London. Speaking tour of U.S and Canada (October); elected to New York Deutsche Akademie.

1937   Finishes speaking tour (February). Goes to California and works on film scripts for M.G.M. Goes to Mexico (November–December).

1938   Attends International Congress of Writers for the Defense of Culture (July); goes on fact-finding tour of Spain (July–September); interviews German and Italian prisoners of war. Broadcasts from Madrid. Campaigns to raise 50 million dollars for food and clothing for Spanish refugees on both sides in Britain, France, Norway, Sweden, and Denmark; in December goes to U.S.A. to obtain support—submits proposals to State Department. Begins *Pastor Hall*. Wife leaves him.

1939   *Pastor Hall* completed. Attends Congress of International P.E.N. Club; visits White House at the invitation of Mrs. Roosevelt. Commits suicide in Mayflower Hotel, New York (May).

CHAPTER 1

The Pattern of Toller's Experience

IT is not my intention to give a full account of Toller's life, an outline of which has already been offered in the chronological table, but to draw attention to those features of it that I consider to be unusually significant. This will inevitably involve me in some biographical narrative, but I want to keep gratuitous information to a minimum.

Even in his boyhood in East Prussia, Toller, as a Jew, was caught midway between two groups, Prussians and Poles, and had the twofold experience of being both persecuted and persecutor—the humiliation of hearing a nursemaid ordering her charge not to play with him because he was a Jew, and the exultation of running after the Poles because "We children believed them to be the descendants of Cain, who murdered Abel and who was branded by God on that account" (p. 31). This meant that Toller experienced, in all its force, the desire of the outsider to be identified with the dominant social group, and yet he was in a position to realize that such solidarity was destructive because it was purchased at the price of antagonism toward other men—a contradiction explored in his first play *Die Wandlung* (Transformation). So while his immediate reaction to the outbreak of the First World War was that it gave him an opportunity "By hazarding my life to prove that I am a German and nothing but a German" (p. 178), the Toller who could later say "meine Heimat ist die Erde, die Welt mein Vaterland" (p. 179) (my home is the earth, the world my fatherland) was already incipiently present.

The way in which he began to turn against the war is interesting by comparison with the received account of British poets of the First World War. In many ways, of course, it follows the pattern we already know so well, but it does contain certain significant features which suggest, I think, that it was profounder than theirs. For Toller

became aware not only of the vast sufferings of others—an awareness which can go, as it does too often even with say, Wilfred Owen,
with the confused belief that one can be the sympathetic observer of
the suffering to which one is contributing—but of the way he had
allowed himself to be alienated from the humanity of other people.
As he says:

> I see the dead and yet I don't see them. When a boy, I used to visit the
> Chamber of Horrors in which the wax figures of emperors and kings, of
> contemporary heroes and murderers were on display. The dead have the
> same unreality, arousing horror but not compassion. (p. 70)

The turning against the war is thus, for Toller, bound up with
recovery of the sense of the full humanity of others which is the
experience of brotherhood; one day a pick he was using caught in a
mass of human entrails and he realized:

> A dead man is buried here . . . And suddenly, like light emerging from
> darkness, a word detaching itself from its meaning, I grasp the simple truth
> which I had forgotten, which had lain dead and buried; humanity, com-
> munity, the only things that really matter . . . At that moment I realize that
> I was blinded, wilfully blinded; at that moment I knew at last that all the
> dead, French and German alike, were brothers, and that I am their brother
> too. (p. 71)

Significantly enough in his autobiography Toller shows how his
awareness of the nature of the war existed on two levels, those of
sensibility and conscious apprehension. Characteristically, the experiences that shocked the sensibility into awareness were subsequently weakened by a process of rationalizing reflection. He
even weakened the significance of the formative experience described above in this way:

> I never ask myself why did you have to die? Never: who is guilty? Each is
> defending his country: the German Germany, the Frenchman France. All
> are doing their duty. (p. 71)

This double development which brings out so well the way in
which the conscious mind can resist enlightenment is one that Toller explicitly realized and, as we shall see, tried to evoke in *Die*

Wandlung. But though his development was slowed down, he underwent a progressive awakening which first led him to a decision actively to oppose the war and take part in strike action (he had, happily for him, been invalided out in the meantime) to stop it; this involved a further extension of his opposition to the war to opposition to all forms of human suffering and a political commitment to Socialism. No English-speaking writer of talent went through a comparable process; it was very much a German experience.

And Toller, like many other Germans, had the experience of feeling that a radical transformation of German society was at hand. The mass uprisings at the end of 1918, which had led to the collapse of the old State structure, and the proclamation of the German Socialist Republic provided the opportunity, and raised the possibility, of being genuinely on the threshold of a new world, which none of us in Britain or the U.S.A. can have experienced. Therefore, the ending of *Die Wandlung*, rhetorical as it is, with the crowd repeating Friedrich's appeal

> Brüder recket zermarterte Hand,
> Flammender freudiger Ton!
> Schreite durch unser freies Land
> Revolution! Revolution! (p. 285)
>
> (Brothers stretch out your tortured hands
> Strike an ardent and joyful note.
> May Revolution! Revolution!
> Stride through our liberated land.)

is not *merely* rhetorical; a stirring but vague call from the study to people who don't, for the most part, feel like that at all, it communicates a genuine excitement, a sense of something really happening.[1] As Toller himself said:

In 1917 the drama was a leaflet for me. I read out scenes from it in the circle of young men at Heidelberg and wanted to stir them up. After expulsion from Heidelberg I went to Berlin and there read the play again. Always with the object of rousing the fainthearted, of getting the reluctant on the move, of showing the way to those groping for it—and to win them all for objective revolutionary tasks. In Eisner's meetings before the January strike in 1918, I distributed leaflets on which certain scenes from *Die Wandlung* were printed; in strike meetings I read extracts from it in my speeches.[2]

There are not many who, living through a time of revolutionary possibility, can have felt, quite justifiably, that by their art they were in a very real sense helping to make the revolution.

The details of Toller's personal participation in the Revolution, his association with Kurt Eisner, with the separatist revolutionary regime in Bavaria, the first phase of which came to an end with the murder of Kurt Eisner by Graf Arco-Valley, his part in the establishment of the first Räterepublik in Munich, of which he was president, until it, in its turn, was overthrown by the Communists; his role under the second, Communist Räterepublik as Field Commander of the Red Army; his victory against the Whites at Dachau; his experience of the bloody massacre of revolutionaries by the White troops under General von Oven; his own narrow escapes from capture, with a price on his head, his trial, his subsequent five-year imprisonment, all make fascinating reading in his autobiography.

It was a series of experiences that tempered his idealism with a sense of practical reality. His levelheaded assessment of probabilities, his quick realization that in Germany the moment of opportunity which he had celebrated in *Die Wandlung* had been thrown away because the desire for radical transformation was more hesitant and superficial than he had thought, and that the attempt to perpetuate the Revolution in Bavaria, necessary as he felt it to be, was doomed, all show a mind with an impressive grasp of what was really happening. He found that an unsuccessful revolution could lead in surviving revolutionaries to the nursing of comfortable illusions, to the formation of futile splinter groups, to egotism, even to treachery; and he experienced at first hand the moral contradictions of revolutionary action itself. Yet he did not allow these experiences to destroy his sense of solidarity with his fellow revolutionaries, or to make him disillusioned with the idea of revolutionary change. It is typical of Toller that he refused the offer, prompted by his growing fame, of pardon from the Bavarian government; he would not be free if others could not be free too. Toller's warm humanity comes out in his generosity to Leviné, the President of the second and Communist Räterepublik, who was a bitter opponent of Toller and who always referred to him contemptuously. Toller was, indeed, twice arrested under his regime.

The rest of Toller's life was a long open-eyed and, in terms of significant results, fruitless struggle to realize his ideals against increasing odds; it was probably the overwhelming sense of that futility that led him to commit suicide. In the Weimar Republic he opposed himself to the apathy, factionalism, and irrationalism of his countrymen. He saw them unlearning the lessons that they should have learned from the war and taking refuge in the cultivation of a selfish sensationalism while the old capitalist power structure reasserted itself more strongly than ever. It is essentially the wasteland experience—*Hoppla, wir leben!* (Hoppla, Such is Life!) can be meaningfully related to *The Waste Land*—but for Toller, unlike T. S. Eliot, it was one that was capable of rational political analysis.

The sense of a society perversely alienated from its proper good, which it had meaningfully glimpsed in the revolution, was of course associated with a sense of impending catastrophe; one remembers from *Hoppla*, Karl Thomas's vision of the inhabitants of the hotel insisting with all the grimaces and gestures of madness that it is they who are sane, not he.

> *Alle Zimmer des Hotels leuchten auf*
> *Chor der Insassen (in hockender Stellung sich ins Unter-*
> *suchungszimmer hinunterbeugend, grinsend nickend):*
> Normal! . . . Normal! *Explosion im Hotel.*
>   *Dunkel.*[3]
>
> *(All the rooms in the hotel light up*
> *Chorus of residents (squatting to look down*
> *into the interrogation room grinning and nodding)*
> Normal! Normal! *Explosion in the hotel.*
>   *Darkness.)*

Again, as in the case of the lines I quoted from *Die Wandlung*, this could be regarded as a piece of sensational dramatic rhetoric, but only if we forget the extremist character of modern German experience. Toller was, indeed, being prophetic.

The rise of Nazism in the 1920s was another complicating factor, of whose significance Toller was very much aware, for he wrote an anti-Hitler play while still in prison: *Der entfesselte Wotan* (Wotan Unchained).[4] For what was particularly disquieting about National Socialism was the way in which it was able to make degraded use of some of the feelings still surviving from the period of the German revolution. Not only did many previous revolutionaries become its supporters, but a dramatist like Hanns Johst, whom, on the strength of *Der arme Mensch* (The Poor Man), written about the same time as *Die Wandlung*, it would be easy to associate with Toller, began to write plays on behalf of the Nazis. National Socialism presented the simulacrum of revolution; it claimed to be opposed to the class structure and to call for a radical transformation of society. It is interesting to note, for example, that in a broadcast discussion between Toller and a prominent Nazi there was some measure of agreement between them in their criticism of bourgeois society.[5] But, of course, Toller, in common with many socialists, saw the spuriousness of the Nazi claim to revolution; despite all its protestations it was in actual alliance with, and helped to perpetuate, that capitalist structure of society against which it claimed to be reacting. To see the possibility of a radical transformation of society disappear when one has, only a few years earlier, believed it imminent is bad enough: to see this spurious and degraded substitute for it is to experience a complex discouragement, particularly as this was taking place at a time when the Left was weak and fragmented—a fragmentation that Toller had already experienced in a grotesquely exaggerated form in prison. What he said in 1927 about the change in the political attitudes of a class of particularly exploited workers has a more general significance:

Today only a small minority keeps up the fight. The majority are once again sectarians, dull and petty men, with no backbone and a will which has been eaten away.[6]

The last phase of Toller's life was the experience of exile: the experience, that is, of being, for all the fame that attended him, cut off from significant participation in the life of the country, either personally or through his art. His plays were, of course, banned in Germany, so that he could neither write in his own language (and he could write in no other) nor reach an audience composed of his own people. And, as Hitler went from success to success in his foreign policy, and his regime became increasingly oppressive, Toller lost what élan he had had in his chosen role of alerting public opinion, chiefly in Britain and the U.S.A.; and he had a growing sense of helplessness and a certainty of catastrophe. The last straw seems to have come when his immense single-handed attempts in 1938 to raise fifty million dollars for food, medical supplies, and clothing for

Spanish children on both sides in the Civil War were frustrated by General Franco's victory.

There was, too, a deliberate simplification of attitude; he often adopted a propagandist hopefulness he did not feel, and sometimes the exigencies of campaigning led him diplomatically to trim his explicit attitudes in a way that compromised his integrity. Being persona grata both in the U.S.A. and the U.S.S.R., he emphasized his noncommunism in the one and his support for the regime in power in the other.

The theme in all of Toller's major works, with the exception of *Die Wandlung*, is deadlock and defeat existing in the context of constant affirmation: "not tun uns, die wollen—obwohl sie wissen"[7] (what we want are those who are resolute despite their awareness). It is one of the most unbearable and characteristic experiences of our time, which is so frequently simplified to defeatism on the one hand and to blinkered optimism on the other. Society, the world, must be changed, but how can it be done? It is a task that should be easy: men stand in their own light and have but to will their happiness:

> Yet, if he chose the earth
> And all her fruits were his;
> And lucky be the man
> Who now unlucky is.

But our experience of men is that they will not do so:

> Bounded is the sea
> And the earth is small;
> Man's stupidity
> Has no bounds at all.[8]

Yet even here it is not so simple; there is, as Toller came increasingly to recognize—as witnessed in *Hinkemann*, much human suffering which it is beyond man's power to alleviate in any conceivable society, however just:

For only unnecessary suffering can be vanquished, the suffering which arises out of the unreason of humanity, out of an inadequate social system. There must always remain a residue of suffering, the lonely suffering im-

posed upon mankind by life and death. And only this residue is necessary
and inevitable, is the tragic element of life and of life's symbolizer, art.[9]

But even granted this, how is the unnecessary suffering to be got
rid of? Only by a radical transformation of society, and how can that
come about unless men themselves change? "Tiefer als je spüre ich
den Sinn des tragischen und gnädigen Worts: Der Mensch wird,
was er ist"[10] (I feel, more deeply than ever, the meaning of the
tragical and merciful saying: man becomes what he is). Men are
always, to a large extent, the victims of the situation they want to
alter, and how can one change it by violence, for violence is the
expression of antagonism and hatred, and how can antagonism and
hatred usher in justice and love?

In life, of course, Toller had to choose, and he chose revolutionary
violence. It was characteristic of the unbearable directness with
which he experienced our common problems that he, of all people,
should have been a commander of the Bavarian Red Army in the
field and have won fame for his victory at Dachau. He knew well the
dilemma of his position and the tragic choice with which he was
faced:

A year ago, when I was arrested during the strike, I refused to wear a
uniform and to carry arms. I hated violence and had sworn rather to endure
it than engage in it. Should I now break this oath because the revolution was
under attack? I had to do so. The workers had given me their confidence,
had entrusted me with leadership and responsibility. Wouldn't I be betraying their confidence if I now refused to defend them, or even called on
them to renounce the use of force? I should have considered the possibility
of bloody consequences before and not taken office. Anyone today who is
willing in the political sphere to struggle for common economic and social
objectives must clearly realize that the course and the consequences of his
struggle will be determined not by his good intentions but by quite different forces, that he will often be compelled to learn the methods of attack
and defense; an experience which he must find tragic, and which, in a very
real sense, can make him bleed to death. (p. 118) [11]

His only solution was to behave as humanely as his role allowed.
He refused to obey the command of Eglhofer, his Commander-in
Chief back in Munich, to bombard and storm Dachau, but the
decision was taken out of his hands by his own troops. He tore up
Eglhofer's order to shoot his White officer prisoners and allowed

them to go free, but "the captured soldiers, who returned home, fought against us again some days later" (p. 122). In Munich itself he had tried to make sure that the Revolutionary tribunals were conducted with the utmost lenience, but again matters got out of hand. During the advance of the Whites on Munich, unbeknown to Toller, ten prisoners in the hands of the Red Army were shot. When he heard it he almost wept.

The profound effect on him of this dilemma is revealed in his account of his mental state when writing *Masse-Mensch* (Masses and Man), the play in which, above all, this particular contradiction is explored. When lying on his prison bed at night he was "as if driven on by visions, by fiendish visions, by visions tumbling over one another in grotesque capers" (p. 293).

In 1926, however, he still expressed the belief that the use of force is inevitable in a revolution, though it must be employed as humanely as possible:

No political revolution can dispense with violence, but as with all political methods there are differences in emphasis. I believe that the Socialist revolutionary never uses force for its own sake. He loathes it, he avoids it, and when he turns to it he finds it a method which, though necessary, is frightful and tragic. On that account he will always use it only in situations where it is unavoidable. It is the virtue of a socialist revolution to be generous and humane.[12]

Until 1933 Toller would have described himself as a revolutionary pacifist;[13] that is to say, he believed, however reluctantly, that revolutionary violence could be justified but war between nations could not. There could be no genuine peace, moreover, until there was a just social order.[14] After 1933 his position changed, and he dropped even his modified pacifism. "Ich war ein überzeugter Pazifist, aber die Wirklichkeit hat mich bekehrt"[15] (I was a convinced pacifist, but reality has converted me), he wrote in 1934. He regarded war with Hitler as inevitable[16] and looked on Hitler's persecution of the Jews as a form of civil war:[17] he wanted the League of Nations to intervene to stop it: "It is its task and its duty to compel states which disregard the basic rights of men, the human rights, to give up this persecution."[18] Similarly he believed that the Western democracies should stand firm against Hitler's flouting of international law and his acts of aggression in a way that inevitably meant war.[19] Toller disapproved too of the European democracies' nonintervention policy in the Spanish Civil War.[20]

But I think he always remained internally divided. It is not that he was not always as explicit as he might have been in what he was asking for—as a German exile in countries which still had diplomatic relations with Hitler this was understandable; but rather that, though fully understanding the significance of the Spanish Civil War, and being capable of shouting "Tod dem Faschismus" (death to Fascism) on a visit to the Republican trenches, Toller did not—like many of those who were far less genuinely committed against fascism than himself—actually fight there, preferring to express his concern through his relief plan. The two plays he wrote in exile, *Nie wieder Friede!* (No More Peace) and *Pastor Hall*, are also somewhat ambiguous on this point. It is possible that he was attracted to Satyagraha, as he appears to have made a study of Gandhi,[21] which unfortunately has been lost.

So far I have, in concentrating on the nature of Toller's experience and the importance of the themes that characteristically occupied him in his work, perhaps begged the question as to whether his plays, whatever the sincerity and intensity of feeling behind them, are successful works of art which do not have to be fitted into the context of a life for us to feel their force and significance. And here, of course, it will not do to say that at the time when they were written they had a considerable impact—appearing to be plays that summed up the feelings of a generation. For even then, despite the popularity of the plays, certain persistent charges were brought against them, which, though sometimes motivated by political prejudices, were of some substance. Toller, it was claimed (I am not asserting that all these charges were made by one and the same critic, I'm merely bringing them together), was not a true dramatist; his gifts were lyrical.[22] This was a way of saying, of course, that he expressed an intensity (or would-be intensity) of feeling that did not arise out of the dramatic action and was, therefore, incoherent. By some he was regarded as one of the inferior followers of Georg Kaiser who "made the drama a dumping ground for the unloading of their undisciplined souls"[23] and who had no artistic discipline. Not only this; but his plays were banal, propagandist, full of slogans, simplifications, and revolutionary sermonizing. They were successful—despite the lack of distinction in, and even the feebleness of, the language—because of the excellence of their directors.[24] Herbert Jhering, rather perceptively one must admit, compares *Hinkemann* with Bertolt Brecht's *Baal* (they were produced at about the same time) in order to bring out Brecht's much greater promise and imaginative resources.[25]

Perhaps it is not altogether possible to discuss those charges in general terms; what is needed in order to do justice to them is to examine particular plays, which I will undertake in the ensuing chapters. Nevertheless, I think some useful general points can be made. Contrary to what is too frequently implied, Toller was a careful artist; not only have we his assurance that he drafted *Die Maschinenstürmer*, (The Machine Wreckers), for example, over five times,[26] but he revised several of his poems and plays after publication, at times substantially: *Die Maschinenstürmer* itself, *Gedichte der Gefangenen*, and *Das Schwalbenbuch* were all treated in this manner.

Although Toller did not see the original production of any of his plays up to and including *Hinkemann*, he was acutely interested in the way they were presented on the stage. He criticized the production of *Die Maschinenstürmer* (The Machine Wreckers) in no uncertain terms,[27] although he must have had only photographs and descriptions to go on. He supported Jürgen Fehling's decision, in his production of *Masse-Mensch*, to give the same visionary quality to the "realen Bilder" (real pictures) as to the "Traumbilder," (dream pictures) stating that not Fehling but those who had criticized the production were at fault.[28] He felt, too, more than half resentful of Erwin Piscator's attempts to turn *Hoppla* into a play different from the one he wrote, not only by unauthorized cuts and rewriting, but also by subjecting it to a mode of production that he felt to be alien to its characteristic structure of feeling. Indeed, he was more than doubtful of the general validity of that favorite theatrical device of Piscator, the mingling of film and play.[29] Further, Toller himself influenced the production of, or took a co-producer's role in, the staging of certain of his plays.[30]

Toller also clearly reflected on his own art even if it could be objected that he did not always live up to his own principles. Thus he drew a clear distinction between art and propaganda though he claimed that all art had a political tendency, whether or not this was recognized. Propaganda he by no means condemned—indeed he classified his pieces for choral recitation *Tag des Proletariats* (Day of the Proletariat) and *Requiem den gemordeten Brüdern* (Requiem for

the Murdered Brothers) as propaganda.[31] Propaganda was directed at
arousing an impulse for immediate action and therefore presented
all problems as completely soluble. It had, in other words, strong
elements of deliberate simplification. Art proper did not work by
this process of simplification; it had to recognize that not all of life's
problems were soluble, eschewing any black-and-white presentation of reality; and it should not be too explicit. Yet the purpose of
such art was to extend consciousness; to stir the emotions in such a
way that intellectual awareness followed; to call forth "buried
streams of feeling and give them a conscious intellectual justification."[32] But art should not merely awaken us to social reality, it
should reveal life's essentially tragic basis—those aspects of the
human condition which are permanent—and reconcile us to our
humanity:

Revolutionary drama and epic will, besides calling forth responses appro-
priate to the time, remind us of that ultimate state in us which Angelus
Silesius calls mystic union and which I would like to call the tranquillity of
Eternity.[33]

But he admitted that this was more a quality of classical art than the
art that he considered appropriate for his own time.

Toller defended Expressionism because it seemed to him a form
that was well fitted to embody a movement of social revolution, for it
represented reality as it appeared to a consciousness that passionately wanted to change it. That is why its manner and style have
such an urgency and why there is an equal stress on the interpreta-
tive presentation of the interrelationships of social reality by means
of a process of abstraction and typification on the one hand, and on
symbolically objectified feeling on the other. He admitted that Expressionism was often fragmentary and chaotic in form but claimed
that for that reason it more faithfully mirrored the confusions of the
time.

In the late 1920s, when Expressionism was on the decline, Toller
came to be distrustful of the *Neue Sachlichkeit* (the New Realism)
because its emphasis on reportage was uninformed by any dynamic
idea:

Objectivity is necessary in relation to things or if men unite for a purpose.
But a true literary work represents the creation of human and social values.
So the more objective it is the emptier it will be.[34]

But though he was opposed to realism for its own sake, he did, in fact, learn from the *Neue Sachlichkeit* (and indeed in exile he was to profess himself an adherent thereof)[35] to develop a "style which is saturated with reality and yet is founded on an idea."[36] *Feuer aus den Kesseln!* (Draw the Fires!) is perhaps of all his later plays the one that most obviously answers to this description (which perhaps explains why it is the only play of Toller's to be highly regarded by Marxists).

Toller was keenly interested too in the organization and function of the theater. He realized that as a concomitant of plays like his own which were aimed in particular at awakening the consciousness of the proletariat there needed to be a theater with this as its objective, in which plays would be performed before a working-class audience.[37] He deplored the way in which the Berlin Volksbühne, (People's Theater) which originally had had such a purpose, had lost sight of it (it even turned down *Hinkemann*); and at a meeting convened to consider the future policy of the Volksbühne he "passionately advocated the cause of a proletarian theatre of struggle."[38] That is why, despite their differences, he was willing to cooperate with Piscator, who intended his newly opened theater to serve a political purpose. He regretted, however, that Piscator tried to attract a fashionable as well as a working-class audience. In reply to a taunt by a Nazi opponent he had to admit that the contradiction between orchestra stalls and stage in Piscator's theater was certainly distressing.[39]

But to show that Toller was a conscious artist who had thought deeply about the possibilities of his medium in relation to what he had to say is not in itself sufficient for a rebuttal of the charges brought against him. And it must be admitted that not all of them can be rebutted: some of them undoubtedly stick. Toller, in fact, admitted that the plays he wrote while in prison had weaknesses owing to inescapable emotional pressures on him on the one hand and to difficulties imposed on him by prison censorship on the other. Indeed the two went together:

As he was shut up in his cell and did not learn what was going on except from the newspapers, as he did not go to the theater and learned nothing from the rehearsals of his plays, he wrote more than one word too much. For example, when he wanted to express a feeling that can be expressed in the theatre in ten words, he wrote twelve or thirteen. Or else he wrote phrases that contained a truth, but one we make use of every day and that, as a result, seems a cliché to us.[40]

And again

The free artist can express in extra-artistic form whatever has excited him, has caused his resentment, whatever he thinks. But my mouth was shut and my pen shackled by the rigid prison censorship.[41]

He was capable too of seeing emotional deflection in his work. He had this to say of *Masse-Mensch*:

I have realized how limited was the form, which can be attributed to what, despite everything, was the inward constraint of those days, a sense of shame which anxiously avoided the artistic embodiment of personal experience, of a straightforward confession and which, indeed, could not bring itself to want clear artistic objectivity.[42]

But Toller insisted that what for his critics was a matter of words was for him and his proletarian audience a matter of experience. Middle-class critics had learned to discuss ideas as if they were counters unrelated to significant experience:

Perhaps a complementary reason is the fact that what for us who are in touch with working people, who know their moral and spiritual world, and *who have derived their creative work from the moral and spiritual world of the working people*, signifies the expression of the most shattering, of the most radical ideological conflicts, signifies for the bourgeois critic, catchwords, newspaper clichés.[43]

While he was in prison Toller had a proletarian audience composed of the fellow prisoners to whom he read his works. He found that they always understood what he was getting at.

CHAPTER 2

Die Wandlung *(Transformation)*

The play concerns the development of Friedrich, a young Jew, alienated from his family, who wants to become a sculptor and, more importantly, to be fully accepted by the community. The outbreak of a colonial war seems a godsend to him, for he sees it as enabling him to realize his major ambition and volunteers immediately. Once in Africa, he insists on going on a dangerous mission knowing that it is likely to lead to his death. He is discovered unconscious, his companions dead, and is taken to a hospital. For his bravery he is awarded the Iron Cross. The war ends, and feeling himself now completely accepted by society, he returns home, determined to make a symbolic statue of the Fatherland. But he still wants something higher, and a crisis is precipitated, first by his jilting by Gabriele, a young gentile girl with whom he is in love, and, more importantly, by his encounter with an old comrade suffering from a general paralysis caused by syphilis in its last stage and his wife, who, being in an earlier stage of syphilis (which she has caught from her husband), is still active enough to beg for him. Friedrich, now thoroughly disillusioned with the war in which he fought, destroys the nearly completed statue of the Fatherland and decides that what he must seek is humanity. There follows a series of scenes which are particularly difficult to interpret, but the upshot of which is an evocation of the suffering of working people and Friedrich's growing awareness of them. At last, though rejected by his family and friends, he speaks to the people and infects them with a belief in his vision of a heaven on earth. The play ends with the people marching to claim their inheritance.

*D*IE *Wandlung* (Transformation) is, one must admit, a work of considerable immaturity. Toller himself recognized that it was: "Every author wants to squeeze into his first work everything that he knows, everything that he has ever experienced. I did the same; and so it is not surprising that its private, lyrical element is much more prominent than the dramatic structure can permit."[1] Elsewhere he speaks of "the problem of form solved with such

uncertainty in *Die Wandlung.*"² The spirit that informs it is based,
at least in those parts which deal with proletarian revolution, on an
inexperience which does not know its own ignorance; a belief in
what he later came to see as "the stereotyped picture I had formed
of the working-man."³ The priggish, if sincere, letter he wrote in
1919 to the anarchist, Gustav Landauer, well conveys its spirit:

To have arrived at the kind of awareness I mean, one must have experienced one's fill of deprivation and suffering, one must have believed oneself
to be uprooted; one must have diced with life and danced with death; one
must have suffered from one's intellect and overcome that suffering through
one's spirit. One must have struggled with man.⁴

But it would be wrong to begin with a detailed account of the
weaknesses of *Die Wandlung.* To do it justice it is necessary to see
what Toller was about. And for this undertaking an examination of
the form of the play is an obvious starting point. *Die Wandlung* is
not divided into acts, but stations, each of which marks a stage in the
spiritual growth of the hero, Friedrich, and associates him with
Christ, though there are six, not twelve, stations for Friedrich's
cross. Each of the first three stations consists of two scenes, one of
them reasonably realistic *(reales Bild)* (real picture), the other symbolic *(Traumbild)* (dream picture). The *reale Bilder* are acted at the
rear, the *Traumbilder* at the front, of the stage and "have a shadowy
reality as if played in a distant, dreamlike consciousness" (p. 239). At
the fourth station, however, the pattern is broken: its only scene
combines elements of both methods. The fifth station has a different
pattern again: there are four scenes, three of which are *Traumbilder.* Then comes a return to the earlier pattern in the sixth station,
though here the order is reversed, with the *reales Bild* being preceded by the *Traumbild.* There is also a symbolic Prologue which
"can also be considered as an epilogue" (p. 241).

The change in the distribution of the scenes halfway through the
play corresponds with a development in its theme. In the first part,
Friedrich tries to give his life meaning and purpose and win the
social acceptance from which his Jewishness has excluded him by
volunteering for a colonial war. He soon realizes, subconsciously,
the inhuman nature of such a war, though his conscious awareness
lags behind and fights a desperate rearguard action. The process is
completed in the fifth station, where his subconscious feelings

finally precipitate themselves into a consciously articulated rejection. In the second part of the play, Friedrich, now the conscious seeker after the goal of brotherhood and community, comes to a full awareness of the suffering inherent in an unjust social order and of the particular deformation of humanity which that unjust social order represents. He also comes to a commitment, which is here seen not merely as personal, but as the commitment of a whole society to revolution, to the establishment of a social order in which the humanity hitherto denied can be fully attained.

In the first part of the play, the *Traumbilder* present the essential reality of war, despite the fact that this reality appears to be distorted. Friedrich experiences the war as a nightmare, but he does so, not because we are to see his responses as subjective and relative, but because that is how it really is. Structurally, Toller has made the matter quite clear by presenting two kinds of *Traumbilder* in this part of the play—one in which a kind of doppelgänger of Friedrich is present (Station I Bild 2: Station 4, Bild 6), and one which, though any surrogate of Friedrich is absent, is still presented in terms of his perception (Prologue: Station 2, Bild 4). The Prologue, which sets the tone of the play, is of this latter kind. It is perhaps characteristic of Expressionism always to present its nightmares, and its rosy visions too, not as a possible response to the world of a particular consciousness, but as objective reality.

Although in the first part of the play the general lines of interpretation are clear, it is not always easy to decide the precise relationships between the experience presented in the *Traumbilder* and that presented in the *reale Bilder*. Toller seems to have gratuitously clouded the issue (though since part of the play was written in prison there may be good extraliterary reasons for doing so) by presenting a different war in the *reale Bilder* from that which is presented in the *Traumbilder*. In the former, Friedrich is fighting a colonial war, in the latter the war of 1914–1918.

But though the result has been to minimize narrative continuity, on the level of character and incident all kinds of connections can be made between *reales Bild* and *Traumbild* in this part of the play. Thus the young girl whose skeleton tells us how she was raped to death in Station 2, Bild 4 *(Traumbild)*, is obviously related to—though not identified with—the woman in Station 4, Bild 7, who was also the victim of mass rape. The doctor in Station 3, Bild 5 *(reales Bild)*, strongly resembles the Professor in Station 3, Bild 6

(Traumbild), and, incidentally, the doctor in Station 6, Bild 13. On a more complex level, the *Traumbilder* in the first part of the play anticipate attitudes and feelings that are developed later in the corresponding *reale Bilder* or deepen those that have already been present in them. The repudiation, by Friedrich's clerical doppelgänger, of the official rationalizations he has been mouthing:

> and whoever should undertake to deceive you with pious words,
> you in whose sight all empty,
> feeble offerings of sympathy are worthless,
> I am not the man.
> I put myself at your head (p. 260)

is realized in actuality only in Station 4, Bild 7, where Friedrich destroys the symbolic statues of the Fatherland on which he had been working and attempts to commit suicide. Conversely, Friedrich's misgivings about the role of the Red Cross Sister in Station 3, Bild 5 *(reales Bild)*, become in Station 3, Bild 6 *(Traumbild)*, the following explicit accusations:

> Nennt euer Tun nicht Nächstenliebe,
> Nennt euer Tun armselig, traurig Flickwerk. (p. 261)

(Don't call what you do brotherly love. Call what you do wretched, sad botching.)

The *Traumbilder* in the first part of the play are still further complicated. Thus in the two scenes in which they appear Friedrich has three doppelgänger. In Station 1, Bild 2, it is "ein stummer Soldat (Antlitz Friedrichs)" (a silent soldier with Friedrich's features); in Station 3, Bild 6, it is first *ein Hörer* (a student) attending a demonstration in a nightmare hospital by a professor who regards the patching up of the wounded as his contribution to the war effort; and afterwards, as we have seen, *ein Pfarrer* (a parson) bringing spurious comfort to the wounded.

It is clear that on each occasion the doppelgänger stands in a different relation to Friedrich: in the first case there is virtual identification between the two (not that the doppelgänger is *merely* Friedrich) because the real Friedrich would, one supposes, travel on a troop train. In the third case, the pastor cannot be identified with Friedrich in the same way: he must represent the impulse in

Friedrich's mind to avoid facing, even subconsciously, the reality of his experience, by trying to adopt the most powerful and subtle evasion open to him. The second case seems to be different again. Had Friedrich joined the German Army medical corps he could be physically identified with the *Hörer* (student). Since, however, he did not, the role of the *Hörer* can be interpreted as a way of representing coherently and consistently Friedrich's dawning realization of the significance of experiences he had obtained as a soldier in a less systematic manner.

The three different types of doppelgänger could, in fact, be said to represent Friedrich's subconscious awareness in his roles of participant, observer, and apologist.

In the second part of the play, the aim of the *Traumbilder* is twofold; to embody Friedrich's further development, his knowledge of reality though the reality not of *Kriegstod* (Death by War) but *Friedenstod* (Death by Peace), to use the distinction made in the Prologue, and to symbolize his Brand-like struggles toward a revolutionary consciousness. It is along with this second motif that a new kind of *Traumbild* appears—one in which the setting and action do not represent, by a mode of heightening and distortion, a reality which is capable of being perceived, though not so clearly and truly, in normal terms, but one which is a completely symbolic projection of a state of mind. Thus in the following excerpt the mountain has, of course, no real existence:

The Mountaineers:	*A precipitous wall of rock which leads up to a narrow ridge. Two men are climbing up the wall of rock.*
First Mountaineer:	(With the friend's face): Stop, I'm feeling giddy.
Second Mountaineer:	(With Friedrich's face): Courage, we'll soon be at the top. (p. 278)

The symbolism here is obviously borrowed from Henrik Ibsen's *Brand,* and it is clear that in this scene (as in the closely similar Station 5, Bild 10, *Der Wanderer*) the doppelgänger is to be identified not with Friedrich's subconscious, but with his conscious self. The impetus for this kind of scene is to be found in the fourth station, the turning point of the play, where the only scene begins realistically and ends symbolically. As the sister, a figure of somewhat mysterious authority, says to Friedrich:

> Der Weg den ich dich gehen heisse
> Führt dich durch alle Tiefen, alle Höhen. (p. 266)

(The way I bid you go will lead you through all depths, all heights); and earlier:

Sister:	Your way leads you upwards.
Friedrich:	Back to Mother?
Sister:	Higher, but still to Mother.
Friedrich:	Back to the Fatherland?
Sister:	Higher, but still to your country. (pp. 265–266)

In this part of the play, the other kind of *Traumbild*, which, broadly speaking, represents Friedrich's awareness of the nature of social reality, is difficult to interpret. There are two such scenes: in the first, which has a slum setting (Station 5, Bild 8), Friedrich's doppelgänger is a *Schlafbursche* (night lodger), in the second (Station 5, Bild 9), set in a prison and suggestively entitled *Tod und Auferstehung* (Death and Resurrection), he is a prisoner who has attempted to commit suicide. It is quite clear that here we have a relationship between Friedrich and his doppelgänger that is different from anything encountered in the first part of the play; it is one of empathy. His doppelgänger is the *Schlafbursche* (night lodger) because he feels with the *Schlafbursche*. In this second half of the play Friedrich is deliberately *seeking* awareness, not *resisting* it as he was in the first half. There is, consequently, no real tension between the *reale Bilder* and the *Traumbilder*.

But the following scene, *Tod und Auferstehung* (Death and Resurrection), presents a more difficult case; for here the doppelgänger seems to exist on two levels: on the one he is, like the *Schlafbursche*, a sign of Friedrich's empathy with the sufferings of others. From this point of view, the prison is really there, just as the room in the slum was, and the suicide is a victim of the prison system and of his own environment.

But Friedrich's doppelgänger is, on another level, more than a simple victim: this can be seen immediately in the stage directions in which he is directly connected with Christ:

On the cement floor, below the shaft, a prisoner (with Friedrich's features) is lying, his head bent back, his arms stretched out as if he had been crucified. (p. 269)

Here the prison is not an actual prison: it is the symbolic equivalent of a particular social condition; and the would-be suicide is not an individual victim; he represents Friedrich's ability to recognize and encompass the essential structure of social experience, that men deform themselves and prevent themselves from realizing their true potentialities.

Yet once the condition is recognized it can be transcended though the way may be the way of further suffering:

> Gekreuzigt wolln wir uns befrein.
> Gekreuzigt wolln wir uns erlösen
> Zu hoher Freiheit auferstehn. (p. 272)

(Through crucifixion we will be free, through crucifixion we will be redeemed, be resurrected to a sublime freedom.)

The scene has, indeed, some of the anticipatory functions of the *Traumbilder* of the first part of the play. The redemption is here symbolically enacted; it is enacted in reality in the last scene. The symbolic action—and here Toller is using a fairly conventional Expressionist one—is the birth of a child, the pain and joy of birth being analogous to the double process of crucifixion and resurrection:

The prisoners look with great reverence at the woman, who holds out the child towards them, with a face distorted by pain but suffused with a joyful radiance. The ceiling arches into the infinite heavens. (p. 273)

It can now be seen that in the second part of the play the two different kinds of *Traumbilder*, the personal and the social, are complementary. For Friedrich the realization of his own human possibility is inseparable from that of others:

> Wer zu den Menschen gehen will,
> Muss erst in sich den Menschen finden. (p. 266)

> (He who wants to reach humanity must
> first find the human in himself.)

And thus it is quite appropriate to have some scenes in which this development is seen in terms of an isolated individual search, and others in which it is seen as a progressive empathic realization not only of the particulars of social experience, but also of the general character of that experience and the need to transform it. The personal and the social feeling are ultimately inseparable; they are part of a single consciousness, just as personal spiritual development cannot take place in isolation from others. Indeed the *Traumbilder* in Station 5, Bilder 8 and 9, foreshadow an emergent consciousness which is not just Friedrich's own. Thus in Bild 8 it is not only that Friedrich becomes enlightened about the *Schlafbursche* (night lodger) through sympathetic identification with his lot, but there appears to be a growth in the consciousness of the *Schlafbursche* himself quite apart from Friedrich. It is, then, the function of the realistic scenes in the second part of the play to show how those fundamental insights work out in terms of the everyday world.

Die Wandlung has a structural design of some complexity, and one which, despite the confusion inherent in the method, is more flexible and organic than has usually been granted. Throughout the play, moreover, the *reale Bilder* are integrated with the *Traumbilder* in mode as well as theme. Toller has made sure, for example, that the movement from realism to symbolism and back again is not too jarring (that is why in the fourth station he is able to move from one to the other within the same scene) while the motifs of the *reale Bilder* are carefully related to those of the *Traumbilder*.

The realism of the *reale Bilder* is, indeed, of a limited kind: the characters in them, other than Friedrich, are never fully developed as human beings. They represent a particular point of view, illustrate kinds of relationships seen as typical and significant, and act as the conveyors of information or the precipitators of decision. And such a rendering of character goes with a particular kind of action, one which is realistic in that what purports to happen could actually happen, but which omits much detail and connection, so that certain of the encounters—that, for example, between Friedrich and Gabriele, the fiancée who deserts him—are presented in outline only. It would be easy to call this mode of presentation crude. But it is not without function; because characters are not developed in detail, the intense concentration on the character of Friedrich, so necessary in the majority of *Traumbilder*, is maintained in the *reale Bilder*, whereas a more naturalistic mode would undoubtedly have led to the development of other centers of interest. It is significant, for example, that in the *reale Bilder* characters can appear from out of the blue, as Friedrich's friend does (Station 1, Bild 5), without our being required to inquire into their antecedents, nor do we ask in the final scene where Friedrich's relatives have suddenly come from. Again it is a realistic mode which makes no real distinction between the representation of public and private relationships. For example, the scene between Friedrich and his mother, which in another kind of drama would be dealt with in a mode of intimate naturalism, even if the issues involved were viewed in a similar way, is not, in its heightened style and in its use of soliloquy, far from the formal rhetorical declamation of the public meetings that conclude the play. But again, this is not necessarily a fault, for it means that in form as well as in theme the difference between private and public life is broken down. They are both parts of a continuous experience: Friedrich's revolt against his family at the beginning is seen as related to his revolt against established society at the end.

Toller also prevents the play from breaking into two parts by allowing the *reale Bilder* in the first three stations to foreshadow, either contrastively or directly, some of the developments in the *Traumbilder* of the play's second half. Thus, when fighting in the colonial war, Friedrich volunteers for a mission "to reconnoiter the strength of the enemy reserves gathering along the enemy front" (p. 251), marches through a desert, suffering from hunger and thirst, and is finally found "bound to a tree. The only survivor" (p. 255). He has undergone a false crucifixion, which contrastively anticipates that in the prison scene later in the play. For in this case the motive was selfish: a mere desire to make himself socially acceptable. Again, whereas the false crucifixion entails a journey through a burning desert, the true one is, by contrast, associated with the ascent of an ice-covered mountain.

Similarly, though here the anticipation is direct and not contrastive, the appearance of Friedrich's doppelgänger as a wanderer in Station 5, Bild 10, and his discovery of the nature of social reality, are anticipated in the opening scene, where Friedrich is talking to his mother:

Wandering, Mother, wandering . . . As always. Don't look at me like that. Yes, I said wandering, like Ahasuerus, whose shadow creeps between streets in bondage, who hides himself in noisome and squalid cellars, and at night comes up to gather rotten potatoes from frozen fields. Yes, I sought him, my mighty brother, him the eternally homeless one. (p. 245)

Again, in the scene in the desert the first soldier criticizes capitalist society: "I don't know any Fatherland, know bosses who do them-

selves well, and workers who slave away" (p. 250), criticisms which
are dropped only to be taken up and developed in the latter part of
the play.

Toller also keeps the *reale Bilder* formally in touch with the
Traumbilder by producing symbolic effects which are then
explained naturalistically. This he does, for example, by the use, in
Station 2, Bild 3, of delirium which relates to the grotesque dance of
death of the Prologue, and anticipates that in the following *Traumbild* (Station 2, Bild 4):

The wounded man: Take the dead man away . . . my foot is always treading
on the dead. Do you think they'll amputate my legs? They hurt me so. But I
did so want to become a dancing master, one two three, one two three, it's
to be a waltz. But take the dead away. I cannot teach them to
dance . . . they torture me . . . I must do it though—will no one strike up?
Sings one two three, it's to be a waltz. (p. 249)

The same scene introduces a madman, whose presence is
naturalistically accounted for and who is, indeed, a grim enough
embodiment of real suffering, but whose function, in part at least, is
that of a mysterious emissary, helping to make Friedrich aware of
his own experience:

Friedrich: Where do you come from?
Madman: A sandstorm drove me here.
Friedrich: You live out there?
Madman: Live? I died over there, hell, many have died out there and let
             themselves be driven . . . (pp. 250–251)

In the same way, some of the *Traumbilder* contain realistic elements. Thus Station 5, Bild 8, *Der Schlafbursche* (the Night
Lodger), is realistic in its presentation of the interior of the slum,
the prostitute daughter, and the drunken mother, though even this
part of the scene is finally marked off from the *reale Bilder* by being
in verse. It is only with the visit of the *nächtlicher Besucher* (nocturnal visitor) that a symbolic mode is adopted, but even this, like the
madman in Station 2, Bild 3, can be naturalistically explained as, in
fact, a dream.

If we look closely at some of the characteristics of the *Traumbilder*, however, we will notice certain weaknesses as well as certain
strengths.

Two dominant emotional modes pervade the *Traumbilder:* the macabre and the pathetic. There are, of course, variations within each mode: the grotesque one of Station 3, Bild 6, *Die Krüppel* (The Cripples) is more strident than that of the Prologue, *Die Toten-kaserne* (The barracks of the dead) or Station 1, Bild 4, *Zwischen den Drahtverhauen* (In No-Man's Land). Indeed, in those latter scenes the use of the macabre, with its deliberate suggestion of the medieval dance of death, is the concurrent expression of satire and compassion:

Death by War: In Companies forward march!
The skeletons, officers, and men, rise from their graves all wearing steel
helmets. They stand to attention in front of their graves.
Death by War: Get your arms!
Each skeleton goes to the cross on his grave, pulls it out of the earth, and
places it by him. (p. 242)

In the first *Traumbild* after the Prologue, Station 1, Bild 2, the mode has already been changed into one of pathos. The men in the troop train lament their fate:

Erster Soldat:	Ewig fahren wir.
Zweiter Soldat:	Ewig stampft die Maschine.
Dritter Soldat:	Ewig gatten sich Menschen.
	Aus gieriger Lust wächst ewig Fluch. (p. 248)

(First soldier:	We travel endlessly
Second soldier:	The engine pounds endlessly
Third soldier:	People couple endlessly
	An eternal curse grows out of lustful desire.)

Toller is, however, already beginning to combine the modes in Station 2, Bild 4, *Zwischen den Drahtverhauen* (In No-Man's Land), even though, as I have mentioned, that scene is primarily macabre in tone:

Skelett: (im Winkel)	Ich weiss noch heute nicht, warum sie's taten.
	Musst' es denn sein, mein Herr?
	Kaum hatt' der eine mich gelassen,
	War schon der andere in meinem Bett. (p. 253)

| *(Skeleton:* (in corner) | I don't know to this day why they did it |
| | Did it have to be like that, Sir? |

No sooner had one left me alone
Than another was in my bed.)

The rationale behind Toller's use of the grotesque and pathetic modes is clear enough: the one expresses, and yet contains, his feelings of horror, outrage, and compassion; the other makes a direct appeal to our feelings. But there is always a tendency for the grotesque mode to collapse into the sensational and for the pathetic to become outright sentimental. The first type of weakness can be illustrated by Toller's use of the death's head *(Totenschädel)*[5] which leads to an effect like the following:

The night visitor enters. A thick scarf is around his death's head. Phosphorescence flickers round the night visitor and the nightly lodger, who stands in front in his overalls. (p. 268)

The end of Station 4 will serve to show the dangerous fluency of the pathetic mode:

Ich will ihn wandern, Schwester,
Allein, und doch mit dir,
Allein, und doch mit allen,
Wissend um den Menschen.
*Schreitet ekstatisch zur Tür hinaus. Schwester lehnt am Fenster,
die Augen geschlossen.* (p. 266)

(I will wander along it, Sister,
Alone and yet with you
Alone and yet with all
In full knowledge of humanity.
*Strides ecstatically out of the door. The sister leans on the window,
her eyes closed.*)

Similar weaknesses become apparent if we look at the modes of presenting characters in the *Traumbilder*. The characters are of two kinds: allegorical like the *Kriegstod* (Death by War) and *Friedenstod* (Death by Peace) of the Prologue, or emblematic like the dancing skeletons of No Man's Land, embodying a way of seeing people in dehumanized terms; and those, in however oblique or exaggerated a way they are represented, who have or could have an existence in the real world. These last, are, of course, frequently given symbolic extension so that the soldiers in *Transportzüge* (Transport trains) (Station 1, Bild 2) are at the same time actual soldiers going to a war and Youth, lonely and oppressed, making a weary journey through the wasteland of modern life.

The importance of the allegorical and emblematic figures can usually be worked out, but, as in the case of Friedrich's doppelgänger, their significance is by no means obvious. They represent a mode that can degenerate into the vaguely pretentious. The *nächtliche Besucher* (nocturnal visitor), for example, seems to be identified with death, or death in life—it is not at all clear which—but in reality he merely provides a vague impressiveness.

Of the characters who are versions of people who could actually exist it is notable that what they say or do is sometimes merely an exaggeration of what such people might very well say and do—a characteristic and acceptable mode of satire—like the Professor in *Die Krüppel* (The Cripples) (Station 3, Bild 6),

> Ja, meine Herren,
> Wir sind gewappnet gegen alle Schrecken.
> Wir könnten uns die positive Branche nennen,
> Die negative ist die Rüstungsindustrie. (p. 256)

> (Yes, gentlemen, we are armed against all terrors;
> We could call ourselves the positive branch,
> The negative is the armaments industry.)

But at other times behavior represents not an exaggeration of what a character could say or do, but is an expression of what he might say if he could articulate his feelings clearly. It is a mode similar to that used by Virginia Woolf in *The Waves*. One can take as an example the speech of the Blind Man in Station 3, Bild 6, *Die Krüppel:*

> Sagt, Brüder, ward es Abend . . .
> Ward es Nacht . . .
> Die Nacht gibt Lindrung mir.
> Die Nacht hat weiche, kühle Hände
> Die streichen meine Augenhöhlen
> Mit zärtlich blauenden Gebärden . . . (p. 257)

(Tell me comrades, was evening drawing on or was it night? Night brings me comfort: Night has soft cool hands, which cover my empty sockets with tender blue gestures.)

That a blind man could feel like this is credible; but already the weakness of this method, the easy attribution of the dramatist's own feelings to others is apparent. Toller is imagining what he might feel had he been blinded in war, rather than trying to get under the skin of someone else who has actually suffered that fate. It might be thought that in this case it does not lead to too much distortion, but when the soldiers on the troop train are made to express a weary collective self-pity one can see how such a method makes for a reckless generalization of feeling.

Fünfter Soldat:	Ewig verwesen wir.
Sechster Soldat:	Ewig Kinder vom Vater geängstigt.
Siebenter Soldat:	Von Müttern geopfert.
	Frierender Not.
Alle:	Ewig fahren wir
	Ewig . . . (p. 249)

(Fifth soldier:	We decay eternally
Sixth soldier:	Children terrified by father
Seventh soldier:	Sacrificed by their mothers.
	To freezing want.
All:	We travel endlessly, endlessly)

In fact, despite its incidental felicities, despite the coherence in general of its thematic design, *Die Wandlung* is not really successful. The fault I have indicated, a confusing method and a tendency toward melodrama, sentimentality, and falsely generalized emotion are signs of a more radical failure of experience and distortion of feeling.

A simple egotism appears in the attempt by Toller to claim for Friedrich, with whom he identifies himself, capacities for understanding and sympathy which are well-nigh godlike. The implied parallelism between Friedrich and Christ, either directly or through one or the other of his doppelgänger, is positively embarrassing and is hardly mitigated by the extension of such an identification from Friedrich to society as a whole:

Der Wanderer:	Mir ist, als ob ich heut
	Zum erstenmal erwache,
	Als ob ich eine schwere Grabesplatte fortgewälzt
	Und auferstehe. (p. 273)

(I feel as if today I am waking up for the first time, as if I had rolled away a heavy gravestone and risen from the dead.)

Indeed, Toller's self-inflation is present, unmediated through a fictional character, in the poem which he intended to be spoken before the play:

> Es schrie ein Mensch.
>
> Ein Bruder, der das grosse Wissen in sich trug
> Um alles Leid und alle Freude,
> Um Schein und quälende Verachtung,
> Ein Bruder, der den grossen Willen in sich trug,
> Verzückte Tempel hoher Freude zu erbauen
> Und hohem Leid der Tore weit zu öffnen,
> Bereit zur Tat.
> Der ballte lodernd harten Ruf:
> Den Weg!
> Den Weg!
>
> Du Dichter weise. (p. 240)

(A man cried out. A brother who bore within himself the mighty knowledge of all suffering and all joy: of hypocrisy and torturing disdain. A brother who bore within himself the mighty will to build ecstatic temples of sublime joy, and to open wide the doors to sublime suffering, ready for action, who ardently urged the stern summons: The way! The way! Oh poet show us.)

No wonder that at the end of the play Friedrich says with sublime self-confidence: "Ihr Brüder und Schwestern: Keinen von euch kenne ich und doch weiss ich um euch alle" (p. 283). (You brothers and sisters, I don't know any of you, and yet I know about you all.)

This egotism leads to a confusion between the personal and social spheres. Although Toller shows that there can be no personal transformation which does not involve commitment to social transformation, he wants to evade the problems involved (he was never able to evade them again) by making Friedrich's growth in awareness of social reality necessarily involve in others a corresponding growth of awareness too. Moreover, he uses the indirect and oblique modes of the *Traumbilder* to conceal from us (and from himself) the arbitrariness of some of the connections he is making. It may be reasonable in Friedrich to become aware of the plight of the *Schlafbursche* (night lodger), but it is a very different thing for the *Schlafbursche* himself to do so; and yet by the use of doppelgänger and *nächtliche Besucher* (night visitor) the connection is made—but only on the level of dramatic rhetoric. Ironically enough in view of Friedrich's own slow growth, there is a tendency for people to be easily converted from one view, or one feeling, to another. Thus, at the end of the play, though we note a token reluctance on the part of the crowd to hear Friedrich, once they have heard him they are affected by what he has to say beyond an orator's wildest dreams:

During the speech there has been a steadily growing excitement among the people. Some have kneeled down. Some, weeping, have buried their heads in their hands. Some, overcome, lie on the ground—they stretch up joyfully. Others extend their hands to heaven. (p. 285)

In this connection Station 6, Bild 12, *Die Bergsteiger* (The Mountaineer), is of significance:

Second Mountaineer:	I will not go any further—
First Mountaineer:	But I will.
Second Mountaineer:	You are abandoning me: me, your old companion.
First Mountaineer:	You are abandoning yourself.
Second Mountaineer:	For the sake of our friendship, stop.
First Mountaineer:	For the sake of our friendship *(climbs higher)*, I am going on.
Second Mountaineer:	You are going too high: Look to yourself: I am frightened on your account.
First Mountaineer:	Because I will not abandon myself *(almost at the top)* I am abandoning you. Farewell. (p. 279)

This, as I have said before, seems to be related to the last scene in Ibsen's *Brand.* But Brand's tragedy was that he was left alone to climb the mountain: his very desire to lead his fellowmen to a fuller and nobler life was what inevitably cut him off from them. Toller, however, is attempting to eat his cake and have it. Like Brand, Friedrich is here a lonely thought-adventurer whose aspirations cut him off from his fellows: elsewhere he has, so to speak, no difficulty in taking others up the mountain with him. That there should be so glaring a contradiction is evidence perhaps of some realization in Toller that things were not as simple as he wanted to present them.

Other contradictions in the play evidence a similar confusion of feeling. Thus, for example, though the play ends with a sense of society moving toward its own emancipation, it is surprising how many people are represented as rejecting Friedrich or misunderstanding him: his mother, his uncle, the doctor, the sick man, the woman. It is true that they do so before Friedrich's speech, but most of them do not seem to be present at it; with the exception of the sick man, they all seem to state their objections and go. Again it is as if Toller were having to recognize the situation in spite of himself. Similarly, in presenting the Communist, whose speech anticipates some features of Friedrich's own, even though Toller tries to discredit it by inviting us to see it as the product of destructive hatred ("Destroy the palaces. Blood will flow, the blood of freedom: I say march, march" [p. 276]), he shows that he is aware of formulations of revolutionary purpose which are alternative to that of Friedrich; but he seems deliberately to close his eyes to the implications.

Those confusions seem to come to a head in Friedrich's last speech. What, one may profitably ask first, is the *Volk* (folk) whom Friedrich is addressing: is it society as a whole or only part of it—the proletariat? Some passages suggest the latter:

I know about you as well, husband, how you have a horror of going home into that room which smells foully, where misery lurks and sickness festers. I know of your hatred of those who can eat and laugh their fill which makes you go into the pub and drink yourself senseless, senseless in order not to think any more, in order not to see any more. (p. 283)

But other passages only make sense if we take them as being addressed to society as a whole:

Und so seid ihr alle verzerrte Bilder des wirklichen Menschen!
Ihr Eingemauerte, ihr Verschüttete, ihr Gekoppelte und Atemkeuchende, ihr Lustlose und Verbitterte
Denn ihr habt den Geist vergraben . . .
Gewaltige Maschinen donnern Tage und Nächte
Tausende von Spaten sind in immerwährender Bewegung, um immer mehr Schutt auf den Geist zu schaufeln.
Eure eignen Herzen sind auf Schusterleisten gespannt. Die Herzen eurer Mitmenschen sind für euch Klingelzüge, an denen ihr nach Belieben ziehen könnt Ihr werft glitzernade Goldstücke euch zu und redet euch ein, es wären Frülingsvögel, die durch die Luft flögen und jubilierten. Ihr pflastert eure Wege mit Goldstücken und redet euch ein, ihr ginget über Wiesen von bunten Blumen überwachsen. (p. 284)

(And so you are all distorted images of true humanity
imprisoned, crushed,
yoked together and gasping for breath,
without pleasure and embittered:
For you have buried the spirit.
Day and night mighty machines thunder.
Thousands of spades are in constant movement, burying the spirit in
    rubbish.
Your hearts are stretched out over a cobbler's last.
The hearts of your fellowmen are bellpulls on which you can tug to your
heart's content. You throw glittering gold pieces to each other, and persuade yourselves they are birds of spring flying, rejoicing, through the air.
You pave your paths with gold coins and pretend that you are passing
through meadows covered with lovely flowers.)

By identifying the *Volk* with society as a whole, Toller is presenting them as their own worst enemies, who must make the revolution
in their own hearts; by identifying them with the proletariat he is
presenting them as having enemies against which the revolution has
to be made.[6] Again the position is paradoxical: it may be that if we
take a sufficiently abstracted view we can say that man is responsible
for his own suffering and that, by a change of heart, he can create a
new world; but in the real world some men are the victims of others
and can hardly be blamed for the conditions of their lives and the
suffering they endure. Toller wants to believe in a collective change
of heart which would make revolution instantaneous and bloodless,
but cannot do so. Despite himself he realizes that revolution involves struggle (and in the prefatory poem allows himself to see it far
more clearly). And so, though it is clear that the revolution is to be a
pushover, the people actually march—had it been completely a
question of a change of heart of the whole people there would have
been no one to march against.
    A similar kind of muddle is to be found in the crucifixion motif
which runs throughout the play;[7] on the whole, it appears to signify
that some (or all?) men must suffer (in the revolution?) in order to
free themselves, though this is made nonsense of by the presentation of crucifixion and revolution as rather painless processes. But
crucifixion also seems to be identified with the sufferings inflicted
here and now by an unjust society, by, that is, the operation of
Kriegstod and *Friedenstod*. The division of the play into stations and
the representation of Friedrich's own progress can, I think, only be

interpreted in this way. But not only does this interpretation conflict with the previous one, for crucifixion is not chosen but imposed, it is naively optimistic: such imposed suffering is not automatically purgative, it is as likely to be brutalizing. And yet Toller, whose finer awareness is always breaking through, cannot but see this—in his portrayal in Station 4 of the husband dying from venereal disease which he had passed on to the woman he had raped, and in Station 5, Bild 8, of the drunken mother and her prostitute daughter.

Toller was not to write another play so muddled in its structure of feeling; by *Masse-Mensch* (Masses and Man) experience had caught up with him.

CHAPTER 3

Masse-Mensch *(Masses and Man)*

It is wartime, and a workers' committee has decided to call a strike both to
end the war and to obtain a just society in the subsequent peace. Sonja
Irene L is one of the leaders, although her husband is a well-heeled
bourgeois who disapproves of her activities. He visits her in the committee
room in an unsuccessful attempt to persuade her to desist from them. Next
day, at a mass meeting of workers, Sonja Irene L calls for the strike, only to
find herself opposed by an unidentified figure who claims that only through
violent revolution will permanent peace and social justice be obtained.
Despite her protests, which alternate with her reluctant acquiescence, the
revolution begins: an enemy prisoner is arrested and shot, and there is a
bloody battle for the city, which the revolutionaries lose. Sonja is captured
and, once in prison, rejects both her husband's attempts at reconciliation
and the offer of the unidentified figure to secure her release (which would
involve killing a warder). She is then executed by a firing squad.

TOLLER'S next piece, *Masse-Mensch*,[1] (Masses and Man) is a
much more significant achievement than *Die Wandlung* and is
still, I think, his most interesting play. In *Die Wandlung* Toller
outran his personal experience—that is the cause of the play's basic
sentimentality—but not in his second play. For between the two lay
the German revolution of 1918–1919 and Toller's agonizing experience not only of its opportunities but also of its ambiguities and
dilemmas. There is, indeed, little in *Masse-Mensch* that does not
reflect, in however indirect a way, Toller's own experience, while
there was an unusual personal urgency about its composition. In his
autobiography and in his open letter to Jürgen Fehling, which
serves as a preface to the second edition of the play, he tells us how,
though he took a year over the revision of *Masse-Mensch*, he wrote
the first draft of the play very quickly in a state of nervous excitement, haunted by visions, and sometimes under great difficulties

52

(he was even reduced to writing it lying down under the table in his cell with the cloth adjusted to conceal the candle he was using).[2]

Toller later came to feel that he had been too close to the experience that had prompted the play, and that through a certain guilt and embarrassment he had failed to present the issues involved as explicitly as he should have done.[3] One sign of this is that the protagonist, who reflects so much of Toller's experience, is a woman (though she was in fact based on a real revolutionary, whose role in the 1918 strike had led to a final breach with her husband which had caused her to commit suicide when in prison).[4] But, though the play seems to have been frequently misunderstood,[5] there is plenty of evidence that the workers who saw it felt its significance for themselves. Jürgen Fehling, who was responsible for the first major production in 1921 at the Berlin Volksbühne, said that it made a more lasting impression than *Die Wandlung* and he attributed that to the socialist character of the audience.[6] The play had been previously staged successfully at a private showing for trade unionists,[7] and Toller also felt that it was understood by his fellow prisoners. He said: "I read the play to an audience of comrades, peasants, industrial workers, laborers, even tough warders were there, and it filled me with real joy when I saw how each understood the play, how each in his own way lived through its experiences and struggles."[8] He was pleased to learn after its staging in Nuremberg and Berlin that "the problems which were touched on in *Masse-Mensch* were passionately and eagerly discussed at Party meetings and in working class pubs."[9]

In stating the theme of the play, Toller showed that the only way he could contain his experience without repudiating it was by positing a duality between man as an individual and man as a social being; for the first his conscience is absolute, for the second it is the goal to be achieved:

Isn't man at the same time an individual and a member of the masses? Does the fight between individual and the mass take place only in society: doesn't it take place in Man's inner being as well? As an individual one acts according to a moral idea known to be right. One wants to follow it even if, as a result, the world is destroyed. As a member of the masses one is driven by social impulses: one wants to reach the goal even if it means giving up that moral principle. Because I have experienced it in actuality, it seems to me that this contradiction is insoluble, and I seek to give it expression. In this way my play "Masse-Mensch" originated. (*Prosa*, p. 175)

And in a letter to Theodor Lessing he wrote:

After experiences, whose burden a man can perhaps only bear once without cracking up, *Masse-Mensch* was a release from spiritual need: a release which did not resolve the ambiguity by some self-deceiving formula, but accepted the ambiguity as fated. The individual can wish for death. The masses must wish for life. And since we are men and masses at the same time we choose death and life.[10]

Toller, in other words, recognized that there can be no revolution without the use of force, and he saw, too, that one cannot even expect force to be rationally applied: its uses will be conditioned by the experience of need and deprivation and will be characterized by hatred and precipitancy. The experience that makes revolution necessary conditions the nature of the revolution itself. Or, as one might put it, the means one takes to become Mensch (Man) involve a further denial of man's humanity and that of other people.

This tension would be felt in all its acuteness by an outsider, a Friedrich (or a Toller), one who, because his commitment arises from moral idealism, cannot but measure the means employed in the revolution against the ends proposed. And yet, if he does adopt these moral principles as absolute, he condemns himself to impotence: he cannot himself take part in the revolutionary process through which alone a more just society can be created. His only way out, as the quotations above suggest, is to accept that it is his fate to be guilty: "There are times when the tragic necessity of taking guilt upon oneself cannot be avoided."[11] Toller saw this as a general human problem of which revolution provided only a particular instance.

How far Toller was from reaching this synthesis by a process of purely intellectual analysis, how far it was with him a mode of seeing and feeling is shown by what he says in his open letter to Jürgen Fehling:

As a politician I act as if men were individuals, members of groups, players of roles, units of power, economic units, as if any and all circumstances were real data. As an artist I see those real data in all their ambiguity.

I see prisoners in a prison yard sawing wood in a monotonous rhythm. Moved, I think: these are men. One may be a worker, the other a peasant, the third perhaps a lawyer's clerk. I see the room in which the worker used to live, see his few possessions, the individual gestures with which, perhaps, he throws away a match, embraces a woman, walks through the factory door of an evening. I see just as clearly the broadshouldered peasant, the small, narrow-chested clerk. Then—suddenly—they are not X, Y and Z any longer but horrible marionettes fatally impelled by a force of whose ominousness one is aware.

Two women once passed in front of the window of my cell when I was clinging to its bars. Seemingly two old maids. Both had bobbed white hair, both were wearing clothes of the same style, color and cut, both carried gray umbrellas with white spots, the heads of both nodded to and fro.

Not for a moment did I see real people in a real Neuburg who were taking a walk in the narrow street. A dance of death of two old maids, the one mirroring the death of the other, stared me in the face. (*Prosa*, p. 293)

But there is, after all, a change of emphasis: Toller is not here speaking of those like himself or like the Sonja of his play who, as non-proletarian idealists, become conscious of contradiction and make a definite choice, but rather of the revolutionary who acts from inside the situation and in whom the relation between individual and social existence takes a different form. The experience is not of a consciously maintained dualism, it is one in which the dualism is only apparent; because the social experience is one of deprivation, its victims cannot be fully human. And yet that lack of authenticity impels them to try to become so, but prevents them from acting consciously, which would suppose the preexistence of the very authenticity. As social beings they lack freedom, as individuals they only appear to have it.

They are, that is to say, *Masse* (Masses) striving to become *Mensch* (Man) in terms of the experience of being *Masse*. But although Toller felt the difficulty of the problem, he did not conceive it to be insoluble. *Masse* can become liberated, can become *Mensch*. But how does Toller resolve the paradox? Here I have to go outside the evidence provided by his own statements and anticipate my exposition of the play by claiming that a growth of awareness of its own condition on the part of *Masse* is possible. For, after all, as Toller realized, his own awareness of duality in the role of revolutionary was not, in fact, entirely different, it was only the basic situation of *Masse* striving to become *Mensch* at a deeper level of self-awareness. The situation of those who become revolutionaries because of conscious idealism and those who do so because they can only will what they must is, after all, only a difference of degree. However, Toller's complete awareness registers itself as a feeling of unreality, of dream, as he holds the perception that his fellows are men and yet not truly so. At first the extension of this feeling to the two old women may seem puzzling. The death they face is inevitable. But what unites them with the prisoners is their lack of awareness of their condition; in an unjust society everyone is, to a greater or lesser extent, alienated from the consciousness even of the unchangeable elements in the human condition. We are, in the last analysis, exploiters and exploited alike, *Masse*.

Looking at the structure of the play will give some idea of its complexity. As in his first play, *Die Wandlung*, Toller divides his scenes into *reale Bilder* (real pictures) and symbolic *Traumbilder* (dream pictures) but here the distinction is not as clear-cut.[12] Toller went out of his way to defend Jürgen Fehling against criticism that in his production he had not sufficiently distinguished between the two types.

The narrowing of the distinction between *Traumbilder* and *reale Bilder* is shown by the use of verse throughout both, though, admittedly, that in the *Traumbilder* is characterized by short lines and a clipped staccato style. Again, there are nonnaturalistic elements in the *reale Bilder*. *Der Namenlose* (The Nameless One), an allegorical figure whose significance I will discuss later, appears in three out of four of these (Bilder 3, 5 and 7) while in Bild 3 the underlying feelings of various groups of workers are expressed in choral speech. Similarly, in the *Traumbilder* the action is not as unrealistic and fantastic as in the corresponding scenes in *Die Wandlung*.

Apart from the elements just mentioned, the *reale Bilder* are reasonably realistic in their surface action: even *der Namenlose*, though an allegorical figure, could still be regarded in those scenes as an actual person, a Leviné, for instance (the Communist leader of the second Munich Räterepublik, on whom he was obviously modelled). But since Toller did not want the action to give promise of close realism he kept it in those scenes unlocalized, unparticularized, and diagrammatically simplified. As he says of the play in general, "The sensuous intensity of the experiences was so strong that I could only master them through a process of abstraction, through the dramatic emphasis on those lines which define the essence of things" (*Prosa*, p. 175).

The *Traumbilder*, on the other hand, which alternate between a pathetic and a grotesque mode, represent the subconscious experience of the heroine, so that frequently the issues canvassed symbolically in the *Traumbilder* are repeated in the *reale Bilder* as the heroine becomes explicitly aware of them.[13] At the beginning of the play, the heroine is in much the same frame of mind as Friedrich at the end of *Die Wandlung*, a state which is now seen to have the sentimentality of inexperience, and which has to be exchanged, slowly and painfully, for a real awareness of the issues involved in revolution. In some ways it is *Die Wandlung* in reverse.

Again, as in *Die Wandlung*, the Sonja of the *reale Bilder* is represented in the *Traumbilder* by a symbolic doppelgänger, who stands for Sonja's subconscious or only half-conscious awareness of her experience, and her attempts to adopt the roles of, or to sympathize with, the lives of people different from herself. Toller has further dramatized Sonja's impulse toward growth and understanding and her desire to identify with others by the use of a symbolic *Begleiter* (companion), a figure who subsumes the role of Friedrich's sister and of certain of the functions of Friedrich's doppelgänger, as he is identified with other people, such as a policeman and a warder.[14]

But because the *Begleiter* is an aspect of Sonja's subconscious and not a separate person, the relation between doppelgänger and companion is not a simple one of master and pupil: growth is through dialectic, and there is frequently opposition and argument. Certain other figures, too, are given doppelgängers to emphasize connections and relations. Thus in Bild 2, *Saal der Effektenbörse* (The Stock Exchange Hall), Sonja's husband is identified with the *Schreiber* (Recorder) to emphasize the relationship between his private and public roles. However he sees himself subjectively, objectively speaking he is a supporter of the capitalist system.[15]

Since *Masse-Mensch* is short enough to make such an undertaking feasible, I intend to give a descriptive analysis of the play to show in detail how the theme is worked out and related to the dramatic form.

In Bild 1 (a *reales Bild*), which continues from where *Die Wandlung* left off, there is a new grasp of the revolutionary situation; despite the lack of particularity in Toller's method, it is clear that we are in the real revolutionary world of committees, pamphlets, and strikes. Friedrich's rhetoric in the mouth of Sonja (though Sonja is more definite than Friedrich: she does call for a strike, i.e., a specific public act) is meant to be viewed critically as the product of enthusiasm without experience:

> Mein Wissen ist so stark. Die Massen
> Auferstanden frei vom Paragraphenband
> Der feisten Herrn am grünen Tisch,
> Armeen der Menschheit werden sie mit wuchtender Gebärde
> Das Friedenswerk zum unsichtbaren Dome türmen. (p. 295)

(I'm so certain of what I know: resurrected, free from the regulations and red tape of well-fed bureaucratic officials, the masses, the army of humanity will, with a mighty gesture, raise up the work of peace into an invisible cathedral.)

Sonja, like Friedrich, imagines that radical change will be easy to accomplish—and yet that easy optimism is qualified by the conspiratorial circumstances in which it is uttered, an optimism that is quite different from the "we'll carry all before us" outdoor meeting in *Die Wandlung*. There is the fear of contingencies:

> If only those on whom we are relying keep quiet.
> Do you think the police know nothing about it?
> What if the soldiers made fast the hall with chains? (p. 295)

Even a knock at the door may mean treachery. The power of the establishment against which the revolution is to be made is subtly indicated from the beginning.

The second part of the scene, enacted between Sonja and her husband (it was he who knocked at the door), further helps to define Sonja's position and the nature of the struggle in which she is engaged. Toller has gone out of his way to present the husband objectively without caricaturing him as he does, say, Friedrich's uncle, a roughly equivalent character in *Die Wandlung*. But in presenting him fairly, Toller is indicating one of the realities of a revolutionary situation: that there are many ordinary decent people who, because they have been brought up to serve an establishment, are incapable of feeling sympathy for the condition of the workers, and even of understanding what the revolution is all about. For Sonja, the shattering of the momentary illusion that her husband has come to help her is the beginning of a long, harsh confrontation with revolutionary reality. And there is something else of which Toller makes us, though not Sonja, aware: how engagement in a revolution may even threaten a revolutionary with a loss of authenticity. Sonja is presented as being very much in love with her husband, as finding her being through him:

> Du, mein Blut blüht dir . . .
> Sieh, ich werde welkes Blatt ohne dich.
> Du bist der Tau, der mich entfaltet.
> Du bist der Sturm, dess märzne Kraft
> Brandfackeln wirft in dürstendes Geäder [. . .]
> Ich glaube, ich werde schwach sein
> Ohne dich . . . grenzenlos . . . . (pp. 298–299)

(You: my blood blossoms on account of you. Look, I become a withered leaf without you: you are the dew which unfolds me: you are the March storm whose power hurls torches into thirsty veins: I believe I shall be weak without you . . . undefined.)

The revolutionary cause can, at present, act as a substitute for this personal need:

> Nicht Wunsch hat mein Geschick gewendet,
> Not wars . . . Not aus Menschsein,
> Not aus meiner tiefsten Fülle.
> Not wendet, höre, Not wendet!
> Nicht Laune, Spiel der Langeweile,
> Not aus Menschsein wendet. (p. 297)

(It is not desire that has changed my destiny: it was need; the need coming from my humanity; the need coming from the depths of my being. Need changes me; listen, need changes me. Not a whim, an idle amusement, need coming from my humanity changes me.)

But there is undoubted loss, and a loss that is bound to prove all the greater if the revolution turns out to be less straightforward, more equivocal, than Sonja thinks.

The purpose of Bild 2 (a *Traumbild: Saal der Effektenbörse*) (The Stock-Exchange Hall) is to show in grotesque form the nature of the social system against which the revolution is to be made. What is stressed in these scenes is not only the inhumanity of that system,

but its entrenched nature, its infinite adaptability. The Recorder has
the face of Sonja's husband, thereby emphasizing, as mentioned
above, the division between his subjective apprehension of his function in society and his objective role, a division which had been
indicated, though not demonstrated, in the first scene. Nor does
Toller necessarily claim that the bankers are consciously unscrupu-
lous; but he represents them as glorying in their heartless manipula-
tions—not only a legitimate way of satirizing a particular social system (which forces people to behave in this manner) but of making
the point that it does not matter whether those playing such oppressive roles do or do not realize what they are doing. That the bankers
are not full human beings, that they are grotesque and one-dimen-
sional is a commentary on the system of which they take advantage.
Their humanity is denied as well: they also are *Masse* (Masses).
Because it treats human beings as objects (*Menschenmaterial/ Wird
schlecht*) (the human material is deteriorating) (p. 33) a society
founded upon private profit is bound to be one in which no one can
be fully human. But it is difficult for people to see the truth about
the system because it habitually claims to be activated by human
concern. Thus the bankers' plan to float a company to provide
brothels to keep up the morale of the troops is called "Convalescent
Home to Strengthen the Will to Victory" (p. 302). The following
exchange brings out the issues involved quite subtly:

Dritter Bankier:	Schwächt Männerliebe
	Die Soldaten?
Vierter Bankier:	Merkwürdig nein,
	Mann hasst Mann.
	Es fehlt.
Dritter Bankier:	Es fehlt? . . .
Vierter Bankier:	Mechanik
	Alles Lebens
	Wurde offenbart.
Vierter Bankier:	Mechanik Alles Lebens Wurde offenbart.
Dritter Bankier:	Es fehlt?
Vierter Bankier:	Masse braucht Lust.
Dritter Bankier:	Es fehlt? . . .
Vierter Bankier:	Die Liebe. (p. 301)

(Third Banker:	Does love between men weaken the troops?
Fourth Banker:	Oddly enough, no. Man hates man. Something's lacking.
Third Banker:	What's lacking?
Fourth Banker:	The mechanism of life as a whole has been revealed.

Third Banker:	What's lacking?
Fourth Banker:	The Masses need lust.
Third Banker:	What's lacking?
Fourth Banker:	Love.)

To the bankers, the only meaning of love is lust and perversion. But throughout the passage, the *Liebe* (love) which to the bankers is synonymous with lust, can be interpreted just as appropriately as the Christian *agape*. But such a love, which would be true *Männerliebe* (love of men), is not only one the bankers cannot conceive of, but one that really would represent a threat to the system:

> Es fehlt? . . .
> Die Liebe.
>
> (What's lacking? Love.)

The existing system appears on the surface to be vulnerable because it seems to be divided against itself by competition (thus the third and fourth bankers attempt to outwit the first and second) and by a dependence on favorable circumstances which cannot always be secured. It would appear to be threatened, for example, by defeat in war. But this is not so; fluctuations in fortune do not really threaten the system as such:

> Die Baisse
> Oder Hausse heute
> Ist nebensächlich.
> Das Wesentliche:
> Mechanisches Gesetz stabil. (p. 304)

(Whether slump or boom today is unimportant. What is really important is the stability of the mechanism.)

Not only is the system incredibly resilient; it is invulnerable to moral appeal precisely because it denies full humanity to those who operate it and are oppressed by it. But Sonja has not learned this lesson, and so the companion who enters with her (whose symbolic function has already been discussed) confidently predicts its destruction:

> Ein Fusstritt,
> Und die Mechanik
> Ist zerbrochnes
> Kinderspielzeug. (p. 304)

(One kick and the mechanism is a broken toy),

while Sonja appeals to the bankers' humanity:

> Meine Herren:
> Menschen.
> Ich wiederhole:
> Menschen! (p. 304)

> (Gentlemen: these are people. I repeat, people.)

We see, however, the confident prediction of the one and the appeal of the other being perverted by an infinitely resilient system (no wonder that the stage direction says *"The companion and the woman fade away"* [p. 304]); their confidence and human appeal are misplaced. Despite defeat in war, peace offers plenty of opportunities for profit which can be dressed up in moral terms that are a simulacrum of those to which Sonja has appealed:

Dritter Bankier:	Hörten Sie? Ein Grubenunglück Scheints. Menschen in Not.
Vierter Bankier:	Ich schlage vor; Wohltätigkeitsfest. Tanz Ums Börsenpult. Tanz Gegen Not. Erlös Den Armen (p. 304)

(Third Banker:	Did you hear? It seems that there is a mine disaster, people in need.
Fourth Banker:	I propose a charity ball. A dance round the Stock Exchange desk. A dance against need. Proceeds for the poor.)

The scene ends in a grotesque triumph of the system: *"The sound of coins rattling: the bankers in top hats dance a foxtrot around the stock exchange desk"* (p. 303).

The system is certainly not going to be overthrown as easily as Sonja (and Friedrich before her) had assumed. But though I think this scene represents in caricature what for Toller was the real truth about the system, for Sonja, following the meeting with her husband, it represents a growing awareness which, even below the level of consciousness, she is as yet unable to face. That is why her subconscious self still speaks in the same kind of language as she had used in the previous scene, and why in this scene the companion, who represents Sonja's impulse to seek out the truth, does not act a part noticeably different from that of Sonja herself.

It is only in the third scene that the theme of the play emerges quite unambiguously. The opening choruses, in which the consciousnesses of various kinds of workers are evoked, serve to remind us that once people are made aware of the deprivation, they will seek to end it, whatever the means. Thus the *junge Arbeiterinnen* (young female workers) soon make the suggestion that the factories should be blown up:

> Und Schlacht speit neue Schlacht!
> Kein Zaudern mehr mit jenen Herren,
> Nicht Schwanken und nicht schwachen Pakt.
> Einer Schar Genossen Auftrag:
> In die Maschinen Dynamit.
> Und morgen fetzen die Fabriken in die Luft. (p. 305)

(and battle spits forth fresh battle: no more shilly-shallying with those bosses, no hesitation and no futile pact. Give orders to a band of comrades: dynamite the machines: and tomorrow the factories will be blown sky high.)

Since this proposal falsely identifies the capitalist system with industrialism as such, it can easily be shown to be politically senseless. Sonja, with support from other workers, thus has no difficulty in arguing successfully against it, though the slightly patronizing tone she uses, even when her arguments are sound enough, reveals the extent to which she is disassociated from a full apprehension of the experience which prompted the demand:

> Es ist ein Traum, der eure Blicke hemmt,
> Ein Traum von Kindern, die vor Nacht erschreckt. (p. 306)

(It is a dream which blinds your sight: a dream of children afraid of the dark.)

For, as *der Namenlose* (the Nameless one) points out later:

> Sie fühlen unsre Not, ich geb es zu.
> Doch waren Sie zehn Stunden lang im Bergwerk,
> In blinden Kammern Kinder heimatlose,
> Zehn Stunden Bergwerk, abends jene Kammern,
> So Tag für Tag das Los der Massen? (p. 309)

(I grant that you feel our need: but have you ever spent ten hours in a mine, your rootless children in windowless rooms: do you know the lot of the masses all day and every day—ten hours working in the mines, evenings in those rooms?)

The moral ideas for which Sonja stands and which cause her to react against the later, more meaningful call for the use of force, could thus be viewed as the result of her being, though sympathetic, a privileged observer.

Consequently, Sonja's call for a strike, though it makes a momentary impression and though it might force a peace, cannot possibly lead to that transformation of society that she obviously wants, though she has not, as yet, fully defined it to herself:

> Wir Schwachen werden Felsen sein der Stärke,
> *Gewaltlos* (my italics) werden wir die Ketten sprengen,
> Und keine Waffe ist gebaut, die uns besiegen könnte. (p. 307)

(We weak ones will become a rock of strength: we will break our fetters *without force*, and the weapon that could beat us has not been built.)

She is easily swept aside by *der Namenlose*, a symbolic figure representing the course of action to which the masses are urged by the nature of the situation and experience ("Ich bin Masse/Masse ist Schicksal") (I am Masses/Masses are Fate), who makes a much more convincing case for the use of violence than we have yet heard:

> Ich rufe mehr als Streik!
> Ich rufe: Krieg!
> Ich rufe: Revolution!
> Der Feind dort oben hört
> Auf schöne Reden nicht.
> Macht gegen Macht!
> Gewalt . . . Gewalt! (p. 309)

(I call for more than a strike, I call for war: I call for revolution. The enemy above us pays no attention to fine speeches. Might against Might. Force . . . Force.)

But though the situation impels the proletarian masses toward violence which is at odds with its proposed ends—a revolution even when made for *Menschheit* (humanity) is still made by *Masse* (the masses)—Sonja is at least partly right when, after registering her moral objection ("Ich will nicht neues Morden" [I want no fresh murder]), she goes on to say:

> Masse ist ohnmächtig.
> Masse ist schwach. (p. 309)

(The masses are powerless. The masses are weak.)

For this last, rather cryptic, statement seems to hint at what *der Namenlose*, for all the plausibility of his arguments, had not recognized: that force of the weak against the strong will not necessarily be successful. But the statement implies another and profound meaning, although it may be one of which Sonja is not yet aware: that the masses are weak precisely because they are masses and have not reached their full individuality as *Mensch*. They are subject to compulsions that arise out of their lack of freedom and that are a sign of weakness.

Moreover, though Sonja decides to throw in her lot with the masses it is with a troubled conscience that she does so:

> Gefühl zwängt mich in Dunkel,
> Doch mein Gewissen schreit mir: Nein! (p. 310)

(Feeling forces me into darkness: yet my conscience cries "no" to me.)

It is obviously a choice that must rob her of what she has of freedom and authenticity, so that the loss she has sustained in the break with her husband will no longer be compounded. No longer will she be able to see a fully human meaning in revolution. Not that this realization emerges explicitly, but it is implied by her forced and mechanically expressed capitulation to *der Namenlose* toward the end of the scene:

> Du . . . bist . . . Masse
> Du . . . bist . . . Recht (p. 310)

(You are the masses: you are law.)

In Bild 4 *(Traumbild)* there is a reworking, through the use of grotesque symbolism and on a profounder level of apprehension, of some of the issues raised in the last scene. Again, like the first *Traumbild*, it is, I think, meant both to be true in absolute terms and also to represent Sonja's growing apprehension of her recent experience and of the problems that it poses.

But, though the general intention behind the scene is clear, the significance of its action is not always so and requires detailed interpretation. The scene is set in *"a yard surrounded by high walls"* in the middle of which there is *"a lantern which emits a scant light. Worker sentries appear from the corners of the yard"* (p. 310). The setting here could easily be accepted as a realistic representation of a typical scene in the middle of a revolution but it is clear that though the setting, initially at any rate, is meant to be acceptable in these terms, it has a symbolic meaning as well. The courtyard with its high walls is meant to suggest a prison—not only the prison of working class deprivation and subjection, but also, perhaps, mental imprisonment within that very experience. The darkness thrown into relief by the meagerness of the light is, one might suggest, also the darkness of the condition of the proletariat and of their feelings and perceptions.

The feelings expressed through the choruses of the preceding scenes have their equivalent in the tunes hummed with grotesque gaiety by the Sentries:

Erste Wache singt:	Meine Mutter
	Hat mich
	Im Graben geboren.
	Lalala la
	Hm, Hm,
Zweite Wache:	Mein Vater
	Hat mich
	Im Rausche verloren.
Alle Wachen:	Lalala, la,
	Hm, Hm. (pp. 310–311)
(First Sentry sings:	My mother gave birth to me in the ditch, Lalala, la, Hm, Hm.
Second Sentry:	My father lost me when he was drunk. Lalala, la, Hm, Hm.)

Why are the plangent complaints of the previous scenes changed into the flippant hardness of these hummed snatches? Because, I think, Toller wants to stress that those moving choruses in which the facts of oppression and aspiration were voiced directly were only part of the truth; there is also cynicism, harshness, and insensitivity: one cannot expect brutalizing experiences not to brutalize. The internal compulsions to which the workers are subject are further symbolized by *der Namenlose* (the Nameless one) playing on a harmonica *"In provocative rhythms which are now soothing to the senses, now passionately exciting"* (pp. 311–312). It is an invitation to a dance of death, for as soon as *der Namenlose* has begun to play, *"a man condemned to death, a noose around his neck, steps out from the darkness"* (p. 312), and later others condemned to death join with the sentries and prostitutes in dance around the Nameless one.

The "man condemned to death" embodies not only the coming deaths of many of the revolutionaries, but also the compulsive inevitability of the action leading to their deaths: their enslavement, in their unfreedom, to their own morality and appetite:

> Leben,
> Aus Tanz geboren,
> Drängt
> Zum Tanz,
> Zum Tanz der Lust,
> Zum Totentanz
> Der Zeit. (p. 312)

(Life born from the dance, urges to the dance: to the dance of lust, to the dance of death of the time.)

One is reminded of the bankers' dance, itself a visual embodiment of what they had said earlier in the second scene:

> So ist der Krieg
> Als unser Instrument,
> Das mächtige gewaltge Instrument,
> Das Könige und Staaten,
> Minister, Parlamente,
> Presse, Kirchen
> Tanzen lässt,
> Tanz über Erdball,

> Tanz über Meere,
> Verloren? (p. 301)

(So is the war lost, that instrument of ours, the mighty powerful instrument that makes kings, countries, ministers, parliaments, the press, the churches dance, dance over the earth, dance over the sea?)

The bankers, as I have pointed out, are, humanly speaking, victims of the situation which they exploit.

In the second part of the scene, in which a figure with Sonja's face enters accompanied by the companion, the contradiction between means and ends in the revolution and the element of compulsive vengeance in it is further explored. The full humanity of those whom the revolutionaries mean to kill, and Sonja's apprehension of it, are brought out by identifying the faceless victims-to-be with her husband ("*A sentry brings in the prisoner, he has the face of the husband*" [p. 313]) with his poignant cry: "Leben! Leben!" (Life! Life!) But a sentry, who has narrowly escaped the same fate wants him shot—revenge, not military expediency being the motivating factor:

> Vergeben ist Feigheit.
> Gestern entfloh ich
> Den Feinden drüben.
> An der Mauer schon stand ich.
> Den Leib zerstriemt.
> Neben mir der Mann,
> Der mich
> Erschlagen sollte. (p. 314)

(To forgive is cowardice. Yesterday I escaped from the enemy over there. I was already standing against the wall, my body beaten sore. Near me was the man [the husband] who was going to shoot me.)

But "*the face of the prisoner turns into that of a sentry*" (p. 314).

The denials of humanity by the sentry and to the sentry are convertible. The lesson is brought out explicitly in Sonja's words:

> Gestern standst du
> An der Mauer.
> Jetzt stehst du
> Wieder an der Mauer
> Das bist du,

> Der heute
> An der Mauer steht.
> Mensch
> Das bist du. (p. 314)

(Yesterday you stood against the wall, now you are standing once more against the wall. You are he who stands today at the wall: humanity, you are he.)

And to the sentry's "Die Masse gilt" (p. 315) (the masses count) Sonja opposes "Der Mensch gilt" (humanity counts). But here again a deadlock is reached. How *is* "masses" to become "humanity"? The masses *cannot* behave as if they were *Mensch* (humanity), and even if they could, they would forfeit their chance really to be *Mensch:* Sonja's desire to obey a categorical imperative merely makes her position socially irrelevant. That is why when she identifies herself with all mankind: "Ich geb/Mich hin . . ./Allen hin . . ." (I give myself to . . . to all), she is met only by *"the evil laughter of the sentries"* (p. 315). But at the end she is beginning to explore a possible answer:

> *Die Frau stellt sich neben den Mann. So schiesst!*
> Ich sag mich los! . . . (p. 315)
>
> *(The woman places herself next to the man.* Shoot now! I re-nounce it!)

To identify oneself with those who suffer, to the extent that one is willing to take the suffering on oneself, may offer some mitigation of the dilemma.

The next scene develops, on the plane of actual experience, some of the issues which had been represented symbolically in the previous one, and with which Sonja was there shown as subconsciously and imaginatively coming to terms. At the opening of the scene, she is still, consciously speaking, at the level she occuped when *der Namenlose* first appeared. She accepts violence and even tries to assimilate it to her previous enthusiasm (*Das Werk! Welch heiliges Wort!* [p. 315]) (The work! What a holy word!) even if it is with a bad conscience: "Kampf mit Eisenwaffen vergewaltigt" (to fight with firearms is rape) (p. 315). It is through the murder of the counter-revolutionary hostages that she finally experiences most sharply the contradiction between revolutionary means and ends:

> Ich rufe:
> Zerbrecht das System!
> Du aber willst die Menschen zerbrechen. (p. 318)

(I cry: smash the system: you, however, desire to smash human beings.)

She clearly perceives the element of vengeance in the behavior of the revolutionaries:

> Die Hälfte ist erschossen!
> Die Tat nicht Notwehr.
> Blinde Wut! nicht Dienst am Werk. (p. 317)

(Half of them are shot: the deed was not self-defense: blind rage, not service to the cause.)

But the scene does more than rework the issues raised in the *Traumbild* on the level of consciousness and realism. It explains them further; the revolution is shown as being overpowered by the superior might of the establishment:

> Der Platz bäumt sich vor Toten.
> Die drüben liegen gut verschanzt,
> Mit allen Waffen ausgerüstet,
> Mit Flammenwerfern, Minen, giftgen Gasen. (p. 316)

(The place is heaped with dead: the other side is well entrenched, armed with all kinds of weapons, flamethrowers, mines, poison gases.)

The process is dramatically illustrated when the singing of the "Internationale" by the revolutionaries is rudely interrupted:

Suddenly there is a short burst of machine gun fire. The song breaks off. The main door and the side doors are suddenly broken down. Soldiers with guns at the ready stand at the doors. (p. 320)

Not only do violent revolutionaries run a considerable risk of being unsuccessful, but unsuccessful revolution leads not to a diminution but to an augmentation of the very suffering it was undertaken to avert:

> Sie metzeln alles nieder.
> Männer, Frauen, Kinder,
> Wir liefern uns nicht aus,
> Dass sie uns töten, eingefangnes Vieh. (p. 317)

(They mow us all down: men, women, children. We shall not surrender for them to slaughter us like penned-up cattle.)

But the element of compulsion in the behavior means that even when it is clear that defeat is inevitable, revolutionaries will continue with violent struggle even though now it is rationally indefensible. Thus, even when it is clear that the day is lost, *der Namenlose* says:

> Aufrichtet Barrikaden!
> Noch sind wir Schützer!
> Trächtig ist unser Blut zum Kampf! (p. 317)

(Erect the barricades: we are still defenders: our blood is pregnant with struggle.)

Such desperation leads to the further illusion that defeat itself is a prelude to victory in the future:

> War heute unsere Kraft zu schwach,
> Morgen dröhnen neue Bataillone. (p. 317)

(If our power was too weak today, tomorrow new batallions will be mustering.)

It also presages a hardening that inevitably causes faction: hostility toward and suspicion of those in one's own ranks. Thus *der Namenlose* refuses to regard Sonja's arguments as even disinterested:

> Wie wagst du, Frau aus jenen Kreisen,
> Die Stunde der Entscheidung zu vergiften?
> Ich höre andern Ton aus deinem Mund.
> Du schützest sie, die mit dir aufgewachsen.
> Das ist der tiefre Grund.
> Du bist Verrat. (p. 319)

(Woman, coming from the class you do, how dare you poison the hour of decision? I hear another tone from your mouth [than the one you intend]. You are defending those who grew up with you: that is the real reason. You are treason.)

The next *Traumbild* examines the nature of human guilt, again through the anguished subconscious of Sonja, and does so in a way that does not limit the problem to the special topic of the play: the guilt of revolution. Again, though the general drift of the scene is clear, certain details of the symbolism are obscure and necessitate a detailed exposition. The setting is, to start with, of considerable significance:

Unbounded space. At its heart a cage illuminated by a spotlight. Inside it is hunched up a fettered prisoner with the woman's face. Near the cage is the companion in the warder's form. (p. 320)

This may be thought sensational, and it is perhaps a general weakness of Expressionist symbolism to have a tendency to be so. But it is certainly a functional use of symbolism. The woman is a fettered prisoner in a cage because her sense of guilt—a guilt which at the opening she does not understand—has deprived her of her humanity. In facing it and understanding its significance, she can become human again and be released from her cage. Sonja's ability to sympathize with the feelings of her opponents—to recognize the existence of a general humanity which others deny—is symbolized in this scene by the appearance of *der Begleiter* (the companion) in the form of a warder.

At first, the sense of guilt issues in a denial which is an acknowledgment of its existence—a state of mind represented theatrically by having Sonja accused by the shades of those who have been killed:

Die Gefesselte:	Ich wollt nicht
	Blut.
Erster Schatten:	Du schwiegst.
Zweiter Schatten:	Schwiegst beim Sturm
	Aufs Stadthaus.
Dritter Schatten:	Schwiegst beim Raub
	Der Waffen. (p. 321)

(Prisoner:	I did not want bloodshed.
First Shade:	You kept quiet.
Second Shade:	Kept quiet when the Town Hall was stormed.
Third Shade:	Kept quiet when the weapons were stolen.)

When the prisoner finally acknowledges her guilt, however, *"The Shades fade away"* (p. 322). To feel guilt in a world which denies its existence is to accept one's humanity:

Erster Bankier:	Aktie Schuldig
	Biete an
	Zum Nennwert.
Zweiter Bankier:	Aktie Schuldig
	Ist nicht mehr
	Zugelassen. (p. 322)

(First Banker:	I offer shares in guilt at par.
Second Banker:	Shares in guilt are no longer admitted.)

But even though it may be necessary not to try to evade it, the question of guilt is by no means all that simple. The life of which the victims of the revolution were deprived was not wholly life after all because it was a life in which men were not wholly free. As the warder-companion says:

> Törin
> Vom sentimentalen
> Lebenswandel.
> Wären sie am Leben
> Sie tanzten
> Um vergoldeten Altar,
> Dem Tausende geopfert.
> Auch Du. (p. 322)

(You are a fool because of a sentimental attitude to life. If they were alive they would dance around the golden altar where thousands have been sacrificed. You as well.)

We had, of course, been reminded of the nature of society by the brief reappearance of the bankers, and because society is what it is, guilt is inevitable. One should say: "I, a human being, am guilty" (p. 322) as if one were a completely free agent, but it must be remembered that "The masses are guilt: life is guilt." Perhaps something in the human condition makes guilt inevitable:

> Der Mensch,
> Wie Baum und Pflanze,

Schicksalgebundne
Vorgeprägte Form,
Die werdend sich entfaltet,
Werdend sich zerstört. (p. 322)

(Humanity, like a tree and a plant bound by a fated form existing before its actualization, in becoming unfolds itself, in becoming destroys itself.)

Life is a process of simultaneous creation and destruction. But Sonja has not yet grasped this fact: she takes things too personally. The fact that *Masse ist Schuld* (The Masses are guilt) and *Leben ist Schuld* (Life is guilt) only increases her sense of guilt: "So bin ich zwiefach/ Schuldig." (I am therefore doubly guilty. [p. 322])

The problem is further explored in terms of visual symbolism:

Prisoners in prison clothes approach, five paces apart. On their heads are pointed caps covering their faces, to which is attached a piece of material with eyeholes. A number is on each prisoner's breast. Soundlessly, and in a monotonous rhythm, they go round the cage in square formation. (p. 322)

The figures are undifferentiated in appearance and movement because they are *Masse* (the masses); but the fact that their uniformity is largely a matter of externals of clothing reminds us of their individuality, the *Mensch* (the humanity), as it were, underneath. They are in prison garb not only to remind us that some of the revolutionaries are actually in prison, but also that they are *Masse* imprisoned in their unrealized humanity by the social structure— and in a third meaning the prisoner's clothes are a reminder of guilt. "Masse ist Schicksal/ Leben ist Schuld" (The Masses are fate/ Life is guilt.)

This prompts in Sonja a deeper perception of the nature of guilt. The masses, because they are masses, are impelled in certain ways, are "guiltless." So much is comprehensible. But when the Warder *(Begleiter)* says "Man is guiltless" this seems at first, in its denial of all human guilt, to be going too far.

But if *Masse* is "guiltless," *Mensch* is "guiltless," too, because in a society where men are not free there is no genuine opposition between *Masse* and *Mensch*. Guilt is inevitable, and its inevitability means that one is in a sense guiltless: guiltily guiltless. Not only can one be compelled to act in a certain way, but there is, in this situation, no effective action that does not involve guilt. But who is guilty? Sonja's doppelgänger blames guilt on God: "Gott ist schuldig!'" (p. 323) (God is guilty). This may seem too facile a conclusion, one which, in absolving man from responsibility, is sentimental. But the conception is more complex than it appears: as the Warder-Companion says "God is in you." In other words, to assert that God is guilty is only another way of saying that it is man's aspirations that are to blame, as he cannot help striving for something higher. This interpretation helps to explain the following rather puzzling exchange:

> *Die Gefesselte:* So überwind ich Gott.
> *Der Warter:*   Wurm!
>   Gottesschänderin! (p. 323)
>
> *(The Prisoner:* So I'll conquer God.
> *The Warder:*   Worm! Blasphemer!)

For to try to root out that aspiration because it is ineluctably involved with guilt is to try to escape from the responsibility of being human, the "ungeheuerliche Gesetz der Schuld" (the monstrous law of guilt), "Darin sich/ Mensch und Mensch/ Verstricken *muss*" (p. 323) (in which man with man is bound to be embroiled). In understanding it Sonja is no longer crippled by it. As the Warder-companion says: "Du bist geheilt,/ Komm aus/ Dem Käfig" (p. 323) (You are healed, come out of the cage). But she cannot be liberated from necessity. To the question "Am I free?" the Warder answers "unfree! free!" Her freedom is to recognize that she has no choice.

What is puzzling about the last *reales Bild* is that issues which have just been closed would seem to be reopened. The first part of the scene is straightforward, for the meeting between Sonja and her husband involves a working out on the conscious plane of issues that had been subconsciously faced in the previous *Traumbild*. Thus the woman recognizes that she is *schuldlos schuldig* (guiltlessly guilty) and:

> Menschen müssen Werk wollen,
> Und Werk wird rot von Menschenblut.
> Menschen müssen Leben wollen,
> Und um sie wächst ein Meer von Menschenblut. (p. 325)

(Men are compelled to want work and work grows red with human blood. Men are compelled to want life and around them grows a sea of human blood.)

There is even a certain serenity in the way Sonja realizes that she
and her husband are united in guilt. Ironically, in view of the
significance of the previous *Traumbild,* her husband had come to
assure her that she is "schuldlos . . . am Frevel der Erschiessung"
(p. 324) (guiltless of the crime of the shooting):

> Gib deine Hand mir . . .
> Gib deine Hand mir, Bruder,
> Auch du mir Bruder. (p. 326)

(Give me your hand: give me your hand, brother: you are my brother too.)

But Sonja realizes that this sense of relationship is won at the cost of
an essential loneliness. Few people can work their way through the
tragic experience she has faced:

> Letzter Weg führt über Schneefeld.
> Letzter Weg kennt nicht Begleiter.
> Letzter Weg ist ohne Mutter.
> Letzter Weg ist Einsamkeit. (p. 326)[16]

(The last road leads over the snowfields: the last road knows no companion:
the last road is motherless: the last road is loneliness.)

But the next exchange between *der Namenlose* (the nameless one)
and the woman is something more than a working out on the conscious plane of the issues raised in the previous *Traumbild.* It contains a surprising and, at this stage in the play, unexpectedly
sweeping denunciation of the use of force:

> Höre: kein Mensch darf Menschen töten
> Um einer Sache willen.
> Unheilig jede Sache, dies verlangt.
> Wer Menschenblut um seinetwillen fordert,
> Ist Moloch:
> Gott war Moloch.
> Staat war Moloch.
> Masse war Moloch. (p. 328)

(Listen: no man may kill men for the sake of a cause. Every cause which
requires it is unholy. Whoever demands human blood in its behalf is
Moloch: God was Moloch: the state was Moloch: the Masses were Moloch.)

It also contains a denial of any significant differences between revolutionary war and capitalist war:

> Ihr mordet für die Menschheit,
> Wie sie, Verblendete, für ihren Staat gemordet.
> Und einige glaubten gar
> Durch ihren Staat, ihr Vaterland,
> Die Erde zu erlösen.
> Ich sehe keine Unterscheidung: (p. 327)

(You murder for humanity just as those who were deluded murdered for the state. Some indeed thought through their country, their Fatherland, to redeem the world. I don't see any difference.)

Again the inevitability of the old deadlock is realized. As *der Namenlose* says:

> Dir fehlt der Mut, die Tat, die harte Tat
> Auf dich zu nehmen.
> Durch harte Tat erst wird das freie Volk. (p. 329)

(You lack the courage to take action, harsh action upon yourself. The people will only be free through harsh action.)

At this point Toller seems to be somewhat evasive, for the woman is shown to project her idealism into a future when it will characterize mankind as a whole—but that, of course, does not solve the problem now:

> Und einst werde ich
> Reiner,
> Schuldloser,
> Menschheit
> Sein. (p. 329)[17]

(And someday I will be purer, more guiltless, I will be humanity.)

But the issues, having been reopened, are genuinely taken further. Thus Sonja refuses to acquiesce in *der Namenlose's* plan of escape, even though she realizes that she is needed by the cause, because it will involve the murder of a sentry.[18] "I have no right/ to obtain my life through the sentry's death" (p. 326), an assertion which is associated with a definite ethical principle: "He who acts may only sacrifice himself" (p. 328). There are, Toller seems to be saying, occasions in a revolution when one can put ethical principles into practice, where necessity and choice are not identical. In situations that concern him directly, an individual can sometimes still be a free agent, in ways not possible for a collective.

And Toller holds out the hope that individual self-sacrifice can contribute to a development of consciousness that will itself help change *Masse* into *Mensch*. Thus, in the fine but subdued ending of the play, Sonja's execution stimulates a growth toward *Menschheit* (humanity) in two of her fellow prisoners (it is significant that it is not clear whether they are in prison for revolutionary or for criminal activities):

First female prisoner:	Did you see the officer?
	What a golden uniform.
Second female prisoner:	I saw the coffin. In the washroom.
	A yellow box of planks.

The first prisoner notices that some bread is lying on the table, she pounces on it.

First prisoner:	Look, bread, hunger! Hunger! Hunger!
Second prisoner:	Bread for me! Bread for me!
	Bread for me!
First prisoner:	Look, a mirror. Oh, how beautiful!
	Hide. Evening. Cell.
Second prisoner:	Look: a silk scarf.
	Hide. Evening. Cell.

The sharp burst of a volley (of rifle fire) is heard in the cell. The prisoners, frightened, throw out their hands, palms extended. The first prisoner feels for the mirror which she has concealed in her skirts, puts it hastily back on the table. Begins to cry: sinks down on her knees.

First prisoner:	Sister: Why do we do that?

Her arms dangle by her side in an immense helplessness. The second prisoner feels for the scarf which she has concealed in her skirts. She puts it hastily back down on the bed.

Second prisoner:	Sister: Why do we do that?

The second prisoner collapses; she buries her head in her lap. (p. 330)

But Toller, I think, realizes—it would make nonsense of his play if he did not—that such an opportunity and development are not symptomatic and that the problem remains. I think he has been at pains at this stage to put so strong and explicit a condemnation of violence into Sonja's mouth and to show the creative possibilities of nonviolent action because he wants the tension of feeling in the play to be maintained. It would be so easy for *Masse-Mensch* merely to underwrite, in a thoroughly complacent way, the position that violence, though deplorable, is necessary. But the last thing that, at the end of the play, Toller wants anybody to be, is complacent.

And it is noticeable that elsewhere in the scene he takes other measures to prevent an easy reduction of the complex theme and feeling he has developed. Thus, through the mouth of the Priest he not only satirizes establishment Christianity but travesties what the play has been saying, in order to try to prevent its being reduced to that very travesty:

> Der Mensch ist gut—so träumtest du
> Und sätest namenlosen Frevel
> Wider heilgen Staat und heilge Ordnung. (p. 329)

(Man is good—that is what you dreamed: and sowed nameless crime against the holy state and holy order.)

Sonja, it may be noted, does not simply deny what he says but retorts: "Man wants to be good" (p. 329). Men want to become good, they want to become really men *(Mensch)*.

But though the formula put forward by the Priest may be resisted, as Sonja's repeated "Ich glaube" (I believe) shows, it is resisted at a price:

> Ich glaube!!!
> Mich friert . . . Gehen Sie!
> Gehen Sie! (p. 330)

(I believe!!! I'm cold. Go away! Go away!)

Similarly, Toller wants to guard against too easy a fatalism about the inevitable role of *Masse* by again presenting a travesty of it in the behavior of the officer, appointed to lead Sonja to execution, who believes himself subsumed to a role that he is forced to play:

Jede Unterhaltung mir verboten.
Befehl Befehl. (p. 330)

(Any conversation is forbidden me. Orders. Orders.)

In no other literary work known to me are such vital themes
worked through in such depth.

CHAPTER 4

Die Maschinenstürmer
(*The Machine Wreckers*)

Die Maschinenstürmer is set in Nottingham in 1815. An Act of Parliament
has just been passed making machine breaking punishable with death. A
group of weavers, led by John Wible, are on strike against the introduction
of power loom weaving, but their strike is having little effect because the
manufacturer, Ure, has obtained blackleg labor. Wible, therefore, suggests
that the weavers destroy the steam engine. Jimmy Cobbett, a politically
conscious workingman who has just returned to Nottingham after travelling
around Britain and parts of Europe, manages to persuade the strikers that
the introduction of machinery is inevitable and that the aim should not be to
destroy it but to take revolutionary political action in order to make workers
its masters, not its servants. He informs the strikers that there is, in fact, a
nationwide political network of workingmen aiming at this goal. Meanwhile, Henry Cobbett, an overseer at the factory, wants to get rid of his
embarrassing brother, whom he and his mother have repudiated, and sends
for Wible, who turns out to be an agent in the pay of the firm. Wible obtains
Ure's approval for the machine wrecking (Ure thinks it will be to his advantage as it will, from his point of view, have a favorable effect on the government), and manages to discredit Jimmy among the men on the grounds
that, being Henry's brother, he is clearly a paid agent. The men break into
the factory, and when Jimmy, having heard what they are going to do,
hurries to the weaving shed to dissuade them, Wible, who is jealous of
Jimmy, encourages the men to murder him as a traitor.

D IE *Maschinenstürmer*[1](The Machine Wreckers), written in the
winter of 1920–1921[2] and first staged in June, 1922,[3] is a
transitional play. Looking backward to *Masse-Mensch* in theme, it
points forward in method and in certain aspects of its outlook to
Hinkemann and *Hoppla!* The distinctive features of Expressionism,
if by no means completely abandoned, have here been subordinated

to a dominant realism. Toller resorts to the traditional five-act structure with a particularized and credible action taking place in a
localized setting at a definite point of time.

Gone in the form in which they existed in *Die Wandlung* and
Masse-Mensch are the distinction between *reale Bilder* and *Traumbilder*, the use of doppelgänger, of allegorical figures, of grotesque
and sensational symbolic action—but they have not disappeared
completely. Thus the scene between Ure and Jimmy Cobbett in
which Jimmy argues against capitalist exploitation and paints a picture of the socialist future (Act 4, Scene 1) is a kind of *Traumbild*, an
ideal confrontation which would be most unlikely to occur in that
form in life itself. Its special status is marked by the use of verse in
what is predominantly a prose scene and by a complete change in
Ure's manner. Further, in the last scene, the Engineer becomes
almost the symbolic embodiment of the machine itself, mocking the
men who have destroyed it.[4] Indeed, much of the machine-breaking
scene has a symbolic coloration, which is further emphasized by the
use of verse. Again, the employment of masks in the prologue[5] can
be seen as related to the devices of identification examined in the
earlier plays.

But even when there is some relationship in technique between
Die Maschinenstürmer and Toller's earlier plays, the former does
not lose touch with Naturalism. However unlikely it may be, the
symbolic action is never quite outside the bounds of probability.
The Engineer's strange behavior in the last scene, despite its obvious symbolic significance, can be viewed as a reasonably realistic
presentation of temporary insanity; the heightened style of speech
adopted by the Beggar and Old Reaper is acceptable because they
are eccentric outsiders;[6] choral speech is naturalized by confining it
to short exclamations and by the use of a theme song sung in unison
by the workers;[7] and verse, though found intermittently throughout, is always, except for the Prologue, mingled with prose.[8] Even
the use of masks in the Prologue is so obviously tacked on (one notes
that it appears to be optional) that it does not interfere with the
mode of the Prologue, which, though in verse, is essentially realistic.

This comparative realism was, of course, necessary for the recrea-
tion of a historical situation, the Luddite riots in the English Mid-
lands in the early part of the nineteenth century, which was unfamiliar to the majority of the audience. Both *Die Wandlung* and

Masse-Mensch, on the other hand, could afford to take a good deal of knowledge for granted.

Unfortunately, however, Toller's history is sadly muddled, and this not only prevents the play from having the authenticity of Gerhart Hauptmann's *Die Weber*, (The Weavers) with which it is often compared, (indeed, many critics have claimed that Toller's play is derivative)[9] but also robs it of internal coherence. Thus, although the play is set in Nottingham in 1815, the action is not about the smashing of knitting frames but of a steam engine newly introduced to power the looms, though the smashing of power looms was the objective not of the Nottinghamshire but of the Lancashire Luddites. It is not just a matter of Toller's having got hold of the wrong lot of Luddites—in itself that would, artistically speaking, be of little importance—but that the action is not coherently conceived at all. The reaction of the Luddites in the last scene is that of men who have not seen a steam engine before, men who are being forced to abandon domestic industry for work in the factories. But this is by no means the case; it is made perfectly clear in the play that a factory system has been in operation for some time, and that what is really at stake is the application of steam, already used for spinning, to weaving. Consequently, the situation was one where the steam engine was not unfamiliar, though for Toller's purposes it was essential for it to be strange and new.[10] Altogether, Toller's realism was not so exacting as to force him to have a lucid conception of the situation he was presenting.

Die Maschinenstürmer is a faulty play in other ways too. The *Traumbilder*-like speeches of Jimmy directed at Ure are a prime example of that occasional tendency toward a boring if sincere didacticism, that banal *Kanzelrede* (preaching) which Toller's critics frequently accused him of having indulged in. Ideas that might well have surprised a historical Ure but that are familiar enough to us are spelled out at inordinate length. The crudity of treatment of which this heavy didacticism is a manifestation[11] is also revealed in Toller's cultivation of a rather cheap and easy irony. Thus Henry Cobbett, extolling the future virtues of mass production, gives the following example of its social utility:

Today you have to pay the parson four shillings for a burial: a plot of earth say, two metres long and another metre broad costs six shillings. Now supposing there came a time which brought with it this joyful news: the parson is asking only two shillings for a burial: the plot of earth costs only three shillings. Wouldn't you die more peacefully in the thought that your family, instead of losing a week's wages from now on would lose only half a week's? (p. 62)

However, despite its blemishes, *Die Maschinenstürmer* is a very interesting play and one that is significantly related to *Masse-Mensch*. But this relationship is perhaps partly obscured by the existence of a subordinate historical theme which Toller presents as its leading idea. The play, according to him, was about the dawning of a modern proletarian consciousness:

The workingman as he is represented in contemporary drama is no longer the workingman of the nineteenth century. That air of "the lower depths" (N.B. a reference to a play by Gorki) so lifeless and hopeless but yet so moving is no longer his. The workingman of the nineteenth century suffered dully under the oppression of his fate: under want, exploitation, overwork, low wages. The workingman of the twentieth century has become a conscious fighter: the champion of an idea. Criticism isn't enough for him: he shapes images of the new realities which he wants to actualize. His language is influenced by editorials in party papers: he is poorer at conveying vivid impressions, but richer in polemical acuteness. Who should be surprised if he rejects on the stage those who oppress him in life too?

In *Die Maschinenstürmer* I tried to delineate the rise of this new type of workingman.[12]

Or, as he says elsewhere, "I wanted, among other things, to embody the first awakening of the people to revolutionary consciousness."[13]

The conditioning factors of the life of the early-nineteenth-century proletariat are sketched in reasonably clearly. It is—if we leave out of account the muddle I have just dealt with—a familiar picture and one that Toller borrowed from Karl Marx and Friedrich Engels,[14] his main sources. There is the oppression of the factory system with its long and exhausting hours, its bullying overseers, its long list of fines and punishments, its exploitation of child labor. There is the poverty and squalor in which the workers live and in which any kind of family life is impossible. There is the oppression of the state, which, as protector of the interests of the manufacturing classes, suppresses not only machine breaking but also strikes in support of higher wages.

Through the impact of the factory system the proletariat are shown as developing a consciousness which prompts them to rebel against their condition and makes them capable of imaginatively responding to a call for genuine revolution. It is, however, something for which they are not really ready. They are capable of taking meaningful collective action, of initiating a strike against the new steam engine, for example, but their actions are vitiated by two considerations: they do not identify clearly the nature of what oppresses them and, consequently, do not appropriately react to it, while that very oppression breeds a hatred, enmity, and suspicion which drive them to acts that give them a temporary emotional satisfaction but that undermine their cause. Their fury, which is frequently expressed in impotent fantasy and ritual, is actually directed against their fellow workers, not only strikebreakers, but even someone like Jimmy, the new socially conscious type of workingman, whom, as an outsider, they can easily be made to think a traitor (not that the fear of traitors is without justification. John Wible is one, though there is more to be said about him).

When the furious resentment of the workers is joined to a faulty analysis of the situation it naturally leads to destruction and murder, to the breaking of the engines, and to killing Jimmy. Not that they are simply mistaken in seeing the engine as the enemy; the matter is more complicated than that. As Ernst Niekisch, with whom Toller, when in prison, discussed the play, says:

He was clear in his own mind that the machine wrecking was, objectively speaking, an attempt to halt technological progress. It cannot be denied, however, that the uprising, subjectively speaking, had a truly revolutionary dynamic. It was this that fascinated him. Couldn't the machine initially be taken as the symbol of the enslaving might of capitalism? Then machine wrecking could be seen as a genuine forerunner of revolution which set itself against capitalist oppression and the destruction of all human values.[15]

In rebelling against the machine the men are really rebelling against the system that uses it to oppress them. Their feelings have been transferred to the machine which is credited with an anthropomorphic malignity ("In my play, too, the machine has more than a material significance. It is a devil, a demon.") Jimmy Cobbett does not have the same reaction: he sees the possibilities of the machine in a different form of society but understands how his fellow workers regard it: "The machine appears like a God to you, a demon, whose cursed hands clutch the human soul" (pp. 42–43). Toller makes quite clear the element of displaced feeling that characterizes this attitude by having the children, who have been taught to put the machine in a different context, look at it in quite another way. To them "It shines like gold" (p. 59), for the parson has told them that "the angels brought it to earth" (p. 59).

So the men, in destroying the engine, are not threatening the capitalist society which uses it as an agent of oppression. Far from it. We know already from the Prologue that machine breaking is a punishable offense and will serve only to bring down the might of the state on the Luddites. Indeed, by a final irony, the decision to destroy the engine is made by the treacherous John Wible with the connivance of Ure, for Ure positively welcomes such a course of action for his own ends:

I am not afraid of machine wrecking. On the contrary. At a time like the present, a machine wrecking could strengthen our position. That would at last open the eyes of this feeble government. (p. 52)

Toller embodies his reading of the situation very effectively in the last, symbolic, scene of the play. When the men first come into the factory to break the machine they are struck with wonder:

The throng catch sight of the machine. Overcome by the marvel of the machine they stand amazed. Sudden stillness.
Ned Lud: So the mills of God may grind. (pp. 104–105)

The fascination here with the machine, the Luddites' sense of its supernatural power, arises from the false isolation in which they see it.

The Engineer defends the machine on what appear to be reasonable grounds:

> Was wollt ihr tun?
> Der guten Vorsehung einfältig trotzen?
> Wie Sklaven tratet ihr den Webstuhl, und harte Fron
> Verkrümmte eure Leiber. Maschine ist Erlösung! (p. 106)

(What do you want to do? Foolishly defy a beneficent Providence? You treadled your looms like slaves and hard toil made your bodies crooked. Machine is redemption.)

But, of course, he is only partly right, and his view is the counter-part of the men's. The machine is not in itself the salvation he promises. In an oppressive society it will be an agent of oppres-sion[16]—and, significantly, the Engineer is in Ure's employ. Thus, as things are, the men are right to see the machine as accentuating their misery. That is why, when the Engineer in a triumphant dem-onstration sets the machine in motion, it "starts up with a sound like a human sigh" (p. 106).

Just as the men see the machine in isolation, so they see the pre-industrial period in isolation, not realizing that it merely repre-sents an earlier stage in capitalist organization:

> *Edward:* We were free men.
> *William:* We were masters at the looms.
> *Albert:* We wove the flowers of God into the work of our hands. (p. 107)

Ironically, when Ned Lud goes to destroy the machine he only succeeds in starting it—a symbolic embodiment of the futility of the whole enterprise:

Ned Lud strikes and hits the starting lever of the machine. The machine starts up. The looms begin to weave. (p. 110)

That Arthur should be killed by the machine is a sign of the gap between what the machine is and what it appears to be:

Arthur hacks at the steam engine. The fly wheel seizes him. (p. 110)

Arthur is killed because the machine is a mere thing without sense and discrimination, but it appears to the men to be an act of malig-nancy with profound symbolic implications:

Edward: The enemy of Man has dashed him to pieces.
Ned Lud: The enemy of Man has drawn him to himself. (p. 111)

Toller uses the pathetic fallacy to underline the destructive futil-ity of the act. A storm symbolizes the self-destructive forces which the men have let loose and of which they are again to become the victims when they murder Jimmy:

*Outside a wild tempest has arisen and continues for the rest of the act. The
storm slams the doors shut. The lamps are extinguished.* (p. 111)

The essential failure of their purpose is brilliantly evoked by the
Engineer who seems, in imitating the sound of the engine, to incar-
nate it. He perceives that the men have not destroyed the machine
but that the order for which it stands has triumphed and will continue to triumph:

Hihuhaha . . .
Ich aber sage euch, die Maschine ist nicht tot . . .
Sie lebt! sie lebt! Ausstreckt sie die Pranken,
Menschen umklammernd . . . krallend die zackigen Finger
Ins blutende Herz . . . Hihuhaha . . . hihuhaha . . .
Gen die unfriedeten Dörfer wälzen sich stampfende Heere . . . (p. 112)

(Hihuhaha . . .
But I tell you, the machine is not dead
It lives, it lives . . . it stretches out its claws
And seizes men: tearing into the bleeding heart
With its jagged fingers. Hihuhaha . . . hihuhaha.
Against the peaceful villages roll on the trampling armies.)

He realizes: "Und die Seele, die Seele . . . ist tot" (p. 112) (And the
soul, the soul, is dead). The Engineer, in incarnating and, in triumphant mockery, praising the destructive power of the machine while
realizing and regretting the human cost, can be said to have gone
mad, to be suffering from schizophrenia. His madness defines that
which has come over the men and has led them to destroy the steam
engine. Toller uses darkness, confused movement, and mode of
utterance in a very effective thematic manner:

*Confusion. An attempt is made to seize the Engineer. Worker collides with
worker in the darkness. The Engineer runs hither and thither. Confusion
worse confounded. Speakers in rapid succession.* (p. 113)

The Engineer, whom they are trying to kill, mocks them like a will o'
the wisp from here, there, and everywhere, "vorne" (from the
front), "aus dem Hintergrund" (from the back), "von oben" (from
above), "wie aus der Ferne" (as from a distance). In the confusion,
one of the workers is killed by mistake in lieu of the Engineer and
the Engineer hangs himself:

Georges: Am Fenster hängt ein Mensch . . .
Charles: Der Ingenieur!
Albert: Der Tod. (p. 115)

(A man is hanging at the window. The engineer. Death.)

Toller's use of theatrical resources to embody his theme is very impressive. The men can destroy this machine but they cannot destroy machinery as such—the futility of their attempt to do so being suggested by the mocking evasions of the Engineer and by their own compulsive behavior which manifests *(Schlag auf Schlag)* (Stroke on stroke i.e. in rapid succession) the rhythms of the machine and leads them, like the machine, to start destroying one another. The Engineer's suicide is interpreted as Death because it is the visible embodiment of the destructive power of machinery in a capitalist society. But the Engineer is not a mere symbol, he is a man whose humanity has been outraged and desolated by the very prospect of the triumph of the machine he seemed to celebrate. In a capitalist society, the humanity of exploiters and exploited alike is outraged. It is a society dedicated to madness and death. All this loads with meaning the supreme madness of the murder of Jimmy at the end of the play. Under the tremendous pressures of this early phase of capitalism, men, though glimpsing the possibility of true revolution, in fact rebel blindly.

Jimmy Cobbett is quite different from the rest. He is the really new kind of workingman who has grasped the nature of the whole social process. Aware both of human need and human potentiality, he sees that the only way for them to be realized is through proletarian revolution: "Ich will die Revolution" (I want revolution) (p. 55). But though Jimmy perceives what the goal should be, he seriously underestimates the difficulty of reaching it. Overestimating the development of consciousness in his fellow workers, he feels that the country is ripe for revolution: "We will lead a struggle, old friend, a mighty struggle. The workers have woken up: they are on the march (p. 31)."

This insight is associated with a sentimentalization of the working class, which prevents him from understanding that his revolutionary eloquence, though it may fire the workers, has no permanent hold on them, particularly since, though a workingman himself (but one who is educated and without family responsibilities), he is an outsider in this community. Jimmy is very much an isolated figure. The other workers, with the exception of John Wible, even at their most enlightened have only a limited awareness. Thus Ned Lud, the most intelligent among them and the most sympathetic to what Jimmy has to say, essentially sees himself as maintaining a traditional (and idealized) set of rights rather than working for revolution:

Every man is born free and has the right to a trade: an inviolable, God-given right. (p. 22)

Consequently, though, like the others, he can be fired by Jimmy's vision, his allegiance to it is uncertain and subject to corruption. He, too, can be persuaded to believe that Jimmy is a traitor, and even strikes the first blow.

The weakness of Jimmy's position is made explicit by the Beggar, who, finding him writing a pamphlet, and realizing, as Jimmy does not, the temporary effect of rhetoric on more traditional ways of thinking and feeling, says: "Pamphlets are like shifting sand. When they move they stop up eyes and ears, but they make no impression on the heart (p. 93)." It is the Beggar too who diagnoses Jimmy's sentimentalization of the proletariat:

Do *all* men keep their word? Are all men brave, upright, loyal, selfless? No. Why should all workmen be like that? Because they are "the workers"? It seems to me that you see them as you want to see them. You have made new gods for yourself: they are called "holy workers": pure Gods, loyal Gods . . . perfect Gods—English workmen of 1815. You dreamer! My dear fellow: to fight in alliance with Gods spells victory—as certainly as an apple blossom spells an apple. (p. 94)

Even the victory of the working class will not necessarily mean justice:

Jimmy: The victory of the worker will be the
            victory of justice.
Beggar: I have experience of three governments.
            All governments deceive the people: some
            more, others less. Those who deceive them
            less are called good governments. (p. 94)

The Beggar even suggests to Jimmy that he himself may be corrupted by a love of power: "Jimmy, you are a well-read worker, an aristocrat: all aristocrats want to govern" (p. 95). Toller does not necessarily mean us to endorse the Beggar's last accusation completely, but he does want us to see that there might be some truth in it.

But it is not I think, merely that Toller wants us to see that there is a certain miscalculation about means in Jimmy: there is something sentimental about Jimmy's whole conception of revolution. Jimmy's rhetoric has a suspicious facility; the speech he addresses to the workers recalls, and is meant to recall, but now in a critical spirit, the tone of Friedrich at the end of *Die Wandlung* (even the instant conviction of the listeners, though in this case temporary, is an ironic reworking of the *Die Wandlung* situation). Jimmy speaks too emotionally, too lyrically:

And yet a dream lives in you! A dream of the land of wonder: a dream of the land of justice . . . of the land of communities bound together in work . . . of the land of creative joyful labor. (p. 44)

while again, reminiscent of Friedrich in *Die Wandlung*, he seems to believe that the workers have only to will revolution for it to occur. He does not, in other words, appreciate how they have been formed by their environment:

An enemy lives in you. He holds your souls in his grip. He breathes in your blood. He has made your spirit rigid and torpid. (p. 43)

So far I have been treating the play as if it were what it claims to be, merely an evocation of a historical consciousness. But as my bringing *Die Wandlung* into the discussion and certain of my formulations have clearly implied, it is not just that. Toller makes all kinds of connections between the situation of the Luddites and the contemporary situation, though not in any crude manner.

First, and most obviously, the characters are made to prophesy a future which is like our present:

The old factories are no longer capable of supplying the needs of the people: new factories, mighty factories, gigantic factories will open their doors to those without bread. England has not anywhere near so many without bread as these gigantic throats of factories will swallow down, swallow down in great mouthfuls. (p. 62)

And in the Engineer's speech, quoted above, he is obviously talking about the use of technology in modern warfare.

But Toller has more subtle means of making the connections. It is quite clear, for example, that he is drawing an implied parallel between World War One and the Napoleonic Wars: "Europe has been bankrupt since the great war" (pp. 62–63). Ure puts his trust in "*Ruhe und Ordnung*" (Law and Order), the watchwords of those who suppressed the German revolution. Jimmy is spoken of as "a foreign agitator" (p. 5), an accusation frequently levelled at the Bavarian revolutionaries, and "ein Kommunist" (p. 51).

To take these two last points further, the strongest connections are made through Jimmy Cobbett himself. He is a just conceivable historical figure, as recent research has shown,[17] there was a real revolutionary element in Luddism (not that Toller would have known this) but Jimmy fits much more clearly into a modern revolutionary context. His exposé of the nature of capitalist production is essentially modern because his formulations outrun the experience that would have been historically available to him. That, for instance, capitalist production is wasteful and does not effectively supply human needs; that it is associated with imperalist oppression; that it involves a denial of humanity even in those who appear to benefit from it—all these are essentially later ideas.

When it is appreciated that Jimmy Cobbett is meant to be a modern revolutionary rather than a verisimilar historical figure (though Toller means him to have some historical validity), the role of John Wible becomes clearer. John Wible is not just the villain of the piece; related to *der Kommis* the clerk (who was a Communist) in *Die Wandlung*, he, like Jimmy, has a revolutionary point of view, but a revolutionary such as Wible would be even less conceivable in 1815 than a Jimmy Cobbett. His attitude involves a complete unscrupulousness about means (which gets confused with the rationalizations of treachery, as with many Communists) and is motivated by hatred, though Toller, in stressing that Wible has been made a hunchback through the drunken cruelty of his father, shows that he too may be considered a victim of his environment. The differences between Jimmy and Wible emerge in open argument. Wible argues, like Brecht in *Die Massnahme*, (The Measures Taken) that it is necessary for the working class to become increasingly wretched in order that a revolutionary consciousness may be engendered in them:[18]

We need defeats. Only abject misery creates rebels. Make them well fed, give them Schnapps, they will repay you by farting on their knowledge, and by wallowing in the troughs like over-fed pigs. They must be stirred up like wild animals. Blood is the whip which will drive them out of their apathetic sleep. (pp. 54–55)

Jimmy sees the fallacy of this kind of reasoning and the destructive hatred which animates it:

How contemptuously you speak of the workers whom you want to liberate! How your eyes glow in spiteful malice! One would think that you did not want to liberate the workingman, but to avenge yourself, yes yourself. Want creates rebels, but let want grow until it is a noose that strangles everyone, so that nobody knows where to get a slice of bread or where to lay his head at night . . . Do you believe that men would then still be rebels? Ask from them solidarity, loyalty, readiness for sacrifice, devotion, renunciation of their own interests, renunciation of their wages: they will laugh at you. (pp. 54–55)

In Jimmy's speech at the end of the play his roles as a historical and contemporary revolutionary are fused:

O Brüder, wenn die Schaffenden von England
Abtrünnig werden ihrer heiligen Sendung . . .
Die Schaffenden des Kontinents, die Schaffenden der Erde . . .
Sich nicht zur grossen Menschheitstat vereinen . . .
Aufrichten Weltgemeinschaft allen Werkvolks . . .
Den Menschheitsbund der freien Völker . . .
Dann, Brüder, bleibt ihr Knechte bis ans Ende aller Tage! (p. 117)

(Oh, brothers: if the workers of England are faithless to their sacred mission, if the workers of the continent, the workers of the earth, do not join together in the great task of humanity, bring into being a world association of all workingmen, the union of all free peoples, then, comrades, you will remain slaves until the end of time.)

Jimmy understands what they have done:

O Kameraden . . . Freie dünket ihr mich und waret Knechte! . .
und eure Tat ist Tat des Knechtes,
Der sich auflehnt. (p. 117)

(Oh, comrades, you seemed to me to be free and were slaves, and your
deed is the deed of insurgent slaves.)

These words are meant to apply not only to the situation depicted in
the play but to that of the working classes of twentieth Century
Western Europe as well, who had constantly betrayed the hope of
revolution. In 1914, for example, the Socialist parties of Germany,
France, and Britain had supported their respective governments at
the outbreak of war. And in so doing, had reneged on a pre-war
decision of the Second International, to which they were parties, to
refuse to support national wars in the interests of working class
solidarity. Further, the German revolution of 1918–1919 had been
aborted because, in Toller's view, the German working class had not
been seriously enough committed to their own ostensibly revolutionary beliefs. These references to contemporary events are not
explicit, but are a kind of shadow cast by Jimmy's words, as Jimmy's
murder seems intended to recall, however obliquely, that of Karl
Liebknecht and Rosa Luxemburg.

But why should Toller use the past in this way to talk about the
present, even when it involved some distortion of credibility? Had
his task been really to concentrate on evoking the development of
the proletarian consciousness, he would, like Hauptmann in *Die
Weber*, have been much more realistic and objective. He does so, I
think, not only to stress a continuity of failure in the achievement of
social change, but also as a way of making tactfully and acceptably an
even more pessimistic reading of the situation than had been found
in *Masse-Mensch*.

Thus the element of optimistic self-deception in the hopeful revolutionary can be both emphasized and distanced by identifying him
with a prototype placed in a situation where we know, as a matter of
historical fact, that revolution did not occur. Similarly, by presenting the failure of the proletariat at a particular moment in time,
Toller is able to present their contemporary failure seen as continuous with it, in terms that are harsh without being too particular. The
historical machine wreckers can be forgiven for their mistakes, since
the pressure of circumstances on them was so great, but there is—
and this is where he is more pessimistic than in *Masse-Mensch*—in
the modern proletariat, who are quite capable of behaving like their
historical progenitors but without their justification, an element of
willful blindness and stupidity which is not forced on them by cir-

cumstances. Like the Luddites, Toller seems to be saying, the modern proletariat is capable of resorting to violence which is not rationally defensible in the cause of revolution as it was in *Masse-Mensch* and which serves no purpose, for the meaning of revolution has been forgotten. Like the Luddites, the modern proletariat is capable of the betrayal and murder of their trusted leaders. Toller is clearly afraid that the workers will follow false gods altogether; a feeling that clearly informs his next play, *Hinkemann*.

Toller was, of course, quite explicit about the lesson he wanted drawn:

Are the enlightened masses of the twentieth century any more reliable than the ignorant ones of the nineteenth century? How easily, even today, the masses allow themselves to be swayed this way and that by moods, promises, hopes of some new advantage. Today they hail their leader: tomorrow they condemn him: today they stand to their task: tomorrow they abandon it: how easy it is for crude demagogues to stir them up to acts of blind passion. I have come to see the social basis of this spiritual instability: desperate daily need, which undermines strength, the dependence of men on the labor market, on the machine. Knowledge is forgotten, experience is forgotten: the road of the people is a difficult one: it is not his opponents who give him the deepest wounds, he gives them to himself. (*Prosa*, p. 177).

But the pattern of feeling is not the same as in, say, George Gissing's *Demos*: revolution is not abandoned as undesirable and impossible, merely as that much more difficult. As the Beggar says to Jimmy even at the moment when he is exposing his illusions: "Wake up, realize that you are fighting alongside ordinary natures: some strong, some weak, some greedy, some selfless, some petty, some magnanimous, and make the attempt nonetheless" (p. 94). Toller had come a long way from *Die Wandlung*.

Jimmy's last speech in which he looks forward to a future that has not yet arrived, does not regard the failure of the proletariat as immutable. As Ned Lud says: "Others will come, more aware, firmer in their belief, more courageous than us" (p. 121). The situation can change. The play is a challenge, not a lament.

Further, it is clear from Old Reaper's last speech that Toller wants to point to that growth of consciousness that he hopes the play will effect. For even the crimes and mistakes of the past, near and remote, can assist in the process of growth if seen in their true light. The ending has, indeed, a clear resemblance to that of *Masse-Mensch*, though the idea of growth is not so clear-cut. Jimmy, after all, did not sacrifice himself, as did Sonja when she refused to escape; he is much more clearly a victim. However, in the closing speech of Old Reaper, Jimmy, like Friedrich before him, is associated with Christ, and his death with the crucifixion. Though Jimmy dies apparently in vain, his death contributes to man's ultimate redemption. And we see the spiritual effect of Jimmy's death on Old Reaper himself: half-crazed with a sense of divine injustice as he has been presented in the play, he begins with unconscious irony by looking on Jimmy's death, as do the workers who had murdered him, as a positive release: God is dead at last:

The children do not need to be afraid any more, want is at an end . . . I have shot the son of God. His burial must be taken care of. To the church-yard? To the knacker's yard with him! (p. 123)

But in the very process of contemplating Jimmy's dead body, his apprehension and feeling change: he is won over to tenderness and understanding. His madness has been healed:

And I shall ask the heavenly Father, and he shall give you another comforter, even the spirit of truth, which the world cannot accept, for it sees it not and it knows it not. Ah you poor dear God . . . His burial must be taken care of. We must help and be good to one another. (p. 389)

Despite its considerable interest, the play leaves an unsatisfactory impression. Some of its faults I outlined at the beginning; there is also the relation to Hauptmann's *Die Weber*, which is rather too close for comfort. Indeed, a comparison of *Die Maschinenstürmer* with Hauptmann's play shows that Toller, in order to give a contemporary meaning to a historical situation, has been involved in distortion in which full justice is done neither to the past nor the present.

CHAPTER 5

Hinkemann

Hinkemann, emasculated in the war, is obsessed by the fear that he will be laughed at. His marriage is under a strain, and his wife, unbeknown to him, is seduced by a mutual friend, Paul Grosshahn. Hinkemann, meanwhile, obtains a highly paid but distasteful job in a fairground which involves biting the throats and sucking the blood of living rats and mice. He does not tell his wife, Grete, about his work, so, when one day, unexpectedly, Grete and Paul see and recognize him in the fairground Grete is ashamed and quarrels with Grosshahn who, having laughed at him maliciously, subsequently pretends to Hinkemann that Grete has done so too. Hinkemann not only loses all confidence in his wife but all desire to live as he has a nightmare vision of what society is really like. Grete tries to reassure him but commits suicide in despair. The play bears a conscious resemblance to Georg Büchner's *Woyzeck*.

T HE disturbances, organized by the Nationalists, that accompanied the performances of *Hinkemann* in Dresden and Vienna early in 1924,[1] as well as being an ironic confirmation of the theme of what is probably Toller's most pessimistic play, were perhaps also an indication of a new departure for the playwright. Set in 1921, it is the first play of Toller's to deal specifically with the postwar world, in which revolution was a virtual impossibility and which was, in his view, sliding downhill toward catastrophe. It is a play which in the nature of its vision of the postwar world invites comparison with British and American writers of the 1920s—with the T.S. Eliot of *The Waste Land* and *The Hollow Men*; the D.H. Lawrence of *St. Mawr*, with Aldous Huxley, Evelyn Waugh, and Ernest Hemingway. Moreover, its central character, Hinkemann, like Sir Clifford Chatterley, or Jake in Ernest Hemingway's *The Sun Also Rises*, has been emasculated in the war.

If we compare *Hinkemann* with Toller's plays which precede it we

97

can observe certain significant shifts in structure and dramatic technique, although there are equally significant continuities. Thus the first two plays involve a situation in which the protagonist is an outsider who attempts to enlighten and control the proletariat: in *Die Wandlung* (Transfiguration) and *Masse-Mensch* (Masses and Man) the outsider is himself middle-class in origin while in *Die Maschinenstürmer* (The Machine Wreckers) he is, though a working man, a "superior" one, who comes from outside the community. In *Die Wandlung*, the protagonist succeeds in asserting control over the proletariat, in *Masse-Mensch* she is controlled by it, and in *Die Maschinenstürmer* the proletariat destroys the protagonist. However, Hinkemann, (and that is part of the meaning of the play), feels alienated from the life around him and is not an active member of any group. Again, though in *Hinkemann* the pattern of transformation, of the growth of consciousness of a central figure, is still present, it is complicated; for whereas in *Die Wandlung* and *Masse-Mensch* the development of the protagonist arises primarily from an identification with the sufferings of others, in *Hinkemann* he arrives at a just insight into the nature of contemporary society because of his own personal sufferings. Furthermore, it is not just one character, Hinkemann, who undergoes transformation, but his wife Grete, too; and it is a transformation that does not lead to a successful call to revolution, to public execution, or even to open murder, but in her case to suicide.[2] It is significant that, at the end of the play, there is no one left on the stage for Hinkemann to talk to: his speech is delivered directly to the audience. All these contrasts with previous plays are a function of *Hinkemann*'s greater pessimism, still to be examined.

In terms of theatrical technique there are again similarities and contrasts. For example, in *Hinkemann* Toller develops—though only for use in certain scenes—a more profound realism, which is indicated in the first words of the play: "Hat Mutter dir Kohlen gegeben?" (p. 397) (Has mother given you some coal?)—a much more natural opening than that found in any of his previous plays. Particularly in the scenes between Grete and Hinkemann, a new sensitivity and complexity appears; in the first, and still more in the last, scenes of the play Toller does justice to the kaleidoscopic changes of feeling and attitude that can take place under tension even when the emotional undertow is steady and coherent. The last scene between Grete and Hinkemann is perhaps the most subtle Toller ever wrote.

The use of such psychological realism was essential for what Toller was trying to do: for in *Hinkemann* he is endeavoring to portray a man who, uneducated and perhaps not even very intelligent, has to struggle to realize the significance of his own experience and the nature of the world around him under the stress of severe personal suffering. The formulation of ideas does not come easily to him.

But besides the psychological realism, in a simpler mode of realism, found before in Toller's work, characters and incidents are exemplificatory—existing to make simple, though credible points. Hinkemann's mother, for example, is brought in only to provide a significant parallel to his own experience (Act 3, Scene 2, p. 426ff) while Fränze, who tries to seduce Hinkemann, not realizing that he has been emasculated, is a conveniently ironic illustration of a world given over to sex and violence (Act 3, Scene 2, pp. 428–429). The scene in the pub with the workers (Act 2, Scene 4) has some of this rather simpleminded, illustrative quality as well, though it operates on a more complex plane.

But the play is not wholly realistic; connections have to be made between Hinkemann and the wider world so that his experience can be used as an acceptable basis for generalization. And for this purpose Toller makes use, in a modified way, of some of the techniques he had adopted in the earlier plays. Though there is only one short passage in verse (p. 418), he still employs the techniques of the *Traumbild*, and one sequence, though its incidents are for the most part exaggerations of the possible, is reminiscent of *Die Wandlung* in its grotesque symbolism:

Enter marching from all sides in a circle one-armed and one-legged war invalids with barrel organs. They sing, unconcernedly, the following soldiers' song. (p. 421)

Nonetheless, Toller is careful to suggest an explanation of the *Traumbild*, relating it, for the first time, to a particular consciousness of which it is a projection. The war invalids, the barrel organs, and the rest of the *Traumbild* exist in Hinkemann's own mind, not in reality:

What follows must be enacted as a nightmare of Hinkemann's. All the figures seem to press in on Hinkemann and, swallowed up by the darkness, to detach themselves from him. (p. 421)

For the most part, however, Toller tries to give a symbolic dimension to action presented realistically. He does this most obviously by using the rather crude device of giving allegorical names to characters realistically conceived: *Grosshahn* (Big Cock), *Singegott* (Sing God), *Immergleich* (Indifferent) and, of course, *Hinkemann* (Hobbleman) himself. But he also does so, interestingly, by attempting to give a generalized meaning to particular incidents or items in the setting. The fair with its din, its lascivious peep shows, its appeal to sadism through Hinkemann's own turn is used as an image with wide implications. It is Hinkemann himself who says: "One has to go round and round like a merry-go-round. Round and round! Round and Round!" (p. 405).[3]

One interesting symbolic extension of the action is Hinkemann's conscious choice of a symbol of his own experience. For Hinkemann, the loveless lust of the postwar world which jeers at a eunuch like himself becomes embodied in a little statue of Priapus which he buys and around which he dances in bitter mockery. This is more effective (and more appropriate) than the insistent spelling out of perceptions that had characterized the earlier plays.

However, despite the considerable degree of success that Toller has achieved in devising a mode of symbolic expression which would be consistent with the claims of realism flexibly interpreted, he has not altogether succeeded: his comparative failure, moreover, particularly affects our view of Hinkemann's character. The trouble with Hinkemann is that the realism with which he is treated is not altogether consistent; sometimes he is an overwhelmingly real, particular man; at other times, while behaving in a way that does not contravene probability, his actions are not, by the most rigorous standards, likely and convincing. Can we believe, for instance, in the objective reality of the distasteful job he is forced to get?[4] But we lower our realistic sights because we see that in these parts Toller is trying to image something through Hinkemann which will be of general application. This flaw comes out, too, in the way in which the author succumbs to the temptation of letting Hinkemann step out of his frame and, abandoning the groping progress toward understanding, allows him to point out the moral of his own predicament in a manner that is appropriate for a much more articulate and informed person. Indeed, it is really the dramatist speaking.[5]

This uncertainty in the use of realism is perhaps not unconnected with the difficulty that has been experienced in interpreting Hinkemann's role. One widely suggested contemporary interpretation was that Hinkemann stood for postwar Germany which "despite its powerlessness to act still intoxicates itself with the language of power and with arrogant gestures."[6] Yet this view was explicitly repudiated by Toller, who changed the title of the play from *Der deutsche Hinkemann* (The German Hinkemann) to *Hinkemann* specifically to guard against it.[7] And one must agree that to see Hinkemann himself as a contemptible fake would make nonsense of the play by endorsing Grosshahn's view rather than repudiating it.

But, despite Toller's denials, there are passages in the text that would appear, at first sight, to support this interpretation. Thus the *Budenbesitzer* (The Showman) announces Hinkemann as *"The* German bear man: *the* German knockout: German power: *the* darling of fashionable women" (p. 406).

To interpret these statements too simply, however, is to lose sight of the context in which they appear, in which their absoluteness is modified by the requirements of character and situation, the requirements, that is, of realism. Thus, it could be argued, it is significant that it should be the *Budenbesitzer* in whose mouth they are placed. It is he who is connecting the brutal sadist, which Hinkemann is supposed to be, with the quality of contemporary German society. What is symbolic, in other words, is not Hinkemann himself, but the role he is supposed to be playing. But if the role forced on Hinkemann is symbolic at this point, his relationship to it is not on the same plane of symbolism at all; it is not, that is to say, a simple antithesis between appearance and reality in postwar Germany, with Hinkemann's role standing for the appearance and Hinkemann himself for the reality. It is essential to remember that Hinkemann is an individual, sympathetic, kindly, agonizingly conscious of the loss of his masculinity, and desperately in need of understanding and affection. Only in this way can we see what the function is of the contrast between role and person: the soulless and brutal world of postwar Germany needs to discover its humanity, but whereas Hinkemann knows it the world does not; and whereas Hinkemann can't do anything about it, the world can. In its symbolic extension Hinkemann's emasculation stands not for inadequacy but for human need.[8]

Similarly, our apprehension of the meaning of the second quotation must be modified by the context in which it appears, though here the case is simple. Hinkemann is talking to Grete:

It's my own fault I have become ridiculous. I should have looked after myself when the mine was lighted by the world's great criminals called statesmen and generals, but I did not do so. I am ridiculous like this age. As sadly ridiculous as this age. (p. 432)

We are not meant to take Hinkemann's words as straightforward exposition: he is savagely exaggerating his own responsibility and bitterly equating his own need with the callousness and brutality of the time.

I have said before that *Hinkemann* was the most pessimistic play Toller ever wrote. So pessimistic is it, in fact, that it is not surprising to find him writing to a friend "the politician in me says you are not doing right in letting *Hinkemann* be performed."[9] The first and most obvious sign of this pessimism is that one of the themes of the play, and one which Toller specifically emphasized, as mentioned in Chapter 1, is that "There are men to whom no state, no society, no family and no community can bring happiness" (p. 418), and, to make matters worse, it is sheer chance who they shall be: "It strikes by chance. It strikes this person and that one. This one and that one it does not strike" (p. 435).

This theme is particularly stressed in the scene in the public house where Hinkemann questions Max Knatsch and Michael Unbeschwert, both of them politically active men. At first he asks, circling round his own case, what the fate of cripples would be in a socialist society. Unbeschwert replies:

Naturally they will be fed, clothed and kept by society, and they will be able to live just as happily as other men. (p. 413)

Then Hinkemann inquires about the mentally ill. Unbeschwert's reply is even less convincing:

They will go into an asylum: but not into the kind of asylum where warders think they have a beast in their charge. (p. 413)

Hinkemann then comes around to his own case:

Now if someone . . . who was in the war (swallowing) for example . . . for example, had his sex . . . his sex shot away . . . what . . . what would happen to him in the new society? (pp. 413–4).

But Unbeschwert, who has at least tried to give an honest answer to his previous questions, has no answer to this one; it is left to Max Knatsch to answer in an unfeeling and doctrinaire manner:

The men to whom such a thing happens are just victims. The proletariat has a right to sacrifices. (p. 414)

No wonder Toller described *Hinkemann* to Ernst Niekisch, his fellow-revolutionary, as "a work that will only be understood after the victory of Socialism."[10] Some suffering arose from the human condition itself and not even a perfect society could abolish it.

Hinkemann, too, seems to mark a change in emphasis, which, though it should give ground for optimism, is decidedly pessimistic in its implications. In *Masse-Mensch,* in particular, Toller had seemed at times to be close to social determinism, the revolutionary working class being presented as virtually compelled to act in certain ways because of the nature of the situation that it faced and its own previous experience. In *Hinkemann,* however, the stress is on freedom of action, on the ability of a society to choose what it wants to be. Hinkemann states this in an extreme form in his closing speech, which obviously (perhaps too obviously) carries the message of the play: "Each day can bring Paradise, each night the Flood" (p. 435). People could be different from what they are by willing it: "Und könnten anders sein, wenn sie wollten" (p. 434). But if this is so, they must be blamed for what they do: ("But they don't want to. They cast stones at the spirit: they mock it: they profane life: they crucify it" (p. 434) or, more explicitly and more particularly addressed to the working class:

How you will have to change in order to build a new society! You fight the bourgeoisie and are full of its arrogance, its self-righteousness, its sloth of heart. (p. 418)

Such a view implies a revaluation of the past and bitter prognostications for the future. For if people are seen as freer agents than Toller had seen them in *Masse-Mensch,* not only were they more obviously responsible for their behavior in the past, but are also responsible for their behavior in the future, which will require a change of heart: "They will suffer again, and hate their rulers again, and obey again and murder again" (p. 434). Toller obviously satirizes

Unbeschwert's belief that circumstances themselves will usher in Socialism without a change of feeling:

Already there is a groaning and a cracking: rifts can be seen opening in the walls: already the knees are knocking of those whose bad consciences make them sleepless, already their teeth can be heard chattering in their pale faces. Light is dawning, comrades. (p. 411)

It is this realization that seems to force on Toller a revaluation of what happened in the revolution, making him fear an aggressive nationalism which would show that the lessons of the war have not been learned. Clearly this is the meaning of the *Traumbild* where the cripples with their barrel organs mime, in sequence, first the war itself:

Suddenly they come to a halt. One after another, in quick succession, they cry it's my pitch. *Not one of them shows any sign of going in another direction. They all yell together:* it's my pitch. (p. 422)

The the revolution seen merely as a continuation of the war-spirit in a purely self-destructive form:

Silence for several seconds. Then, since no-one gives way, as if at a word of command, they all start moving forward again, playing and marching, against one another. As if, fired by revolutionary ardor, they wanted to storm a barricade of reaction, they sing the following song, turning the barrel organ like mad:

> Down with the dogs, down with the dogs,
> Down with the dogs of reaction. (p. 421)

and, finally after the suppression of the revolution a mindlessly aggressive nationalism:

The barrel organs crash together with an awful din. Thrown back by the rebound, the men march on one another again. Some policemen come running. The shouts of the policemen can be heard:

> Law and Order!
> Officers of the State!
> Old soldiers!

*A sudden stillness falls, as if a well-known sound commanding silence had
reached the ears of the invalids. There is a military about turn. The invalids
march away stiffly in different directions but always at the same radius*
(from the center). *All the time playing on and singing in a military manner:*
All-conquering we'll beat the French . . . (p. 422)

To see the revolution not as representing a change of feeling on
which society has turned its back, but merely as a change in the
form of aggressiveness, and as leading to renewed nationalism, is a
view that for Toller was the apogee of pessimism. Unfortunately it
was to prove only too true. What Toller could see more clearly in
this play—and this note he strikes for the first time—was the ease
with which the idea of social determinism could be used to justify
practically anything. Paul Grosshahn, perhaps the most detest-
able character he ever created illustrates its dangers most
clearly,[11]—Grosshahn, who laughs at Hinkemann's disability, who
seduces his wife through blandishment and threat, who scoffs at
Hinkemann when he discovers him at the fair, who torments him
with the lie that Grete had laughed at him, who, when Hinkemann
generously offers his wife to him, says that she was only after her
pleasure, and if he doesn't satisfy her he'll let her be a prostitute;
Grosshahn who, as a final act of callousness, exposes Hinkemann to
the mockery of his fellow workers in the public house.
Yet the irony of the matter is that Grosshahn is a verbal
revolutionary, one who is sometimes made to speak in a way that
recalls Toller's enlightened protagonists:

Poor people are worse off than cattle: they at least are fattened and driven to
pasture, and only when they are fat enough, when they are nicely covered
in fat, are they slaughtered. (pp. 399–400)

But those sentiments are used by Grosshahn to justify his callous
womanizing which, in treating women as exploitable objects, is the
equivalent, on the level of intimate personal relations, of the
capitalist system whose oppression he has evoked:

He sells his labor, as a gallon of gasoline is sold, and belongs to the entre-
preneur, to the head of the business. He becomes, so to speak, a hammer,
or a chair, or a steam lever, or a fountain pen, or he becomes an iron. It's
quite true. What's the only pleasure he's got left? Love! (p. 401)

Grosshahn's use of *Liebe*—so richly ambiguous a word—recalls that of the bankers in *Masse-Mensch*. It is not for nothing that Toller hints that a man like Grosshahn is a Nazi at heart, for when he puts a coin in the juke box the latter *"bawls, stutters and drums out a military march"* (p. 416).

Nor is this mode of reasoning limited to Grosshahn. Unbeschwert, who is a much more decent man, says, as a way of escaping from his own responsibility for laughing at Hinkemann: "It's the fault of this lousy world we live in" (p. 419), while one of the signs that Grosshahn has corrupted Grete is that she says as an excuse for her own betrayal: "I'm only a poor woman and life is so complicated" (p. 404).

Even when the views expressed lack this element of rationalization, Toller shows that too many utterances are mere words which can easily go with an unregenerate heart. Unbeschwert, for instance, has the dangerous fluency of a platform orator mouthing sentiments that, though hypocrisy is not in question, he does not really feel: *"With the pathos of the platform orator:* Out of the womb of the historical development of circumstances the new order of society will be born" (p. 411). We have already seen his inability to face the problem with which Hinkemann presents him and the easy way in which he predicts the inevitability of revolution. Then there is the *Schieferdecker's* (slater's) insistence on his status in relation to the *Ziegeldecker* (tiler), even though, finally, he claims to believe in a classless society:

I don't care if there is revolution a hundred times over. No revolution can alter the fact that a painter and decorator is better than a whitewasher, a printer of books than a printer of wallpaper; a newspaper compositor than a timetable compositor; a coppersmith than a tinker; a lordly chauffeur rather better than a common carter. We remain slaters and you tilers. (p. 410)

Indeed, the existence of political factions in the working class shows how little there is of the true revolutionary feeling. Max Knatsch, for example, in many ways the best of the bunch, can be referred to by Unbeschwert as one of "those radical messengers and fanatics from the East who want to replace faith by science" (p. 412).

Yet Toller is far from discrediting revolutionary sentiments. Hinkemann himself has them, but in his case they come from the heart and contrast with the bad faith or, at least, the superficial fluency of those around him. This is revealed not only in the question he asks Unbeschwert, but in the way in which, before he has been tragically enlightened, he takes the dross of Unbeschwert's rhetoric for pure gold. To Hinkemann it really means what it says:

Much of what you say is dead right . . . you have spoken exactly what I was thinking . . . that about the woolen shirts and the silk shirts . . . Man is not good if he is hungry. (p. 412)

And it is Hinkemann who reveals that questing openness before life that the others so conspicuously lack:

Life is so odd . . . So much presses in on you which you don't understand, don't get hold of—and are even frightened of . . . You see absolutely no meaning . . . you ask yourself whether life can be really understood. (p. 413)

Despite the insistence in *Hinkemann* on responsibility and choice, Toller does not go to the opposite extreme. He does, of course, still emphasize the conditioning factors that predispose people to act in certain ways. And it is clear, for example, that Max Knatsch's formulations, apparently so near to those of Hinkemann in his closing speech, are meant to be understood as too extreme in their assertion of voluntarism, an upside down mirror image of Unbeschwert's insistence on revolutionary inevitability: "If men have no will to revolution, all your 'circumstances' are of no help, and if men have the will to revolution, they can begin a new life no matter what the circumstances" (p. 412), particularly since it is Knatsch himself who realizes the significant effect of circumstances in his own life (he doesn't use it as an excuse; he knows that he doesn't have to behave in this manner):

When I see the kitchen at home, which is our parlor and our living room, our washroom and our drying room, when I see the miserable children . . . when I think about my wife and her perpetual nagging, then I turn back on the staircase and go my own way of salvation. (p. 411)

Similarly, though nothing compels Grete, the quality of her whole life makes it more likely that she will succumb to Grosshahn's blandishments. She is more open to them because of the very frustration that her life involves:

It's surely only a dream . . . like a fairy tale . . . A working class girl finds
out at home what is in store for her. If all goes well, a life of hard work until
you're old and have to rely on the children. If it goes badly, quarrels, fights,
beatings. (p. 407)

And, of course, the proletarian may be forced to serve a function
that he himself loathes, just as Hinkemann is compelled by
economic circumstances to take a job where he has to suppress all
his normal feelings and pander to the bloodlust he hates. And once
in it, he cannot get out of it; the full weight of capitalist society is
behind the *Budenbesitzer's* (the showman's) threat of legal proceedings:

I'll call in the police to force you to work, man. Contract, man, the basis of
bourgeois society, man. You're threatening the most cherished values of the
nation, man: I have behind me the power of the state, man. (p. 421)

The view of society that is presented in *Hinkemann* needs to be
stated rather more fully. It is in the *Traumbild* and the scenes
between Hinkemann and the *Budenbesitzer* that the explicit terms
of the diagnosis are given. This is a society—and it is clear that
Toller is thinking of Western society as a whole—that has no moral
center. It is characterized by a selfish unfeelingness which affects all
but the best even when they think they are presenting a fundamental challenge to it, and in the majority involves a search for sensation
and a turning to loveless sex, and to cruelty, vicarious if not direct,
to obtain it. Society has a restless, destructive energy that Toller
sees as intimately linked to its capitalist structure:

You've got to achieve something. Achievement. That is the key to our time.
It doesn't matter what. A champion boxer; a popular leader; a currency
swindler; the director of a speculative bank; a cyclist in the six-day race; a
fake general; a ballroom dancer; a cabinet minister; an agitator for national
vengeance; a champagne manufacturer; a prophet; a leading tenor; a half-
baked Nationalist Messiah (literally a little Nationalist Wotan-in-Chief)[12]; a
Jew baiter. Business is booming. (p. 420)

It is a society where people seem to have no authentic life but are
subdued to an inhuman or subhuman function; here is a deepening
of that way of seeing which Toller had described in the preface to
Masse-Mensch. As Hinkemann himself says,

And all at once you *see*. Knatsch, what you see is terrible. You see the soul. And do you know what the soul looks like? It's got no life in it at all: one soul is a lump of fat (lit.: a neck of bacon), the second a machine, the third an automatic regulator, the fourth a steel helmet and the fifth a rubber truncheon. (p. 425)

The outward symbol of that inhumanity is the laughter of the unconcerned and isolated ego which replaces any kind of involvement or compassion, an ego which can even engage in its own self-destruction without realizing it: "Die Menschen morden sich unter Gelächter!" (p. 420) (Men laugh as they murder one another). And it is an inhumanity that is looked on as normal, that receives political expression in the state. Not for nothing does the *Budenbesitzer* invoke "Kontrakt, das Fundament bürgerlicher Gesellschaft" (contract, one basis of bourgeois society) especially when he is dressed in "Frackpaletot und Zylinder" (dress overcoat and top hat). Elsewhere, he says "Kings, generals, priests and showmen are the only politicians: they know how to appeal to the instincts of the people" (p. 405).

This inhumanity of society and state represents a willful self-immolation in the denial of human possibility: "And many men are free, and yet they are sitting in prison and have not done anything wrong, like animals in cages. There is a window with bars, which lets no light in. There are walls against which life dies. There are chains which eat into the flesh" (p. 421). And so society is fundamentally dissatisfied, as is proved by its clutching at ersatz remedies for its condition, whether economic, religious, moral, or religious cum-political.

Toller makes the artistic embodiment of this view of society more convincing because it is seen as an extension of Hinkemann's own case. For the structure of Hinkemann's experience is characterised by the realisation of individual isolation and an awareness of what society could be and what it is. His physical emasculation has made him sympathetic to the sufferings of others, whether men or animals, but that very sympathy makes him aware of how indifferent society as a whole is to them. Gradually, through the play, the experience is deepened until it becomes unbearable. His feeling that there are exceptions to what he considers a general state of affairs is expressed in a willed confidence in his wife's love, which is seen as giving back meaning to the life of such an unfortunate as himself, but this disappears before the contempt of Grosshahn, Grete's alleged laughter, and the actual laughter of the men in the pub. And this growing disillusion is accompanied by an increasing ability to generalize his experience into an absolute and detailed insight into the nature of society. Ironically enough, Hinkemann has been helped to this insight by the *Budenbesitzer* who exploits the weaknesses of the society he sees so clearly, and by his own unwilling part in that exploitation. This insight is accompanied, first of all, by a feeling of shocked and bewildered concern, which gradually hardens into the isolation of despair and contempt. And as the last scene with Grete shows, even though Hinkemann can be brought back from despair to compassion, even though he learns that his wife did not laugh at him, this does not alter the absolute and disabling nature of the insight. It does not really matter if there are a few people here and there who are exceptions: if Grete is better than he supposed, if Max Knatsch is ruefully aware of his own shortcomings and those of the proletariat: these don't change the nature of the society as a whole. The full awakening is an awakening to defeat, which Toller tries hard not to see as absolute, but which has that effect. Grete, when she is enlightened by Hinkemann's insight, commits suicide, ironically after he has told her: "kämpf für eine neue Welt" (p. 434) (fight for a new world)—something which he himself is not able to do. He knows too much. This conclusion is given further authenticity by Toller's refusal to sentimentalize even at the end the relation between Hinkemann and Grete. Grete is quite incapable of loving Hinkemann: she can only think of sacrificing herself to him, or of looking to him to help her face that loneliness of which he has made her aware.

But Toller did not consciously want the play to be so pessimistic; rather, he wanted it to help people carry on the struggle free from illusion:

Nonetheless, and despite everything, we have to struggle, and the more clear-sighted we are, the more persistently will we do so. Isn't it already a good deal if social misery is got rid of and care is taken to give Old Adam and Old Eve a chance—to use an American expression.[13]

Toller, however, knew that what impelled people to work to change society was the strength to dream. He takes as his epigraph to the play an extract from one of Hinkemann's speeches: "Wer

keine Kraft zum Traum hat, hat keine Kraft zum Leben" (p. 393)
(He who has no strength to dream has no strength to live); but he
was eager to stress that the necessary dream should not be illusion,
though he was uneasily aware that it might be:

But just as to a religious sensibility the welfare of the soul seems more
important than happiness in the world, so the artistic sensibility does not
close its eyes to the illusions which sometimes give it strength and driving
power. Out of a deep necessity it urges him to shatter human illusion.[14]

And as Toller shows us, in spite of himself, when Hinkemann
finally knows the world and no longer has the illusion that his wife
loves him, he is a completely broken man.

CHAPTER 6

Hoppla: Wir Leben!
(Hoppla! Such Is Life!)

The play opens with a prologue. It is 1919: six revolutionaries, including Karl Thomas, Eva Berg, Wilhelm Kilman, Albert Kroll, and Frau Meller, are waiting to be executed. At the last moment the death sentence is commuted to imprisonment except in the case of Kilman, who is secretly allowed to go free, as he has claimed that his part in the revolution was involuntary. The sudden release of tension drives Karl Thomas mad, and he spends the next eight years in a mental hospital in complete ignorance of what is going on in the outside world. When he is released, it is 1927 and Kilman is Prime Minister of the Republic. Thomas becomes disillusioned with him and also with his former associates who, though working in the Communist Party, have, in his view, lost their revolutionary enthusiasm. Increasingly disturbed by the madness of the society he sees around him, he decides that he must do something and plans to assassinate Kilman. Unbeknown to him, a right-wing nationalist, though for different reasons, has the same plan. Thomas uses his job as waiter in a luxury hotel as a means of gaining access to Kilman, but just as he has decided not to murder him after all, the right-wing assassin enters the room and, having shot Kilman, flees. Thomas is arrested, charged with the murder, and committed to prison, as are Albert Kroll and Frau Meller on suspicion of being accomplices (Eva Berg is already there for different reasons). Just before the news comes through that the real assassin has been caught Karl Thomas commits suicide.

*H*OPPLA was the first play written after Toller's release from prison; it was also his first play to be commissioned, as Erwin Piscator had asked for a play with which to open his new theater in Berlin in September, 1927.[1] Piscator had a very definite idea of what he wanted from *Hoppla*—an objective and unemotional analysis of postwar German society; and he saw to it that, as far as possible, he got it:

112

All our efforts in the course of further work on the play were to give the piece as realistic an underpinning as possible. You can't prove anything against the bourgeois world if your evidence is not accurate, and it is not accurate if emotion is the decisive factor.[2]

The play, as Piscator produced it, was certainly different from the text that Toller had written (and published) before the production. Piscator and his team were responsible for interpolations, substitutions, and omissions which aimed to fit the play to his conceptions of realism and his method of production.[3] But Piscator's influence went further: even the text as we have it was, to some extent, tailored to meet his demands. Toller had to provide opportunities for the exploitation of Piscator's favorite theatrical techniques, notably the film,[4] providing brief outlines of its content, while Piscator was responsible for its detailed conception and production. When, shortly after Piscator's production, another one was mounted by a different director at Leipzig, in October 1927, Toller made sure that the film was cut out.

But it is Piscator's influence on the basic conception of the play which is most serious and which causes difficulties in interpreting it. The ending as we have it, in which Karl Thomas commits suicide, is, in fact, the one Piscator insisted on, whereas in the Leipzig production Toller substituted the ending he preferred. The situation is not entirely clear, for both Piscator and Toller give differing accounts as to what happened. According to Piscator, Toller experimented with several endings: the third is the one we have; in the first Karl Thomas is arrested and sent back to the asylum: in the second Thomas, though not arrested, goes voluntarily to prison. Toller confirms that he had three possible endings in mind, but claims that the second attributed to him by Piscator was one that he had never considered. One of the rejected endings, and the only one that Toller describes in detail, is different from any of the three indicated by Piscator, for it involves Thomas's voluntary return to the lunatic asylum, which gives him the chance to perceive the madness of the world and to appreciate the work of those comrades he had despised; but this time he is never allowed out: "Only now has he become 'dangerous to the state'; previously when he was a restless dreamer he was not."[5] This seems to have been the ending adopted in the Leipzig production.

But, masterful director though he was, Piscator was unable to subdue Toller's play entirely to his own conception. Consequently, the dramatic critics were aware that even though Toller had come so far to meet Piscator, there was a discrepancy between play and production: "He (Piscator) imparts to Toller's cosy style the iron scaffolding of his scenic construction", said Herbert Jhering revealingly.[6] The deliberate underplaying of emotion in the acting, particularly that of the central character, though it had greater objectivity, was quite unsuited to *Hoppla* in general, and to Karl Thomas in particular.

It is possible, too, to overstress the importance of Piscator's influence on the play, for *Hoppla* is a logical extension in method of Toller's previous work and is in conformity with his growing realization that a greater realism was necessary, provided, of course, that it was at the service of a central idea. Toller's next play, *Feuer aus den Kesseln!* was much more rigorously realistic even than *Hoppla*, and this time with no prompting from Piscator.

It would be a mistake, too, to see Piscator as opposed to any use of dramatic symbolism. It is clear that as long as such symbolism was underpinned by an overall realism, he welcomed it; thus those elements in *Hoppla* which can be related to Toller's early work are not necessarily there despite Piscator. For we discern, even in *Hoppla*, at least the remnants of Toller's earlier *Traumbild* technique, deployed in a way not dissimilar to that used in *Hinkemann*. For instance, in the scene between Professor Lüdin, the psychiatrist, and Karl Thomas (Act 4, Scene 4) various people and situations we have met before appear in caricature, which is meant to stress the madness underlying their apparent normality. And as in *Hinkemann*, it is clear that the symbolic scenes represent Karl Thomas's vision of society (which Toller endorses) for Professor Lüdin does not see them. It is a neat, perhaps too neat, reversal; the man accused of madness is sane, whereas the people who accept the existing state of affairs as normal are mad. The fact that scenes like these, which Thomas sees in a way that reveals their inner reality, have already been portrayed for the most part in purely realistic terms represents an advance over *Hinkemann*: we don't depend on them for a detailed analysis of society as we do on their equivalents in the earlier play.

And besides this scene there is another, which if not related to the *Traumbild*, even indeed apparently realistic, is still basically non-naturalistic (though this is owing as much to Piscator as to Toller): the scene in the hotel, where the wireless operator obtains trans-

missions from all over the world for Karl Thomas. For those transmissions in their concentrated geographical miscellaneity and
exaggeration sacrifice realism to the necessities of the theme: "Attention! Attention! Unrest in India, unrest in China, unrest in Africa" (p. 97). Significantly, certain of the transmissions are accompanied by television pictures of the events described though television was not invented until 1929, and the worldwide coverage that
Toller's television obtains was not possible until the invention of
transmission via satellite. By employing these hyperbolic devices,
Toller was, of course, able to generalize the experience contained in
Hoppla: to suggest that what he found wrong in Germany was not
confined to it, but could be met with all over the world. And by
using wireless and television as the vehicles of his symbolic exaggeration, Toller was emphasizing the possibilities given to man by the
new means of communication as well as their actual misuse, their
being employed to titillate people's desire for sensation, and their
bombarding the hearer and viewer with so many different items on
so many different levels of importance that they are not really involved
in the news of human suffering of which the new media make them
aware.

But it is the increased realism of the play that is most significant.
Hinkemann represented an advance in psychological realism, particularly in the intimate scenes between Grete and Hinkemann, but
the wider social scene was nonetheless presented in terms that,
though barely consistent with realism, were not notably realistic. In
Hoppla, however, we encounter, particularly in certain scenes, a
psychological realism which is similar to that in *Hinkemann* and a
realism of speech which goes beyond that of the earlier play. This is
especially noticeable in the prologue, where several revolutionaries—it is just after the German revolution—are waiting to
be shot. Toller carefully discriminates between the characters of
each and displays their different reactions to the terrible tensions
they are under, which break out into insensate quarrelling. The
prison scene is, in fact, comparable to that in Jean-Paul Sartre's *Men
without Shadows.* A short extract will suffice to illustrate what I
mean. The prisoners are sharing a cigarette which one of them has
discovered in his pocket:

All smoke. Each takes a drag. They watch one another closely.
Albert Kroll: Karl, you mustn't take two drags.

Karl Thomas:	Don't talk rot.
Albert Kroll:	Are you calling me a liar?
Karl Thomas:	Yes.
Wilhelm Kilman:	(to Albert): You pulled on it much longer than we did.
Albert Kroll:	Shut your trap, you coward.
Wilhelm Kilman:	He called me a coward.
Albert Kroll:	Where did you slink off to when it came to the crunch? Where were you sitting on your arse (lit.: giving a shine to the seat of your pants) when we stormed the Town Hall—enemies behind us and the prospect of a common grave ahead? Where did you hide out?
Wilhelm Kilman:	Didn't I speak to the crowd from the Town Hall balcony?
Albert Kroll:	Oh yes, when we were in control. Before that you sat on the fence: but then quick as a flash you saw there was something in it for you (lit.: you poked your nose in the trough).
Karl Thomas	(to Albert Kroll): You've no right to talk like that.
Albert Kroll:	Mother's little middle-class darling!
Mother Meller:	What a set: to start rowing fifteen minutes before we're up against the wall.
Wilhelm Kilman:	He called me a coward . . . For fifteen years I've . . .
Albert Kroll:	(Imitating him) For fifteen years . . . The big shot . . . It's not much of a privilege to be shoveled into the same grave as you.
Eva Berg:	Shame!
Karl Thomas:	That's right. Shame!
Albert Kroll:	Shame. What for? Lie down with your tart in the corner and give her a kid. Then in the grave it can crawl out and play with the worms.

Eva Berg cries out. Karl Thomas jumps at Albert Kroll. (pp. 17–18)

One of the signs of Toller's realism is an increased objectivity: an ability, revealed perhaps for the first time, to present characters of whom he disapproves, whom he even detests, in their own terms and from their own point of view. Thus Kilman, the gradualist Social Democrat, whom Toller obviously sees as having betrayed his former ideals and being hand in glove with the forces of reaction, is allowed to have quite an honorable way of regarding his activities;

this comes out notably in the conversation between him and Karl Thomas:

Wilhelm Kilman:	In a democracy I have the rights of the employers to look after, just as much as the rights of the employees. Utopia isn't quite here yet.
Karl Thomas:	But the others have the press, money, weapons, and what have the workers got? Empty fists.
Wilhelm Kilman:	Oh, all your lot is interested in is armed struggle, hacking, stabbing, shooting. To the barricades! Comrade workers to the barricades! We repudiate a brutally violent struggle. We have said, over and over again, that we will conquer with moral, with spiritual weapons. Force is always reactionary. (p. 46)

That last sentence presents a view with which Gustav Landauer would have agreed, and there is obviously some sense in the rest of what Kilman says, too. Toller's fairness and objectivity, however, emerge most strikingly in the understanding way in which he presents the motives of a right-wing nationalist who wants to murder Kilman, motives that involve a view of military honor and of the revolution which were anathema to Toller himself:

I hate the revolution as I've never hated anything. From one particular day. My uncle was a general. We youngsters worshipped him like a God. At the end he was in charge of an army corps. Three days after the revolution I was sitting beside him. Someone rang the bell. A private bounced in "I'm a representative of the soldiers' council. We have been informed, General, that your epaulettes have been found offensive by people in the street. As from today there are to be no more epaulettes. We're all to have bare shoulders." My uncle stood bolt upright. "I'm to give up my epaulettes?" "Certainly." My uncle took his sword which was lying on the table, and drew it out of its sheath. I was terribly afraid. I pressed nearer so that I could stand by him: then I saw the Old Man give a dry cough while his eyes became moist. "Mr. Representative of the Soldiers' Council, for forty years I have worn the uniform of my supreme Commander in Chief with honor. I remember how a non-commissioned officer had his stripes torn off in disgrace. What you want me to do today is the worst that anyone could want me to do. If I can't wear my uniform with honor any longer . . . here," and with that the old man bent his sword, broke it in two and threw it at the feet of the representative of the Soldiers' Council. That representative was Mr. Kilman. (p. 90)[7]

Even in the scenes that are realistic in technique, however, the realism is not absolute; not until *Feuer aus den Kesseln* did it become that. Toller cannot resist the use, from time to time, of a rather simple mode of caricature as in the presentation of Pickel, the innocent up from the country with a touching faith in the powers that be,[8] or in that of "the discussion evening of the Circle of Intellectual Brainworkers" (p. 99). But, nonetheless, the Germany of 1927 is presented as Piscator had wanted it to be presented, in terms of a much more explicit and objective social analysis than Toller had ever tried before. This analysis was given theatrical objectivation in Piscator's multilevel tripartite stage building, which could serve as prison, ministry, Grand Hotel, and asylum.

But, although the character portrayal is much more realistic—and in being more realistic more detailed and specific than it was in *Hinkemann*—*Hoppla* is written in terms of a similar structure of experience. As we have seen, the symbolic devices are very close to *Hinkemann* in the emotion they communicate, presenting a society where human feeling has broken down and which is largely bent on its own destruction. In more narrowly political terms—and Toller's method naturally encourages a political diagnosis of a general malaise—the society is one in which the Social Democrats, who are identified with a policy of socialist gradualism, though nominally in power, are actually the creatures of a variety of coordinated reactionary forces. Such forces include: the financiers, the older generation of whom are in favor of a kind of guided democracy, while their juniors are explicitly in favor of dictatorship; the military, who are willing to cooperate with a Social Democrat like Kilman, whom they despise, but who are actively preparing the way for a Fascist dictatorship, being in league with the right-wing nationalists, although they do not actively support the latter's use of violence and political assassination. Thus, though the state is officially democratic, its power structure reveals that nothing has changed. Kilman, the Social Democratic Prime Minister, however plausibly he argues in favor of his official creed (as above), is always yielding to pressure to take action against the workers by shabby electoral maneuvers, by interfering with the right to strike, and by repression.

The analysis is done in terms of representative fictional figures:

the financiers, father and son, the old Hindenburg figure, His Excellency von Wandsring, the right-wing Count de Graf, and so on; but though it is a just analysis, it is hardly profound—it was, after all, a fairly commonplace type of socialist analysis. One feels some sympathy with contemporary critics who found a certain staleness in the play;[9] it is as if Toller, in being encouraged by Piscator to spell out his analysis in detail, had become more obviously orthodox, and in consequence, less interesting. Sometimes too great a clarity can deprive a work of depth.

However, in the presentation of the revolutionaries (here clearly members of the Communist Party [K.P.D.], though this is not made explicit) we have the more genuine and interesting Toller. The revolutionaries are depicted, for the first time, in historical perspective; we see them first in the prologue, just after the failure of the revolution, where, though they are presented in defeat, they are still near enough to the high hopes with which that revolution was made to bring those home to us. We see them again eight years later when the most craven of them, Wilhelm Kilman, has become Prime Minister and when the rest, who unlike Kilman have remained true to the cause, are still doggedly working by what political means they can to change a society in which not only is revolution impossible, but which is actively becoming more reactionary; the election of von Wandsring as president shows this only too well. The difference between 1919 and 1927 is thrown into relief by Karl Thomas, who, having spent the intervening years in an asylum, returns to society not realizing how much it has changed.

But it is clear that though revolution is impossible, there is no alternative to continuing with political activity in the hope that someday revolution will be possible. Toller respects the activities of Eva Berg, Mutter Meller, and Albert Kroll, their attempts to make the system work in their favor, their protests to officialdom, their distribution of leaflets, their meetings. But though he sees this as the only thing to do, he shows that it is bound to fail; for to work in terms of the system in order to alter it radically is inevitably to be contained by it. In the election scene in the public house, the remark of one of the anarchist workers "Huh! It's going swimmingly: the racket's booming" (p. 67), is shown as only too justified despite all the efforts of Kroll and his friends.

In showing the continuing existence of honest, hard political work to change society, Toller would not seem to present as hopeless a

picture as he had done in *Hinkemann*. But in those who carry on
with political activity, however honorable, there is not only a touch
of dogged futility—which it is not in their power to do anything
about—but also a certain dulling of perception as to what society is
really like—in human terms. None of the continuously active revolutionaries, Albert Kroll, Eva Berg, Mutter Meller, has the kind of
perception of the quality of society that Hinkemann had; i.e., of its
true inhumanity and madness.

Toller is reverting to a view of behavior less voluntaristic and
more socially determined than that which informs *Hinkemann*. He
shows, for example, how Eva Berg, who was only an adolescent
when she took part in the revolution of 1919, is now, in 1927, part of
the world she wants to alter. She has been hardened by the values of
that world and by her continuing expenditure of energy in an effort
to change it. Significantly, sexual relations no longer mean anything
more than a bit of off-duty relaxation; the promiscuity of the 1920s,
and the excessive sacrifices which can make a stone of the heart,
have taken their toll:

Karl Thomas:	You love me, don't you?
Eva Berg:	Because I've slept with you? Is that it?
Karl Thomas:	Isn't that a bond?
Eva Berg:	A glance exchanged with a stranger on a windy street can bind me to him more closely than sleeping with anyone. That doesn't need to be anything more than a very nice game. (pp. 56–57)

It is nonetheless through Eva Berg that Toller insists on the admirable toughness and resilience that have gone into that political campaigning:

We can't throw away the clear-sightedness, the knowledge that we've
gained, into a corner as if it were a plaything that we didn't want any more.
Experience—oh yes—I've had a good deal of experience of men and circumstances. For eight years I've worked the way only men used to work.
For eight years I've had to plan every hour of my life. That's why I am as I
am . . . Do you think it was easy for me? Often when I was sitting in one of
those loathsome furnished rooms I've thrown myself on the bed and cried as
if I were finished . . . and thought I couldn't go on living. . . . Then I found
I had work to do. The party needed me. I gritted my teeth and . . . . (p. 59)

Albert Kroll, Eva Berg, Mutter Meller, and the rest are contrasted with those would-be reformers who like to play with preposterous and crankish schemes of reform which they haven't the courage to put into practice and which, though they think of them as progressive, are, in fact, deeply reactionary, betraying the unregenerate feeling that actually inspired them.

Thus, at a meeting held, revealingly enough, in a room in the Grand Hotel, Philosopher X puts forward eugenics as the cure for the ills of society: "In conclusion: if quality is lacking, you won't be able to substitute quantity for it. So here's my proposal: nobody must marry below his station in life" (p. 99).

Philosopher X thinks he is being progressive, even, as it turns out, Marxist, but, of course, he is deeply implicated in society as it is, and his ideas point forward to the Nazis. The real feelings of him and his fellow reformers come out well enough in the following dialogue with Karl Thomas when he laughs at a question that Philosopher X has put to him:

Chairman:	It is not a laughing matter. The question is serious. And remember we're guests and you're a waiter.
Karl Thomas:	Oh ho! First it was comrade waiter. But now look at the big boss. You're going to redeem the proletariat. Here in the Grand Hotel, eh? Where were you when it happened? Where will you be? Still in the Grand Hotel? Phoneys!
Voices:	Disgraceful! Disgraceful!
	Karl Thomas goes.
Philospher X:	Petit-bourgeois ideologist!
Chairman:	We come now to the second item on the agenda. Working class free love and the duty of the intellectuals. (p. 102)

Here the points are made rather too obviously in a very simple mode of caricature. It is, indeed, Karl Thomas who sees and feels what society is like with an unblunted intensity of perception which is reminiscent of *Hinkemann,* and many of his insights are endorsed by the play's structure. Thus his belief in society's fundamental madness is emphasized by the staging that collapses the distinction between Ministry, Hotel, Prison, and Madhouse. It is Karl Thomas who listens and watches while the Radio Operator unwittingly brings him further evidence of a world that is at once cruel, trivial,

sensation-seeking, indifferent. It is Karl Thomas who argues with
Professor Lüdin and whose points are endorsed by the grinning
antics of the "normal" people. It is Thomas again who realizes with
the utmost keenness how much has been forgotten: in conversation
with the landlady's two children he discovers how little the war and
the revolution mean to the rising generation (and it is significant that
once Toller attributes to Karl Thomas one of his own experiences of
the front).[10] And Thomas's speech before he commits suicide has
undeniable authority even if, as we shall see, it may have to be
finally qualified; it is indeed reminiscent of *Hinkemann*, and
Thomas, unlike Hinkemann, commits suicide on stage:

Is the dance starting all over again? . . . Once more it's wait, wait,
wait . . . I can't . . . Don't you really see anything? . . . What are you doing? . . . Defend yourselves! . . . Nobody hears, nobody hears, nobody . . . We speak and do not hear one another . . . We hate and do not
see one another . . . We love and do not know one another . . . We murder and have no feeling for one another . . . Must it be like that for ever
and ever? . . . You, there, will I never understand you? . . . You there,
will you never understand me? . . . No! no! no! . . . Why did you lay
waste, burn up and gas the earth? . . . Is it all forgotten? . . . All mean-
ingless? . . . Go on, make the merry-go-round whizz faster, dance, laugh,
cry, marry and much good may it do you. I'm jumping off . . .
Oh how mad the world is! . . .
Where is it going? Where? The stone walls are moving closer and closer.
I'm freezing and it's dark and the ice-cold darkness grips me without mercy.
Where are we going? Where? Up the highest mountain, the tallest tree, the
flood. . . . (pp. 138–139)

Karl Thomas is, of course, the figure who undergoes transformation and, as with Hinkemann, it is a transformation in reverse. Full
of high hopes when he leaves the asylum, he ends, as we have seen,
in complete despair. But Karl Thomas is to be viewed much more
critically than any other Toller hero; he may have more insight than
do the others into what society is like, but his proposals as to what to
do about it are most emphatically wrong. At first he wants to escape,
to flee with Eva Berg away from it all:

Karl Thomas: Are you convinced now, Eva? Come. Here's a timetable.
                    We can still go tonight. Away, away, away.

Eva Berg: You're talking about both of us? Nothing has changed. Do
                   you really think I would leave my comrades in the lurch?
                   (p. 65)

Eva Berg's response with its strong appeal to comradely solidarity
sufficiently places Karl Thomas's escapism.

Thomas's second plan is to do something that he thinks will be
decisive: assassinate Kilman. He mentions the plan first to Albert
Kroll, though what he exactly envisages is not at this stage revealed:

Albert Kroll: What's your idea? What are you going to do?
Karl Thomas: Something must be done. Someone must give an example.
Albert Kroll: Someone? Everyone. Every day.
Karl Thomas: I don't mean it like that. Someone has to sacrifice himself.
                   That would liven things up a bit. I've been racking my
                   brains day and night. Now I know what to do.
Albert Kroll: I'm listening.
Karl Thomas: Come closer. I don't want anyone to hear.
                   Speaks in a low voice to Albert.
Albert Kroll: You're no use to us.
Karl Thomas: That's the only way I can help myself. It's made me
                   physically sick. (pp. 75–76)

Though the nature and details of the plan are not yet clear, it is
obvious what is going to be wrong with it: it is essentially romantic,
i.e., arising from the belief that the act of a single man can fundamentally alter the state of society, a belief that alternates with, and
significantly shades into, the idea that his act is one of self-expres-
sion. Even if it does not change the world it will express Karl
Thomas's feelings about it.

For the act is not in itself commendable; it could only be justified,
and then in terms of a largely expedient morality, if it made political
sense. But its futility, which Kroll is quick to see, is underlined by
Toller's making Thomas's plot coincide with that hatched by the
extreme nationalists, who want to assassinate Kilman because he is
too much of a socialist for them and therefore in the way of their
plans. This use of simultaneous assassination plots may be considered a rather clumsy and obvious device to make an ironic point.
But the point is well taken for all that: in this society the use of
violence for political ends is as much the prerogative of the Right as

of the Left, and each will tend to have some enemies in common. If Thomas had murdered Kilman, the chief beneficiaries would have been the nationalists (and it is they, of course, who do assassinate him). And so Thomas, far from furthering his own cause, was going to aid the cause of his bitterest opponents.

So Thomas is deeply and ironically mistaken in his solution, which he actually doesn't adopt. By the time he has an opportunity to shoot Kilman, he no longer wants to do so, as he feels that it does not matter any more. Just as he had progressed beyond wanting simple escape, he progresses beyond the romantic illusion that an assassination would be both satisfying and effective. But what *is* his final solution? In the play as we have it, it is suicide, withdrawal. In the ending that Toller preferred it would seem that Thomas was converted to Kroll's point of view; but the intense and passionate insight that would inform it, and that Kroll and his comrades do not possess, makes him so dangerous to the establishment that he is incarcerated.

Toller's preferred conclusion seems even more pessimistic than the one embraced in the printed text. But Toller is fair. To revert to the conclusion as we have it, justice does still operate, to some extent at least, even in this society:

Eva Berg:	(*knocks*) We're all going to be free. It wasn't Karl who did the shooting. They've got the murderer.
Frau Meller:	(*knocks on the other wall*) Are you there, Karl! Are you there! Are you there! Are you there! (*Knocks on the floor*) Eva, Karl isn't answering.
Eva Berg:	(*knocks*) Knock louder.
Frau Meller:	(*knocks*) Karl! Karl! Karl!
Eva Berg:	(*knocks*) Albert, there's no reply from Karl.
Albert Kroll:	(*knocks*) Let's all knock. It doesn't matter now. *They knock* *All the other prisoners knock* *Silence* *The whole prison is full of knocking* *Silence*
Eva Berg:	He isn't answering. *Warders are running in the passages.* *The cells become dark.* *The prison is dark.* (p. 141)

Those who are knocking are showing their human concern, which if it does not completely negate the speech that Karl makes before committing suicide—and I don't think it can be said to do this— seriously qualifies it, particularly since these are his political comrades who will be released to carry on the struggle.

From what Toller said of the play his sympathies were clearly rather against the Karl Thomas of the published version. His play, as he said, is about

The clash between the man who wants to realize the unqualified absolute here and now, the forces of the time and his comrades who abandon the attempt out of weakness, treachery or cowardice, or prepare themselves for the time to come out of strength, loyalty and courage. Karl Thomas understands neither, views their motives and deeds in the same light and goes under.[11]

Toller has, I think, simplified his play here: it is true that Karl Thomas is shown as not discriminating between the renegade Kilman and Albert Kroll. As he says to the psychiatrist "I first went to see Wilhelm Kilman as you had suggested. He had been sentenced to death like me. I found him a cabinet minister hand in glove with his old enemies. I went to my best friend, a chap who, by himself, with only a revolver in his hand forced a company of Whites to retreat. And what did I hear "One has to know how to wait"; nonetheless he swore he had remained true to the revolution" (p. 130).

It is also true that, in his exchange with Karl Thomas, Albert Kroll comes off best, showing himself both aware and constructive:

Albert Kroll:	We know. We know a lot more. Those who let us down when it came to the crunch are making a good deal of noise again today.
Karl Thomas:	And you put up with it?
Albert Kroll:	We fight. There are too few of us. The majority have forgotten and want peace and quiet. We have to get other comrades.
Karl Thomas:	Hundreds of thousands are out of work.
Albert Kroll:	When hunger slips in by one door sense slips out by another.
Karl Thomas:	You speak like an old man.

Albert Kroll: Years like these are of tenfold value. You learn.[12]
                    (pp. 73–74)

But despite what Toller says, the truth does not lie only with
Albert Kroll whose arguments make sense only if a revolution is
coming, if not today, then tomorrow or the day after. But it is this
which the play fundamentally questions, as its bitter shoulder-
shrugging title suggests. Continuous political activity such as Albert
Kroll and Eva Berg engage in may be the only self-respecting thing
to do, but on the evidence of the play it seems to offer little prospect
of success. Indeed, it depends to some extent on the activists not
realizing to the full the true state of the society that they are trying
to alter—not having a deep inward sense of what society is like. For
those who have such a sense, like Hinkemann and Karl Thomas, the
knowledge is disabling and ultimately leads to withdrawal. Toller is
pulled in two directions: intellectually he is on the side of Albert
Kroll, but it is through Karl Thomas, despite the qualifications that
are introduced into his position, that much of the structure of feeling
is articulated. It is significant that twelve years later, and for similar
reasons, Toller was to imitate Karl Thomas by committing suicide.[13]
The play is ambiguous in a way that none of Toller's earlier plays
had ever been, even when, like *Masse-Mensch,* they faced an unre-
solvable ambiguity in experience itself. It marks, perhaps, the first
signs in Toller's work of bad faith: the attempt for expedient political reasons to put a better face on things than he really felt they
warranted, one sign of which is the play's all-but-explicit support for
the Communist Party. The K.P.D. in return responded with
greater, if still qualified, approval than it had given to any previous
work of Toller's. It really felt, with reservations of course, that he
was making progress.[14] Ultimately, the theatrical pressures from
Piscator, who supported the K.P.D., were really transformed political ones. Naturally Piscator would view suicide as ideologically
appropriate for a hero who, to his way of thinking, was at heart a
bourgeois individualist: naturally too, he would see that Karl
Thomas was represented on stage as not of working-class origin,
though this was against Toller's intention.

CHAPTER 7

Other Plays

I   Der Entfesselte Wotan (*Wotan Unchained*)

Wilhelm Dietrich Wotan, a romantic megalomaniac of a barber, founds a company to encourage emigration to Brazil for those who are disillusioned with modern Germany. His scheme is a fraud, for Wotan has neither the permission nor the loan he claims to have received from the Brazilian government. However, he manages to attract enormous support until the whole thing is blown up by a message from the Brazilian government. He is arrested but given assurances that he will be treated leniently and released soon. It is astonishing to discover that the play was apparently written before Hitler's unsuccessful putsch of 1923. Significantly Wotan's headquarters are in Bavaria.

*D*ER ENTFESSELTE WOTAN, (Wotan Unchained) the last work Toller wrote in prison (it was composed in the early spring of 1923,[1] but not performed in Germany until February, 1926)[2] was his first experiment in a purely comic mode,[3] which did not come naturally to him and which he was to attempt only once more, if we except the abortive *Bourgeois bleibt Bourgeois* (Once a Bourgeois always a Bourgeois),[4] in *Nie wieder Friede!* (No More Peace). The play was less successful than Toller's other works and was badly received by the critics, who detected in it echoes of Carl Sternheim and Georg Kaiser.[5] Because it predicts the rise of Hitler, however, it has been successfully revived in West Germany.

Nonetheless, the play is of some interest, if only because it shows a further development of the experience embodied in *Hinkemann*; for here society has no redeeming feature at all.[6] As Rudolf Jentzsch, one of the few critics who liked the play, said:

So here as well that inner emptiness, loss of instinct, soullessness of our immoderately busy age is once again revealed. It is the same heartlessness

which in *Die Wandlung* Toller still hoped that the revolution would overcome, and which receives its heaviest indictment as the guilt of our age in
Masse-Mensch, Die Maschinenstürmer and *Hinkemann*.[7]

Moreover, the society depicted in this play is willing to lend an
ear to a pseudorevolutionary rhetoric:

The man of character is wasting his time in Europe! Scoundrels flourish
here: hypocrites grow fat: black marketeers stuff their guts with French
bacon. Women clothe legs eaten away with syphilis in silk stockings. Marie,
my sweet, there is no god in Europe any more. (p. 13)

And it is a deeply reactionary rhetoric, thriving on illusion and
exacerbating the worst features of the present society:

The officer is deprived of his right to war. In Brazil he can make war on the
natives to his heart's content. The idle rich are deprived of their right to
dividends in gold. Where will they find them? In Brazil. The official is
deprived of his titles and orders, the nobility of ministerial appointments,
honorable young ladies of the mission against the Jews. (p. 15)

Wilhelm Dietrich Wotan, the barber with his "Auswan-
derergenossenschaft" (p. 10) (Society for Emigrants), which is to
establish a new Germany in Brazil, is a megalomaniac charlatan, a
pseudosavior. As Toller said when he was asked against whom the
play was directed: "Whom am I lamming out at? At those types who,
I am convinced, have led us into the most frightful mess and who
will push the people further into it unless they free themselves from
their influence."[8] But as he saw, such a pseudosavior was likely to
have the powerful support of business (Wotan is actually manipu-
lated by Schleim after the latter has called his bluff) and of the
military (in the shape of von Wolfblitz), and to be treated leniently
by the political establishment (Wotan, at the end, though arrested,
is told that he will not be treated harshly). It seems to be clear that
in creating Wotan, Toller had Hitler in mind. Significantly, Wotan,
when led away after his arrest, says: "I will write a book, in prison,
in the galleys, in exile" (p. 60).

So clear seem the intentions of the play that it is rather surprising
to find that what gave Toller the idea for it was the activities of a
fellow prisoner and revolutionary in Niederschönenfeld, who, incapable of distinguishing fantasy from reality, elaborated in all seri-

ousness a harebrained scheme to save Germany by founding a colony abroad.[9] *Der entfesselte Wotan* was meant to represent tendencies to be found in Europe and America: "The figure of Wotan, although one that flourishes in a German context, is a universal phenomenon or, at least, a European and American one."[10] But this does not quite fit the play. Wotan is apparently meant to represent in the fullest sense "the combination of idealist and whimperer"[11] in those who do have not the strength to turn their wishes into actuality and to act with any kind of force and determination: "This is what has happened to Don Quixote in the new age: he no longer has the strength to live his dream and believe in it: nor is he a virile hustler who is always aware of what he has done."[12]

But the Wotan of the play, in contradistinction to his historical prototype, does not have this significance. He is shown as having considerable success in obtaining power over others by an appeal to their irrationality and confused emotions. Far from being futile, Wotan, though treated comically, is sinister, and the play a warning:

> O Publikum! Lach nicht zu früh!
> Einst lachtest du zu spät
> Und zahltest deine Blindheit mit lebendgen Leibern.
> Lach nicht zu früh!
> Doch-lach zur rechten Zeit! (p. 8)

> (O public, don't laugh too soon: once you laughed
> too late and paid for your blindness with your
> living bodies. Don't laugh too soon: but laugh
> at the right time.)

II   Feuer Aus Den Kesseln! *(Draw the Fires!)*

Reichpietsch and Köbis, two stokers on the battleship *Friedrich der Grosse* in 1917 are critical of the war and discontented because they and their comrades are not allowed to receive socialist newspapers, and contact U.S.P.D. (Independent Socialist Party) deputies in the Reichstag, who encourage them to proselytize among the fleet to strengthen the hand of the forthcoming peace conference of socialist parties in Stockholm. Discontent with the poor quality of the food and with their treatment by the officers is becoming widespread among the enlisted men in the fleet, and on *Friedrich der Grosse*, Köbis, Reichpietsch, Beckers, Sachse, and Weber are elected to an unofficial food commission. There is a meeting on shore of the enlisted men, at which Reichpietsch puts forward the U.S.P.D. peace proposals, but an *agent provocateur* planted by the officers suggests that the sailors mutiny and sail for England. The members of the food commission are arrested for high treason: Reichpietsch and Köbis are executed; the death sentence on their colleagues is commuted to fifteen years' imprisonment.

Feuer aus den Kesseln! (Draw the Fires!), which was first staged in 1930,[13] is the first of Toller's plays to be completely realistic in style. There is no use of *Traumbilder*, of symbolism, of nonnaturalistic action, as there had been even in *Hoppla*. For the first time no character appears who is a surrogate, of however qualified a kind, of Toller himself; nor is there any of his usual plangent rhetoric. Indeed, the unsentimental realism with which he depicts the mutinying sailors resembles throughout the mode of the prologue to *Hoppla*. This is, moreover, the only Toller play that is a faithful depiction of history[14]—the Kiel naval mutiny of 1917. Many of the characters are historical personages, whose names remain unaltered, and some of whom were alive when the play was first staged.[15] Toller even made use of the findings of a Reichstag investigation of 1927–28 into the causes of the mutiny.[16] The play opens with a representation of a meeting of the committee, and the action is presented as if it were a dramatized result of those findings on which the audience is implicitly invited to pass judgment.[17] And, in an appendix to the first edition, Toller reproduced a good deal of documentary material, much, though by no means all, of which was taken from the proceedings of the official inquiry, to demonstrate the basis in fact of many of the incidents depicted in the play. Even Reichpietsch's last letter before execution is merely a shortened version of the letter written by the historical model.[18]

The object of the play is to show the beginnings of the growth of a revolutionary consciousness among the enlisted men, particularly the stokers, of the German Navy; the strengths and limitations of that consciousness; and their relationship to the limitations and strengths that had manifested themselves in the German revolution. At first the enlisted men are divided into a handful who have an explicitly political consciousness and the majority, who have not. But under the stress of just treatment from the officers, particularly over the misallocation of food, there is a growth of political awareness, not only in those who already have it, but in the others as well. The men begin to see their interests as opposed to those of the officers and to band together to protect them.[19] When once the reality of class conflict is felt in a military setting, where the facts of injustice and exploitation can be very much more obvious than in civilian life, the way is open for fresh connections to be made, for the war to be identified as a class war and, therefore, to be opposed.[20]

But Toller shows that the growth of this consciousness is very imperfect. The connections that are made are not made consistently and are still capable, even when acquiesced in by the majority, of being formulated only by a small minority. Further, the conception of the appropriate political action to be taken is somewhat ineffectual: the most that the revolutionary enlisted men do in strictly political terms is to collect signatures of support for the Stockholm International Peace Conference of Socialist Parties, to recruit for the Independent Socialist Party (the U.S.P.D.), to distribute socialist literature, and to encourage others to take out a subscription to the leading socialist newspaper. Their other actions, the setting up of a food commission and the mutiny over shore leave, are not in themselves revolutionary but rather means to the development of such a consciousness, and are always capable of being defined in isolated and purely local terms.[21] And so when, at the end of the play in 1918, decisive action appears to be taken and the stokers draw the fires to prevent the officers from engaging in a naval Götterdämmerung, there is a hollowness about the apparent triumph.[22]

That hollowness reverberates more clearly in Toller's presentation of the power of the establishment, which executes Köbis and Reichpietsch and imprisons Beckers, Sachse, and Weber because it is able to detach them from the rest, which can use informers and *agents provocateurs*,[23] and which can bully revolutionaries to deny their vision in the hope of saving themselves.[24] Even the meeting in the Rüstersiel pub where the sailors get nearest to revolt has been connived at by the authorities. It is another of the ironies of the play that the authorities see the sailors' movement as potentially more effective and revolutionary then it really was—as the prologue to a strike for peace in alliance with the U.S.P.D. Köbis himself says, "We were too stupid and cowardly to do what the Prosecution is accusing us of" (p. 324).

But despite its considerable distinction, *Feur aus den Kesseln!* (Draw the Fires!) is a disappointing play. Indeed, it is possible to imagine it as having been written by another dramatist. Friedrich

Wolf's *Die Matrosen von Catarro (The Sailors of Catarro)*, for example, has a similar subject—a mutiny in the Austrian Navy—and comparable merits. The play lacks consistent evidence of Toller's finer consciousness; in one sense it represents not development but retrogression, an act of piety toward the past, which does little more than show why some kind of German revolution was possible. Insofar as the play has a more general contemporary theme it is that of *Die Matrosen von Catarro*, which is summed up by one of the characters as "Next time better." But the pessimism in *Hinkemann* and *Hoppla* casts doubt on whether there will be a next time at all.

In his presentation of Köbis and Reichpietsch, the two sailors who were shot, we can see, however, touches of Toller's distinctive consciousness. Through these two characters he appears to be working over again the central theme of *Masse-Mensch* and the effect of the realistic method used in *Feuer aus den Kesseln!* is to emphasize what had been presented in abstract terms in the earlier play: the dependence of an effective revolutionary consciousness not on ethical conversion but on an experience of oppression and injustice which will repudiate ethical absolutes. We should note, however, that a shift seems to have taken place in Toller's attitude: the figure who most nearly resembles *der Namenlose* (The nameless one) in *Masse-Mensch* is Köbis, who refuses to defend himself at his trial, who utterly despises his prosecutors, and who (in the English version) dies cursing the German military state.[25] The play obviously invites us to admire Köbis intensely: his effectiveness, born of controlled hatred, is contrasted with the more ineffective and soft-centered Reichpietsch, who has some distant kinship with Sonja in *Masse-Mensch*, who repudiates violence on religious grounds[26] and is capable of being bullied into temporary collapse. But Toller is able to evade what appears, emotionally speaking, to be a clear and unreserved underwriting of violent revolution, by not allowing the distinction to be developed in explicit terms: violence is not immediately in question, though it is obvious that Köbis would have had no hesitation in resorting to it if it were: his whole attitude implies it.[27]

III   Wunder in Amerika *(Miracle in America)*

Wunder in Amerika (Miracle in America) is about the life of Mary Baker Eddy. It begins with her establishing contact with the hypnotic faith-healing methods of Quimby and her imitation of them. It deals with her treatment of a small band of associates whom she ruthlessly dominates, quarrels with, and, if necessary, appropriates for her sexual needs; her development of the distinctive doctrine of Christian Science; the founding of a church to propagandize that doctrine; and her self-exaltation to semi-divine status. The play ends with a sordid squabble as to who is to inherit her money and power as she declines rapidly into senility. Forced, while totally unfit for the task, to preach a sermon to multitudes of her followers by those who have a financial interest in proving that she is not senile (as against those who have a similar interest in proving that she is), she dies while proclaiming that there is no death.

At first sight Toller's next play *Wunder in Amerika*, written in collaboration with Hermann Kesten, looks like a complete withdrawal;[28] a signalizing of defeat by turning the eyes elsewhere. And so Friedrich Wolf in his article, "Zehn Jahre zehn Dramatiker" (Ten Years, Ten Dramatists) seems to regard it.[29] At first sight it is an exposé, easy enough to make and perhaps too crudely biased to be effective, of the pretensions of Mary Baker Eddy. Toller had visited the U.S.A. in 1929—a visit that is chronicled in *Quer durch (Right Across)*. While there he saw Aimee Sempel McPherson at work and became fascinated by the way in which so obvious a charlatan could not only succeed, but could apparently survive a scandal involving a staged disappearance, living in what for her official creed was certainly sin, and a pack of what should have been obvious lies to cover it up.[30] Though there is no external evidence to prove it, I suggest that it was Toller's experience of Aimee Sempel McPherson that gave him the idea for *Wunder in Amerika*.

But it would be wrong to see this play as representing complete withdrawal. However, it is certainly not one of his best and, since it was written in collaboration, it is always difficult to be certain when one is reading the work of Toller rather than his collaborator's. For it is clear that in *Wunder in Amerika* Toller returns to the theme of *Der entfesselte Wotan*, exploring the liability of capitalist society, conscious always of deep human need, to go whoring after false gods, to work out not its own true salvation but to snatch at an ersatz substitute, which, far from being a challenge to society's values, is a manifestation of them. In *Wunder in Amerika*, what Toller sees Mary Baker Eddy as embodying, even when she claims to be liberating others from it, is that inhuman drive for money and power that motivates much of society. And in her old age she herself becomes the victim of other people's drive for money and power. The language she speaks is, ironically enough, often close to that of *Die Wandlung:* Friedrich, if he had been a thought more priggish than he was, could well have said: "I have a mission. Only a few people really know that I can free men from their error. If the truth is known there is no sickness and no want" (p. 34),[31] or "We want to abolish the burdens of illness, unhappiness, restlessness and fear in face of death and life" (p. 34).

Mary Baker Eddy, in other words, tries to make people believe in the illusion that their lives are changed in a way that is related to what is genuinely offered by a socialist society. Moreover—and here *Hinkemann* is of obvious importance—she ignores the limits on happiness set by life itself through illness and death. Indeed, going far beyond orthodox Christianity, she preaches that "there is no life after death, because there is no death, because this corporeal frame which torments us is only a bad dream" (pp. 40–41).

What fascinates Toller is not only that Mary Baker Eddy is the kind of false prophet thrown up by advanced capitalism—a false prophet whose operations and appeal he clearly saw were, like Wotan's, analogous to Hitler's—but that she is successful. True, in her old age, she becomes a victim of the very drives which she herself has exploited, and the death she had denied stops for her; but she is not discredited in the eyes of her followers. Time and again Toller presents her as seemingly on the verge of exposure and defeat, only to show her bouncing back higher than before. After the nadir of her fortunes at the end of Act III, she is shown, without explanation, at the beginning of Act IV as the wealthy, powerful, and idolized head of a national, even international movement. (The suddenness and lack of explanation are here legitimate theatrically because we have seen the essential process in operation before.) Her success, indeed, is in ironic contrast to that of the revolutionary leader, who, trying to bring radical change to society, is suppressed and discredited very easily, and never makes a comeback. The false prophet—Wotan as well—is resilient and his followers difficult, perhaps impossible, to disillusion.

Wunder in Amerika is a pessimistic play: its demonstration of the deadly power of illusion is not presented in terms of any significant countervailing power. One or two workmen are not taken in, however, among those who help to erect Mrs. Eddy's Christian Science center:

First Workman:	She's got what it takes. A few years ago she was still in a small way and now she has her big house in the finest street in Boston.
Third Workman:	The factory owners pay her to promise the poor heaven on earth, so that they won't notice that the rich have heaven on earth here already. (p. 50)

Insofar as they can see this there is a hope; but even here irony enters. In this society, despite their clear-sightedness, these workmen—paralleling Hinkemann's situation—are working for Mary Baker Eddy. They are helping her to perpetuate illusion.

After *Wunder in Amerika* there was really nowhere left for Toller to go. From *Die Wandlung* onwards he had examined, with urgency and against a constantly deteriorating situation, the nature and difficulty of revolutionary change; in *Feuer aus den Kesseln!* (Draw the Fires!) he had written a kind of epitaph of the revolution, and in *Der entfesselte Wotan* (Wotan Unchained) and *Wunder in Amerika* (Miracle in America) he had analyzed and explored in particular the forces of unreason. And so in his next play, *Die blinde Göttin* (The Blind Goddess),[32] it is not surprising that there are signs of a loss of direction. The play, though theatrically effective, makes its diminished point in a muddled and halfhearted way.

IV Die Blinde Göttin *(The Blind Goddess)*

Dr. Färber is unhappily married and is in love with his secretary, Anna Gorst, with whom he is having an affair. Frau Färber dies, and a postmortem examination establishes that the cause of death was arsenic poisoning. Dr. Färber and his mistress are found guilty of murder and are imprisoned. The crucial evidence against them is that of a pathologist who categorically maintains that Frau Färber could only have died from accumulated doses of the poison, and that therefore suicide must be ruled out. Later, however, Frau Färber's diary is discovered. Not only does it contain a stated intention to commit suicide but further research convinces the pathologist that death from a single large dose of arsenic is perfectly possible. After having already served a term of imprisonment of four years, Dr. Färber and Anna Gorst are released. But Anna no longer loves him.

In *Die blinde Göttin* (The Blind Goddess) Toller is trying to abstract from the complex of society one particular element: the

nature of justice, die blinde Göttin (the blind goddess) of the title.
But the trouble is that he, unfairly, takes a special case (the play is
based on a contemporary cause célèbre) and seems to be trying to
argue that Justice as a social institution is as haphazard in its workings as the Goddess Fortune. It is not clear, however, whether he is
arguing this in absolute or contingent terms. It is true that he does
appear to imply that justice is like this in presentday capitalist society because of that preoccupation with power, wealth, and status
which leads to breaches of duty, bias, and bad faith; but it is difficult
to see that even in a capitalist society miscarriages of justice of this
nature are common, or that any conceivable society could guard
against them. The play is a piece of special pleading, which even
vitiates its own thesis by allowing justice to be done at last.

Nonetheless, the play has its moments. What interest there is in
it centers upon Anna Gorst, Dr. Färber's mistress. Like so many of
Toller's characters she undergoes a transformation. What she has
suffered at the hands of justice and what she has seen and heard in
prison (Toller is again drawing on his own experience) cause her to
grow away from the selfishness of Färber, and from the selfish
claims implicit in his love to a sense of social responsibility.[33] But—
and nothing could show more clearly how far we have come from
Die Wandlung—it is not clear what she has learned or what she is
going to do. She remains an isolated figure, and the play ends not
with a subdued hope (except insofar as her commitment is itself a
hope), but even more than in *Hinkemann* and *Hoppla* with waste
and isolation.

V   *Plays of Exile*

Toller wrote two plays in exile: *Nie wieder Friede!* (No More
Peace)[34] and *Pastor Hall*.[35] Both suffer from the fact that under the
circumstances they could be performed only in translation before a
foreign audience and had to be written with this limitation in mind.
Further, Toller's energies, particularly in the later years of exile,
were concentrated on exhausting practical activities: campaigning
against Nazism, helping his fellow exiles, raising money for the
relief of victims of the Spanish Civil War. It was not only that he had
little energy left over for dramatic creation, or that his plays could
not be performed in Germany before German audiences, but there
is in them an ultimately dishonest simplification of attitude which,
considering the exigencies of the time, was understandable but,

now that that time is mercifully over, has drained the plays of real interest and has left *Pastor Hall*, in particular, stranded.

Formally speaking, *Nie wieder Friede!*, a satirical musical comedy with a deliberately fantastic action (some of the scenes are laid in heaven) is a new departure for Toller, but it cannot be claimed to be original. Not only does it owe something to the example of Bertolt Brecht and Kurt Weill but also to that of his friend Walther Hasenclever, in whose play, *Ehen werden im Himmel geschlossen*[36] (Marriages are made in Heaven), the heavenly powers manipulate human beings into situations that will illustrate their weaknesses and the intractable problems arising from them.

Nie wieder Friede! has as its theme man's self-destructive irrationality; in particular, his ability to do a complete aboutface, to be all for peace one minute and all for war the next. The satire is meant to be universal, though clearly Toller was thinking of the Germany of 1933 as opposed to that of 1918. And because he had to universalize the idea for an English audience, the ostensible theme of the play is empty and even at odds with his belief that a European war was inevitable, not because of a general willingness to go to war at the drop of a hat, but because of Hitler. Indeed, in many respects, *Nie wieder Friede!* is the sort of antiwar comedy that could have been written by a member of the Peace Pledge Union who happened also to be a gifted dramatist. For the belief that war is always a murderous fuss about nothing grounded on a mutual illusion about the intentions of the other side has always been the bane of British pacifism. Toller knew better than that.

A brief account of the play may bear these observations out. It opens in heaven where Napoleon wagers with St. Francis that despite the talk of peace on earth people are as ready as ever to go to war. To prove it, he dispatches a fake telegram stating that war has broken out to Dunkelstein, which is just celebrating a League of Nations peace day. Everything is immediately put on a war footing. Nobody knows who is fighting whom about what, but everyone gets to work organizing, commandeering, arresting spies under the direction of their capitalist ruler, Laban, who makes a dictator of Cain the Barber—until as the result of further supernatural intervention the situation is reversed. Napoleon has won his bet.

Of course, Toller's real theme does show through, and the play as a whole reflects a deep pessimism about Germany. Napoleon and Cain are surrogates of Hitler (there is clearly a reference back to *Der entfesselte Wotan*), and so that pessimism is given a historical dimension which belies the apparently exemplary nature of the satire. It is St. Francis, the greatest of Christian saints, who is deluded whereas Napoleon and Cain are right:

St. Francis:	Whoever is in possession of the truth is invincible. The mind is greater than force.
Napoleon:	But people *like* force.
St. Francis:	No, people love freedom.
Napoleon:	Not even the illusion of freedom. (p. 48)

In Dunkelstein, Socrates underlines Napoleon's point; he is powerless in his wisdom while Rachel who, like Toller's earlier heroes, thinks and feels on a deeply sincere human level is more isolated than any of them had ever been. Toller, in interpreting German experience was right to see it as a particular example of what human beings in general can be capable of and have done before; but he could not, in this play, face the tragedy of that knowledge. He even makes use of a vulgar Marxism which sees capitalism as the sole cause of war; but he knew that Hitler, unlike Cain, might receive support from big business although he was not its tool. That was the mistake that the K.P.D. (but not Toller[37]) had made when Hitler became Chancellor in 1932.

The basic propagandist intention of the play, however hopelessly obscured, is nonetheless present. There is a covert appeal to Communists and Christians to unite against Hitler and a contempt for the League of Nations. St. Francis finds "die Internationale" "very sweet" and is finally convinced by Marx's famous statement (Marx is in hell) that it is necessary to change the world. But in cutting this statement adrift from Marx's specific doctrines Toller assimilates Christianity and Marxism far too easily. For a Christian could well see in Marx's adjuration, taken in isolation, an ethical idea in complete conformity with Christianity (Toller once tricked a Nazi who did not know its source into agreeing with it too).[38] St. Francis's interpretation of it evades the very problem that the real theme of the play has set. Things will change "when the clever stop talking and the wise begin to act" (p. 103). This would make nonsense of the ostensible theme of the play if it were interpreted as a call to prepare for war; but in terms of its real theme it is a solution that has already been discredited.

Unlike *Nie wieder Friede!*, Toller's next play, *Pastor Hall*, is set in Germany and is a return to dramatic realism.[39] The bare bones of the plot are as follows:

Friedrich Hall, a Lutheran clergyman, has been preaching against the Nazi regime and has been in correspondence with those who are oppressed by it. Hall's daughter, Christiane, is going to marry Werner, the son of General Paul von Grotjahn, himself, though a monarchist, a friend of Friedrich and critical of the Nazi regime. The local Storm Troop leader, Fritz Gerte, is in love with Christiane, and Ida Hall, the pastor's wife, has been stringing him along so that he may help to protect Friedrich from the consequences of his own actions. But the proposed marriage between Christiane and Werner leads Fritz Gerte to blackmail Ida into pressurizing her husband to call off the match.

By corrupting the Hall's family servant, Jule, he has managed to get hold of some correspondence which will incriminate Friedrich, and he has an extra hold over Ida, as she has been involved in a currency offense. Friedrich, refusing to be blackmailed, is arrested and put in a concentration camp, to which, meanwhile, Fritz Gerte is transferred as the new Commandant. After the brutal punishment of a Jewish biblical scholar, Johann Herder, Friedrich denounces Fritz Gerte publicly and is himself sentenced to be severely punished. Before the beating is to be carried out Hall's nerve fails him and with the help of a friendly guard, who is shot for his pains, he manages to escape. Friedrich goes to von Grotjahn's house and when Fritz Gerte comes looking for him there, von Grotjhahn, without betraying the presence of his friend, orders Gerte out at pistol point.

Friedrich is ashamed of his weakness and wishes to atone for it by inviting arrest when preaching against the Nazis from his pulpit. Von Grotjahn volunteers to stand beside him and we are led to understand that Hall is arrested and taken back to the camp by a posse of storm troopers. (There is an earlier ending, rejected by Toller, in which Hall escapes rearrest by a fatal heart attack in von Grotjahn's house.)

It is not surprising that, though the play was not staged until 1947, it formed the basis of a wartime British propaganda film directed by the Boulting brothers in 1940. However worthy its intentions, it suffers from the fact that Toller did not know Nazi Germany at first hand, and the play was also in some respects out of date. The Germany of 1938 was not that of 1935, the time at which the action takes place. It was worse. Even some of the material on which the play is based was provided by a fellow refugee who had spent ten months in a concentration camp and who told Toller about the case of "des siebzigjährigen Bibelstudenten Albert Einst der gewagt

hatte, ein Wort des Apostel Paulus zu zitieren"[40] (the seventy-year
old biblical scholar, Albert Einst, who had dared to quote a saying of
St. Paul). Pastor Hall himself was probably modelled on Martin
Niemöller.

If now a dated propaganda play, *Pastor Hall* has still a good deal of
interest, even though, more than in the case of *Nie wieder Friede!*,
much of it would be lost on an audience or reader, German or
otherwise, who knew nothing of its author. For, through the figure
of Friedrich Hall, Toller is really testing himself, trying to find an
answer to a question that could have no firm answer. What would he
have done had he been arrested as the Nazis intended on the day
after the Reichstag fire instead of, by a stroke of the merest good
fortune, being safely in Switzerland making a broadcast? He would
have remembered how hard Niederschönenfeld (the prison) had
been for him to bear, and knew well enough that, however harsh it
had seemed, it was nothing like a concentration camp. Would he
have been able to hold out, have shown the heroic bravery of his old
friend and comrade of Munich and Niederschönenfeld, Erich
Mühsam, who defied his tormentors to the end and who, having
refused to commit the suicide to which they deliberately tempted
him, was hanged and the report put out that he had done it himself?
Mühsam's heroism is described and saluted in *Pastor Hall:* dramatically, the reason for introducing it is to show that heroism is possible, and if Mühsam had been heroic, so could Hall be.

That Toller was aware of the challenge with which Mühsam presented him, and that in *Pastor Hall* he was trying himself out receives clear support from the play. The three female characters are
named after women who were important in his own life: Ida Toller,
his mother, who had recently died in Germany; Christiane, his wife,
who had recently left him; and Jule, the family cook of his boyhood,
whom he describes so touchingly, yet understandingly, in *Eine
Jugend in Deutschland* (Growing up in Germany). Then, too, Friedrich Hall is given some of Toller's own personal background: he was
a volunteer in the 1914–18 war, was invalided out through nervous
trouble and decided "from now on to preach love and not force" (p.
145). The concentration camp guard who is killed when Hall escapes
can be related to the warder whom Toller would have had to kill for
his plan of escape to succeed, (this caused him to abandon the plan,
an incident reflected in *Masse-Mensch*). But it was not a concentra-

tion camp he had wanted to escape from, and if we look back on *Masse-Mensch*, it is clear that there too he had asked himself a similar question: could he have faced a firing squad with the bravery of Eugene Leviné, the leading Communist revolutionary in the Munich Soviet Republic, who had died shouting 'es lebe die Welt revolution!" (Long live the world revolution!) at his executioners? In *Masse-Mensch, der Namenlose*, the Leviné figure escaped. It was Sonja Toller who was executed. Toller was fantasizing to comfort his self-doubt.

Toller (as will be shown in a subsequent chapter) was, too, aware that his nerve had failed him on two occasions, when there was nothing like this kind of challenge, to be at all sure that he could have done what the real Mühsam did or his fictional Pastor Hall proposes to do at the end of the play. The fact that Hall cracks once and cannot live up to his brave words shows that in his heart Toller doubted himself. But he could not understandably in *Pastor Hall* face up to what he knew was the likely answer.[41] He tried to escape from it in the first version of the play by Hall's providential heart attack, a deus ex machina which evades the problem. In subsequent versions he tried to evade it by giving himself a false answer: Hall will go back to camp and face his beating. But Toller betrays himself by the rhetoric he allows Hall to use: "The cell will not silence my voice. Even the block on which you stretch me out will be a pulpit, and the congregation so huge that no church in the world could hold them" (p. 177). Brave words. But it is easy to give oneself promissory notes in stagy rhetoric, knowing that one will never have to pay. Toller was not, however, really deceiving himself: he knew better. In a concentration camp you would have to be heroic alone, without support, uncertain as to whether people outside would ever hear about you, let alone respond. Toller knew that he had heard of Mühsam only because a fellow inmate who knew how he died had been released. The heroism required was almost out of this world. Well might Toller say through Hall: "in Mühsam lebte der Geist" (p. 165) (in Mühsam the spirit lived), the supreme tribute that one man can pay to another. It was Toller's misfortune that he had to ask himself what he would have done had the Nazis arrested him. Perhaps when he decided to commit suicide shortly after completing *Pastor Hall*, aware as he was that Mühsam, when deliberately ill-treated and encouraged, had not done so, he knew the answer.[42]

But is is just at this point in the play that for those who are not aware of its esoteric personal meaning the dishonesty of *Pastor Hall* is most apparent. For the rhetoric gets worse:

I will live. It will be like a conflagration which no worldly power can extinguish. The oppressed will pass it on to one another and will take new heart. One will say to another that Antichrist reigns, the adversary of mankind, and they will pool their strength and follow my example. (loc. cit.)

What exactly does this mean? That the example of people like Pastor Hall will lead to widespread resistance against Hitler which will be successful? Will it be by war and will that take the form of intervention by other countries or of an internal rising, or both? At whom is the rhetoric aimed? At his fellow countrymen?—but they are not there to hear it. At Britain and America?—but how could anyone there follow Hall's example? When one tests rhetoric in this manner its poverty and evasiveness are revealed.

Toller, of course, could hardly call for war against Hitler in countries which still had diplomatic relations with Germany. No theatrical management would have produced such a play, and, as it was, he could not get *Pastor Hall* accepted for production. Even the British film based on the play ran into a good deal of trouble in the United States where attempts were made to ban it, precisely because the U.S. was still neutral when it was released.[43] One has to allow for the extreme difficulty that Toller was in artistically speaking: he could not have spoken out for prudential reasons, even had he wanted to.

But, as a matter of fact, the whole drive of the play shows that Toller did not want to face up to this question.[44] The answer that the play appears to give is that opposition inside Germany is potentially strong enough for Hitler's regime to be overthrown from within, and all that is needed is the example of men like Hall *pour encourager les autres*. But what is it to encourage them to? A repetition of the Spanish Civil War, or is Hitler to be puffed away in the same way as Eisner's march had sent the King of Bavaria packing, an example which had been followed with similar success throughout Germany in 1918?

Toller could not have believed that. Even in 1920 he had referred to Eisner, the revolutionary president of the Bavarian republic, as belonging to what seemed prehistoric times.[45] The real question was whether Hitler could be overthrown by any internal opposition, using any means whatsoever, however bloody the outcome. But Toller could not face even that: he was still, in this play at least, clinging to the idea of successful nonviolent collective action; that is, if we are to take the play seriously at all. Even in relation to a much more intractable situation he turned his back on the insights of *Masse-Mensch*.

An exchange in the camp between the Communist Hofer and Pastor Hall faces, it is true, more frankly than *Nie wieder Friede* had done the rift between Christianity and Communism. Hofer, the last incarnation of *der Namenlose*, is quite frank: what his party would do only sounds humane because the Nazis are worse:

When we are in power things will be different. I reject whippings, concentration camps, condemnations without a trial, secret beatings to death and all the rest of it. Our enemies will be brought before a people's tribunal, tried, and, if necessary, shot. (p. 164)

But in the exchange between Hall and Hofer about the use of force, the play, through its ending, seems to endorse Hall, while allowing Hofer to get the best of the argument:

Hall: Today I believe only in the way of understanding.
There's no question on earth so hopeless and
perplexed that it could not be solved.
Hofer: It takes two to make a solution without force,
your reverence. We don't ask for force. It's
the others who do that. Should I be robbed of
my right and say thank you very much? I'd rather
die.
Hall: The courage to die has become cheap. So cheap
that I often ask myself if it is not really a
flight from life. (p. 164)

Hall, of course, does not answer Hofer's argument, but merely pounces on "Rather die." Nonetheless, in doing so, he has a point: that force would not succeed if used by Hitler's opponents, and that it would lead to defeat. But Hofer reminds us that Hall's way is even more unrealistic.

But Hall's way or Hofer's way, to be successful, would depend on there being widespread opposition to Hitler within Germany on the part of a representative cross section of the German people. And there is another significant and related falsity in the play in the figure of General von Grotjahn, the old monarchist military aristocrat, who still supports and respects the Kaiser and his war—a kind of figure which, in his earlier plays, Toller had seen very differently. Of course, astonishingly, there is a sense in which Toller showed prescience, but the von Grotjahns only took action against Hitler when he was losing the war. But at the end of the play von Grotjahn is shown as opposing Hitler on principle and following Hall's example. That was quite inconceivable, and Toller must have known that it was.

It is true that Toller's quite admirable campaigning against Hitler had led him to make common cause with, or to enlist the support of, people with political beliefs very different from his own; and no doubt there was in him a genuine broadening of sympathies to enable him to make von Grotjahn a sympathetic figure at all. But that prudential compromise and dishonesty which his campaigning had led him into, I think, affected the integrity of his creative imagination. To make his past acceptable to the American public he had allowed himself to be described in a brochure advertising his lecture tour in 1936–37 as the commander, not of the Bavarian Red Army, but of the army of the Bavarian Free State.[46] He clearly wanted to make use of the widespread sympathy in the United States for the Irish Free State and the armed resistance of the Irish to the British by a process of verbal confusion. He emphatically objected to being called a Communist, too,[47] which in an American context gave a misleading impression, in view of his cooperation with Leviné, *Hoppla*, and the fact that he used to speak at elections in the Weimar Republic on behalf of K.P.D. candidates.

Like other exiled German writers, Toller wanted to reclaim the German cultural tradition from its appropriation by the Nazis. In 1934 he had written an article attempting to show that Carl von Stein was a courageous democrat and not the forerunner of the Nazis, who had made much of his "I know only one Fatherland called Germany."[48] It was in the same propagandist spirit that in 1938 the Schutzverband Deutscher Schriftsteller (Protective union of German writers) adopted an anti-Nazi resolution, which, by quoting Fichte's patriotic call to Germans to resist Napoleon,[49] attempted to make Hitler appear an alien intruder. The portrayal of von Grotjahn reflects the same impulse.

Other signs of this kind of cultural propaganda appear in *Pastor Hall*. The real-life Albert Einst is renamed Johann Herder, no doubt in deliberate allusion to the famous eighteenth-century man of letters. A portrait of Frederick the Great, so closely connected with the period of German culture to which Herder belonged, hangs over Paul von Grotjahn's desk (p. 170). A stanza from a patriotic lyric of the Napoleonic period is quoted: at first it was Max von Schenkendorf's "Freiheit, die ich meine" (Freedom, which I love) (p. 154), later Ernst Moritz Arndt's "Der Gott, der Eisen wachsen liess" (God, who created iron) was substituted.[50]

And what is it that Albert Einst-Johann Herder is represented as quoting from the Apostle Paul? Naturally a text which fits in with the rhetorical ending of the play: "Es wird gesäet in Unehre und wird auferstehen in Herrlichkeit. Es wird gesäet in Schwachheit und wird auferstehen in Kraft" (p. 159). (It [i.e. the seed] is sown in dishonor and will arise with honor. It is sown in weakness and will arise in strength.)

That is Hall's message too. Toller, however, can be allowed the silent comment of his earlier self on it. He had used this quotation as the epigraph for the first edition (Berlin, 1920) of *Der Tag des Proletariats*, (The Day of the Proletariat) the *Sprechchor* (a chorus for speaking) which, in its structure of feeling, resembles *Die Wandlung*. By the third edition (Potsdam 1925) it had been removed. In *Pastor Hall* Toller could be said to be pretending to believe some of what he had believed when he wrote *Die Wandlung*. But, in reality, he was in deep despair.

VI Die Rache Des Verhöhnten Liebhabers
(The Scorned Lover's Revenge)

This chapter would not be complete without an account of one play by Toller which is something of a sport, *Die Rache des verhöhnten Liebhabers*,[51] described by the author as "ein galantes Puppenspiel" (a puppet play about gallantry). It is a dramatization in two acts and in stylized verse, rhyming in couplets, of the third novella in the first book of Bandello's collection of tales (Bandello was a sixteenth century imitator of Boccaccio).[52] It has no obvious connection with any other play of Toller in subject matter or style, though it was his third, being written in January, 1920, when he was in the fortress prison of Eichstädt, but not published in book form until 1925.

Why did Toller dramatize this bawdy story which culminates in rape, and the exposure of the body of the woman who has been raped (and liked it) to the friends of the rapist seducer and her husband, who, since his wife's head is concealed, does not recognize her? Toller himself in his dedication referred to it as "Spiel einer heiteren Laune" (a good-humored play). But the place and date of composition strongly suggest that he had an ulterior motive. For it was in Eichstädt that the sexual pressures on Toller and his fellow prisoners were at their greatest because there were women prisoners there as well. Men and women prisoners developed crushes on one another, men sent the women specimens of their semen: the women sent pubic hair, and a woman prisoner was accustomed to expose herself while her lover masturbated.[53]

Toller describes in detail what went on in his essay on the sexual life of prisoners but is naturally completely silent about his own behavior. He seems to have been a man of strong sexual feelings, however, even something of a womanizer, and it would not, I think, be going too far to see *Die Rache des verhöhnten Liebhabers* as essentially pornographic, a masturbation fantasy disguising itself as a work of culture and taste. The stylization of the language, so exaggerated as to be self-mocking in its sensuousness and sensuality, seems to indicate that Toller was both indulging his imagination and yet protecting himself at the same time against a full awareness of what he was doing:

O Mona! Schlürfe ich den Duft der Augen, die ich dürstend trinke,
In die ich wie in hyazinthne Juninacht versinke,
Strom von roten Flammenfackeln stürmt mein Blut,
Ihr seid der Kelch, in dem der Unrastpilger ruht. (p. 16)

(Oh Moon, I sip the flavor of eyes which thirsty I drink, into which I sink as a hyacinth in a night in June. A stream of red flaming torches rushes through my blood. You are the grail in which the weary pilgrim finds peace.)

Most significant of all is the description of Elena's body after she has been raped:

Ihr starken Lenden. Ihr Gefäss der fruchtbeschwingten Welle,
Du blonder Märchenhain, gelobtes Land der heilgen Schwelle,
Ersehnter Altar Du, in dem der heisse Kämpfer selig ruht,
In Dir zerbrechend löst sich Gott in keuscher Liebesglut . . . . (p. 52)

You sturdy loins. You vessel that receives the fertilising wave. You blond fairy-tale grove, promised land with the sacred threshold. You, the wished for altar in which the struggler finds a blessed peace. Bursting within you, God is released in a chaste glow of love.

and so on, bodily item by bodily item until her neck. It is all very obvious, very coy, and rather corrupt. The mockingly exaggerated erotic metaphors, the self-conscious misuse of religious language are ultimately distasteful. No wonder the woman is a body without a head.

Toller would not be Toller, however, if he did not leave in the play at least a trace of his characteristic themes. The cuckolded husband, Giuseppe (Pompeio in Bandello), is a Venetian senator through whom he satirizes German nationalists by giving him some of their sentiments:

Immorality is growing among the people: usury is triumphant. There is no man who respects the laws fully, though the judges are on our side as they should be. Whomever I pay I have to demand that he take an oath on it to me. Jews and Germans are fools (p. 23)

It is very simple in its method, of course, using the well-tried idea that you are more likely to recognize your own prejudices if someone else expresses the same prejudices against you.

But this very minor theme is itself tangled up in the impure feelings that inspired the play. That Giuseppe is impotent (he has given his sword away), does not even recognize the naked body of his own wife, and is cuckolded is, I think, Toller's fantasy revenge on the prosecutor, who, at his treason trial in 1919, had asked what Toller considered irrelevant questions about his sexual life, and tried to prove he had VD[54]. Lorenzo's exploitation of Elena is not essentially different from Paul Grosshahn's of Grete Hinkemann. Impotence is not funny. In one way Toller could be said in *Hinkemann* to be trying to make amends.

CHAPTER 8

Poetry

TOLLER wrote a good deal of verse, which is unequal in quality. His first volume *Gedichte der Gefangenen: Ein Sonnetenkreis,* (The Prisoners' poems-a sonnet cycle)[1] consisting for the most part of poems written during imprisonment, was published in 1921 at about the same time as two poems especially written for choral recitation: *Tag des Proletariats* (Day of the Proletariat) and *Requiem den gemordeten Brüdern* (Requiem for the murdered Brothers).[2] In 1924 appeared *Das Schwalbenbuch* (The Swallowbook)[3] and *Vormorgen* (Tomorrow),[4] a revised edition of *Gedichte der Gefangenan,* to which an early group of poems, now collected for the first time and entitled *Verse vom Friedhof,* (Verses from the Graveyard), had been added. After 1924 Toller wrote little verse; only another piece for choral recitation, *Weltliche Passion* (Secular Passion)[5] an elegiac celebration of Karl Liebknecht and Rosa Luxemburg, and *Die Feuer-Kantate* (The Fire-Cantata),[6] a propagandist poem on the burning of the Reichstag, which was set to music by Hanns Eisler. Neither was republished in book form.

I *Poems written for public performance*

These poems are the least interesting. The last two, *Weltliche Passion* and *Die Feuer-Kantate,* even more clearly than the plays of the last period, evince a willed simplification of experience; and the mode of retrospective elegiac celebration in *Weltliche Passion* is reminiscent of that in *Feuer aus den Kesseln! (Draw the Fires!).*

Even *Die Feuer-Kantate,* however, shows skill in getting its simple point across effectively by a deliberate exploitation of the antinomies, Helios (sun) and hell, latent in the concept, fire. Through their use of the swastika the Nazis identified themselves (falsely of course) with regenerative fire and by burning down the Reichstag

148

tried to associate the Communists with destructive fire. But the poet predicts that their stratagem will rebound on themselves and the Reichstag fire will become a symbol of the fire of regeneration which is to destroy them.

Weltliche Passion, however, is a much more accomplished work and might be genuinely impressive in performance, though there is no evidence that it was performed. It recounts Liebknecht's opposition to the First World War, the outbreak of the German Revolution, and Liebknecht's and Rosa Luxemburg's part in it and their subsequent capture and murder. The story is narrated by a "Chronist," a chronicler, with interventions from a choir, which is, where necessary, divided into different sections and various voices.[7]

It opens with a celebration of achieved revolution. Since *Weltliche Passion* appeared in a periodical published in Moscow, it is not surprising that the Russian revolution is made to stand as the type of inevitable world revolution. Despite failures elsewhere and, more particularly, the failure in postwar Germany, celebration of the failure of Liebknecht and Luxemburg will hasten arrival at the goal for which they strove.

As with *Die Feuer-Kantate*, Toller constructs his poem out of simple antinomies. Successful revolution is associated with natural growth, harvest, and purposeful work. By contrast, capitalist war is regarded as a perversion of meaningful human activity. In his opposition to the war, Liebknecht revealed both the power and the powerlessness of the spoken word. And Toller makes use of the choral mode to oppose these differing conceptions; the women emphasize its powerlessness (wie fallendes Laub/ Im Sturm der September/ Sie weht vergeht [like a falling leaf in a September storm it is blown away]) and the men its power (Eines Menschen Stimme/ Ist gewaltiger/ Als des Himmels Donner [the voice of a human being is more powerful than the thunder of Heaven]). The contrast is not merely locally effective; it embodies the central concern of the poem, the tension between elegy and celebration.

Two sets of oppositions—the true harvest and the deadly harvest, immediate failure and ultimate success—are then developed in terms of an implicit but increasingly obvious parallel between Liebknecht and Christ.[8] The informer who betrayed Liebknecht and Rosa Luxemburg is clearly identified with Judas (Ich werde Euch sagen/ wo sie schlafen [I will tell you where they sleep]) and the capitalist ruling class with Christ's persecutors. For them "money is power," and with this power they can corrupt those who have neither "bread" nor a "a full belly," to betray their leaders.

In *Weltliche Passion* an allusion is made through an adapted quotation to the second poem in the diptych for the Sprechchöre *Tag des Proletariats* and *Requiem den gemordeten Brüdern:*

> Senkt die Fahnen
> Fahnen des Kampfes
> Fahnen der Freiheit
> Senkt sie zur Erde
> Zum Schoss der Mutter.

(Haul the flags down, the flags of struggle, the flags of freedom; haul them to the ground, to the mother's womb.)

Of Toller's propaganda poems these two are the most interesting, for though they are simplifications of, they are related to, Toller's deeper experience. As pieces intended for public performance they are more elaborate than *Weltliche Passion*, the first particularly so. In *Tag des Proletariats* not only are parts taken by a full choir and various of its subdivisions and several soloists, but there are musical interludes for orchestra or organ.

Tag des Proletariats, unlike *Weltliche Passion* written in regular rhyming verse, opens with a call by the full choir for centuries of oppression to end, a process that is associated with struggle: "Erkämpft! Erkämpft, Erkämpft euch den Tag!" (p. 11) (Win, win, win the day for yourselves). But, as in *Die Wandlung*, the struggle is not envisaged at all. By some mysterious process "Fesseln zerfallen/ Gebändigter Wucht" (mastered, the fetters' burden collapses into fragments). It is just a matter of holding up the Red Flag and "Der Tag bricht an! Die Fackel loht" (The day dawns: the torch blazes).

But the meanings of *Tag des Proletariats* are deliberately qualified by those of *Requiem den gemordeten Brüdern*. And this poem, because of its somber nature, has none of the musical accompaniment of the first and is mostly in unrhymed verse. *Requiem den gemordeten Brüdern* begins with the chorus, quoted in a slightly adapted version in *Weltliche Passion*, which is repeated twice, each time with an accession of meaning, once during and once at the end of the poem. The failure of the revolution is admitted at the start, and this colors what follows, while it alters the meaning of *Tag des*

Proletariats, the achievement celebrated there now appearing premature or perhaps merely an anticipatory triumph of the imagination.

In the first poem there had not been a clear distinction between the roles of men and women, but in *Requiem den gemordeten Brüdern* they are differentiated. This differentiation, which is absent from *Masse-Mensch* because the protagonist is herself a woman, enables Toller to present a diagrammatic version of the experience embodied in the play while pushing the poem toward the simple elegiac pathos of which the title gives earnest; for the women, since they take no active part in the revolution, become the guardians of that pathos.

But Toller is thereby enabled to eat his cake and have it. For while the men insist on the tragic necessity of revolutionary war:

> Nicht Jubel grüsst den Krieg,
> Die Waffe blinder Unvernunft (p. 21)

(Rejoicing does not greet the war, the weapons of blind unreason),

the women (or at least some of them) condemn violence altogether:

> Zerbrecht die Eisenwaffen, Männer!
> Zerbrecht die Waffen der verwesten Zeit! (p. 21)

(Smash the weapons of iron, men; smash the weapons of the rotten epoch.)

The problem of revolutionary violence is further glossed over by Toller's evident wish to contrast oppressor and victim in the simple manner promised by the title. The fate of the revolutionaries after the revolution receives the stress:

> Wie Sklaven tragen sie die Hände überm Haupt,
> Wie Sklaven werden vorwärts sie gestossen,
> O Schwestern,
> Nacht erwürgte Licht. (p. 21)

(Like slaves they hold their hands above their heads: like slaves they are thrust forward. Oh, sisters, night has swallowed the light.)

Further special pleading occurs with the evocation of the brutal murder of Gustav Landauer, the anarchist pacifist who withdrew from active participation in the Räterepublik when the Communists

came to power. Landauer was not at all typical of his fellow revolutionaries.[9]

Toller cannot allow the role of defeat to become dominant in a
propagandist piece, and so the poem ends with the chorus of young
people predicting the future success of the revolution and with the
repetition of the opening chorus, which by now sounds sentimental.

II   Vormorgen

Verse vom Friedhof (Verses from the Graveyard), the first section
of *Vormorgen* (Tomorrow),[10] is an impressive cycle of poems. By
what must have been careful arrangement, Toller has given to these
poems, written between 1912 and 1918, the effect of a sequence.
There are weak poems in *Verse vom Friedhof*, but these cannot be
isolated from the context, which by juxtaposition and implicit allusion qualifies that weakness, so that they emerge as records of a state
of feeling whose limitations are known to the author.

The sequence begins with *Der Ringende* ('The Striver'), which is
about the adolescent's struggle to achieve self-sufficient manhood by
transcending both alienation from and lingering dependence on the
mother. The stages in Toller's experience of and attitude to the war
are then systematically embodied. First in *Marschlied* ('Marching
Song'), which denies the self-fulfillment glimpsed in *Der Ringende:*
for the young there is only a common fate; a perversion of childhood
brought about by a Germany which is symbolized as an unfulfilled
mother. The next five poems *Morgen; Geschützwache* ('On Duty by
the Cannon'); *Gang zum Schützengraben* ('On the Way to the
Trenches'); *Gang zur Ruhestellung* ('On the Way to Rest Quarters');
and *Stellungskrieg* ('War of Attrition') evoke different but typical
aspects of the war, in consonance with the consciousness expressed
in *Marschlied,* in a bare imagistic manner. Then with *Konzert,* written almost certainly out of an experience Toller had when on leave,
there is a countermovement of feeling, a vision of a fundamental
change of consciousness wrought by music, which though temporary, is an earnest of what human life could be. The note of explicit
rhetorical protest against the war is heard first in *Leichen in Pries-
terwald* (Corpses in Bois le Prêtre) and is continued and extended in
Alp ('Nightmare'), an exercise in the symbolic grotesque which can
be related to *Die Wandlung*. The mode is used again, but with a
more explicit didacticism, in *Menschen,* which attacks the society

back home. Then follow three weak poems of political protest
against the war: *An die Dichter* ('To the Writers'), *Den Müttern* ('To
the Mothers'), and *Ich habe euch umarmt* ('I have embraced you').
In the first two poems there is an embarrassingly emotional stri-
dency and in the last, which is about Toller's contact with the workers, an equally embarrassing emotionalism. But the last two poems
in the collection *Über meiner Zelle* ('Over my Cell') and *Deutschland*, written clearly when Toller was in a military prison for his
political agitation against the war, in their somber but wistful acceptance of defeat, imply a criticism of the simple stridencies of the
poems that have immediately preceded them.

The finest poems in the collection are undoubtedly *Morgen*,
('Morning'), *Geschützwache*, ('On Duty by the Cannon') *Gang zum
Schützengraben*, ('On the way to the Trenches') *Gang zur Ruhestellung*, ('On the way to Rest Quarters') and *Stellungskrieg* ('War of
Attrition'). Their poetic method is unlike that used in any other
of Toller's poems. They are economical; direct and rhetorically
heightened statements of feeling are usually absent; and their
meanings develop largely by implication. They are examples of
expressive form; their indirect method notates the partial anaes-
thesia of feeling consequent on an attempt to believe that what is
happening is inevitable. The imagic collocations and implications,
however, exhibit the subterranean workings of a sensitive and
humane feeling.

The best of these poems, *Geschützwache* ('On Duty by the Cannon') is worth analyzing in full.

> Sternenhimmel.
> Gebändigtes Untier
> Glänzt mein Geschütz.
> Glotzt mit schwarzem Rohr
> Zum milchigen Mond.
> Käuzchen schreit.
> Wimmert im Dorf ein Kind.
> Geschoss,
> Tückischer Wolf,
> Bricht ins schlafende Haus.
> Lindenblüten duftet die Nacht. (p. 50)

(The starry sky: my cannon gleams, a tamed monster, gapes with black
barrel at the milky moon: a little screech owl cries. A child whimpers in the
village: a shell, a malicious wolf, breaks into the sleeping house. The night is
fragrant with lime blossoms.)

This poem consists of a series of statements in six sentences, one of which is verbless and none of which contains any subordinate clauses. The form is significant. Toller, on duty by his cannon at night, naturally has to keep his senses alert, but this alertness is inimical to reflection. His consciousness is heightened, but in terms of a specialized attention. The external world impinges upon him as a succession of apparently discrete experiences registered by different senses: sight in the first two sentences, hearing in the next three, smell in the last. Only in "Gebändigtes Untier" (tamed monster) and "Tückischer Wolf" (malicious wolf) is there an explicit judgment on what he sees, hears, and smells.

The poem begins and ends with, and is punctuated halfway through by, an evocation of aspects of the natural world: the starry sky and the moon, the cry of an owl, the smell of lime blossom. Since each of these is registered by a different sense, they impinge with all the more force. The phenomena of war are then presented as perversions of this natural world. The blackness of the barrel of the cannon contrasts with the whiteness of the moon; the moon is, through "milky," associated with motherhood, while the cannon is unnatural, an "Untier" whose destructive sterility is implicitly mocked by the fact that even at the front the owl cries and lime blossoms fill the air with scent.

These antinomies are beautifully exemplified in the ambiguous implications of "Wimmert im Dorf ein Kind" (a child whimpers in the village). Is the child's whimpering natural, analagous to the cry of the screech owl? Or is it the manifestation of a fear that is both unchildish and only too justified? Toller does not oppose man and nature too simply, however: a shell has something in common with a wolf; but, even so, the differences between them are more important than their similarities. Even if the predatoriness of a wolf is regarded anthropomorphically as voluntaristic rather than instinctive ("Tückischer"), yet, nonetheless, a wolf must be in contact with its victim, and its acts are not only the direct embodiment of its purpose but are limited by its bodily strength. A wolf cannot break into a house at all, let alone do so by "accident" (for it is implied that the house was not the shell's target).

We do not even know whether the shell has been fired by a German or an Allied gun, for that does not matter. And we are implicitly invited to connect the detonated shell with just such a cannon as the one that "mit schwarzem Rohr" (with black barrel)

Toller is guarding. In judging the "Geschoss" (shell) as a "Tüc-kischer Wolf" (malicious wolf) Toller is not judging an activity sepa-rated from himself: it is a type of that in which he is engaged, if, at the present, only potentially. The sensuous experience evoked by the last line is a submerged human protest. The smell of the lime blossom had, no doubt, been present all the time, but only now, in reaction, does he become aware of it. The economical artistry of the poem renders effectively the destructive alienation of the war from the natural world, of which human beings are a part because they are living things.

The poems that Toller wrote in prison, with the exception of the concluding poems in *Verse vom Friedhof,* (Verses from the Graveyard) can be found in the *Lieder der Gefangenen* (The Prison-ers' Songs) section of *Vormorgen* (Tomorrow) and *Das Schwalben-buch* (The Swallowbook). On the whole, the first of these covers the earlier period of his imprisonment, *Das Schwalbenbuch* the later.

Like *Verse vom Friedhof, Lieder der Gefangenen* is intended as a sequence: its subtitle, when published earlier and separately as *Gedichte des Gefangenen,* was *ein Sonettenkreis* (a sonnet cycle). Two plaques ("zwei Tafeln") serve as a prelude to the volume: 'Den Toten der Revolution' and 'Den Lebenden' (To the Revolutionary Dead: To the Living), while 'Unser Weg, dem Andenken Kurt Eis-ners' ('Our Way: to the Memory of Kurt Eisner') forms a kind of epilogue. The theme of the collection is indicated in the first prison poem proper ('An alle Gefangenen') ('To All Prisoners') with its key line "Wer kann vom sich sagen, er sei nicht gefangenen" ("Who can say of himself that he is not imprisoned?").

But as a sequence, *Lieder der Gefangenen* is not successful. In the body of the work we fail to note the dramatic progress discoverable in *Verse vom Friedhof,* while the framing poems mentioned above exhibit the simplifying histrionicism of Toller's public manner. The poems in the body of the volume reflect various aspects of the strain of prolonged imprisonment, which are vividily evoked in Toller's prose works, *Eine Jugend in Deutschland* (Growing up in Germany) and *Briefe aus dem Gefängnis* (Letters from Prison). The extreme strain meant that Toller's emotions were frequently feverish. In particular, the perpetual struggle to adjust himself to his situation and his inability to do so for very long together led to emotional oscillations. To communicate feelings in an extreme situation to those who have not experienced it is always difficult, of course, but a heightened emotionalism acts as a further barrier to empathy and too frequently leads to a detached, patronizing pity in the reader: "poor chap, he must have been in a state to write like that." Moreover, Toller is constantly attempting, through a projected generalization of his own emotions, to articulate what he thinks is a common feeling among his fellow prisoners.[11] No doubt there were correspondences, but Toller does not seem to have allowed for differences.

Nonetheless, there is a handful of impressive poems: 'Nächte' ('Nights'), 'Gefangener und Tod' ('Prisoner and Death'), 'Verweilen um Mitternacht' ('Watch at Midnight'), 'Gefangener reicht dem Tod die Hand' ('A prisoner shakes hands with Death'). An analysis of the first of these will perhaps indicate the quality that, particularly as a result of late revision, Toller could achieve:

> Nächte bergen stilles Weinen,
> Pocht wie Kindertritt an Deine Wand,
> Lauscht erschreckt: Will jemand Deine Hand?
> Weisst: Due reichst die nur den Steinen.
>
> Nächte bergen Trotz und Stöhnen,
> Wilde Sucht nach einer Frau,
> Not des Blutes bleicht Dich grau,
> Blecken Fratzen, die Dich höhnen.
>
> Nächte bergen niegesungne Lieder,
> Nachttau blühn sie, samtne Schmetterlinge,
> Küssen die verborgnen Dinge,
>
> Willst sie haschen, sind verweht. (p. 81)

(Nights conceal quiet crying. There's a knock like a child's footstep on your wall. You listen, frightened: does anyone want your hand? You know you will give it only to the stones. Nights conceal defiance and groans, a frenzied search for a woman. The needs of your blood bleach you gray: grimacing faces show their teeth and mock you. Nights conceal songs which have never been sung: in the night dew they blossom, velvet butterflies, and kiss hidden things. If you want to catch them they are blown away.)

What is striking is the way in which the simple rhetorical framework of the poem, with the repetition at the beginning of each stanza of the formula "Nächte bergen" (Nights conceal) plus (syntactical) objects, is used to control the articulation of what, at first glance, might appear to be a chaos of feelings. Thus the second stanza, where the feelings are particularly excited and inchoate, is separated by unique variations in its syntactical structure from the first and third; whereas the structure of these last is "Nächte bergen" plus adjective plus noun, that of the first line of the second stanza is "Nächte bergen" plus noun plus noun. Similarly, "Blecken Fratzen die dich höhnen" is the only line in the second stanza to begin with a verb; but in the first stanza there are three (Pocht: Lauscht: Weisst) and in the final stanza two (Küssen: Willst). This means that, particularly since the second stanza has no medial caesuras (as has the first) or pronounced terminal pauses (as has the last stanza), it drives on to the climax of feeling represented by its last line. Further, the beautiful effect of the concluding line of the poem is created by its deliberate separation from the rest of the third stanza, not only typographically but structurally. Instead of the rhyme scheme *abba,* to which the reader has become used with the preceding stanzas, there is instead *abbc,* with a functional frustration of expectation. The consequent pause between the final and penultimate line of the stanza enacts by analogy the attempts to catch a butterfly, a pursuit that often leads to a momentary belief that one has caught it before realizing that, after all, one hasn't. Again, in the first stanza, the beginning of a new sentence in the third line enforces a heavy caesural pause which analogously evokes the hallucinatory start described by the sense. This is echoed in the following line by the early caesural pause after "Weisst" in the fourth line. The realization of reality does not rush back, it returns only reluctantly.

Nächte gives unity to what appear to be diverse feelings—grief, loneliness, longing for parenthood, desire—a vision of ungraspable harmony and beauty, because they have a common element, illusion, and a common cause, unfulfilled sexual need.

III   Das Schwalbenbuch

Without doubt *Das Schwalbenbuch* (The Swallowbook) is Toller's most celebrated collection of poems. More explicitly than either *Verse vom Friedhof* (Verses from the Graveyard) or *Lieder der Gefangenen* (The Prisoners' Songs) it is a poetic cycle, though even the finest poems are inferior to the best in these earlier collections. Moreover, *Das Schwalbenbuch* contains poems that, isolated from their context, would be too frail and vague to be considered poems at all.

But the observation of nonhuman creatures gives Toller, on the whole, a discipline of feeling too often absent from *Lieder der Gefangenen*. Just because the swallows are fundamentally different from himself he cannot use them as easily as he can other human beings as pegs on which to hang his own emotions. Nonetheless, an occasional archness of tone indicates a lapse into anthropomorphism, and sometimes Toller forces his feelings or becomes crudely didactic. Moreover, the cycle is in free verse, which because it is not a disciplined form—and some of the less successful pieces not surprisingly move toward prose—offers a strong temptation to emotional indulgence, even though at the same time it enables Toller to cultivate a fuller tonal range in poetry than ever before. But whatever the faults of the cycle, they are held in sufficient check to ensure its success as a whole.

Toller responds to the swallows in three ways; as creatures different from men with ways of their own from which men can learn; as creatures whose behavior is analogous in certain respects to human behavior; and as repositories of symbolic meaning—or, to put it more technically, as vehicles for new tenors. The flexibility of method enables Toller to notate the trajectory of his own feelings with spontaneity and naturalness as they change from despair to something akin to joy and finally to a quiet stoical strength:

> Zum Winterflug
> Sammeln sich die Schwalben.
>
> Zur Winterstille
> Sammelt sich mein Herz. (p. 52)

(The swallows gather for their winter flight. My heart gathers itself for winter stillness.)

And this inner change is accompanied by, indeed depends upon, the wider meanings learned from the swallows. This involves a renewed commitment to revolution,[12] whose significance the poet becomes more fully aware of through the swallows:

> Bevor nicht die Menschen wiederfinden den Grund ihrer Tierheit,
> Bevor sie nicht sind
> Sind
> Wird ihr Kampf nur wert sein
> Neuen Kampfes,

Und noch ihre heiligste Wandlung
Wird wert sein neuer Wandlung. (pp. 54–55)

(Unless men rediscover their creaturely basis, unless they are Are, their struggle will lead only to a fresh struggle, and their holiest transformation will still need a fresh transformation.)

The natural, spontaneous, creative fulfillment of being characteristic of the swallows, an implied concept which has all the authority of close observation behind it, painstakingly and lovingly built up in the cycle, is the goal for men, too.

The first part of the sequence deals with the abyss of spirit from which the swallows were to rescue Toller. The tragic death of a friend has made the loneliness and oppression of prison almost unbearable (p. 5). The pressures of imprisonment have attacked his soul:

> Und wohin Du blickst,
> Überall
> Überall siehst Du Gitterstäbe (p. 6)

(And wherever you look, you see barred windows.)

But there is an explicit recognition of need and desire, which aches so much to find release that it is afraid to recognize itself too fully, and so expresses itself in fragmented particulars (p. 7). Books, his only remaining resource, begin to fail him as his consciousness begins to go to pieces (p. 8). Suicide (or perhaps just lying down and giving up) tempts him (p. 8). It is at this moment, however, that he hears the swallows' song (p. 8) and life and hope begin to return (p. 9). A self-given invitation to a life-enhancing, disciplined abandonment of spirit is embodied in the idea of the dance:

> Tanze meine atmende Brust,
> Tanzet Ihr wunden geketteten Augen,
> Tanzet! Tanzet! (p. 10)

(Dance my heavy breast, dance you wounded fettered eyes, dance, dance.)

But in his isolation of spirit the prisoner identifies the swallows with writers like himself. The swallows come to Winter expecting Spring: the poets, who are essentially lonely, love men and yet suffer from them (p. 11). At one point he thinks that the swallows have abandoned him and when they return part of their latent metaphorical significance becomes patent. They become vehicles for the Spring of the revolution, the renewal of life which is what revolution is about (p. 16). Through the freedom of the swallows, which is contrasted with the oppressed condition of men and domestic animals, he realizes the significance of the free human spirit (pp. 17–18). Further, whereas cathedrals are dedicated "Dem Jenseits / Dem Tode" (to the beyond, to death) (p. 19) because built by oppressed labor from costly materials, the swallows dedicate their nest "Der Erde / Dem Leben" (p. 19) (to the earth, to life). The swallows' eggs are "Fünf festliche Tempel keimenden Lebens" (Five festive temples of germinating life) (p. 22), whereas human motives are "Beschattet von täglicher Not" (overshadowed by daily need). Moreover, even the extremest of human joys, because defined in relation to inhumanity and oppression, never have the spontaneous creativity of a swallow's flight (p. 24). Nonetheless, through the swallows he begins to feel himself in significant relationship to the whole cosmos (p. 28).

It is from this inner stillness that the poet is able to launch an attack on contemporary German society. Moreover, the swallows provide a paradigm of revolutionary activity. He describes how, in the prison yard, he saw a crowd of swallows attack a sparrow hawk, making it disgorge its prey: "In seligen Flügen feiern die Schwalben den Sieg der Gemeinschaft" (In happy swoops the swallows celebrate the victory of community) (p. 31). The application is obvious.

There follow a number of poems describing the hatching of the swallows' eggs and the nurture and growth of the nestlings. What is implicitly stressed is an ideal of parenthood and family life naturally realized by the birds: "Geheimes Gesetz / Waltet" (A secret law rules) (p. 37). However the swallows are subject to the primeval curse; they must destroy other creatures to live ("Weh uns! Was lebt mordet"—Alas, any being that lives murders) (p. 38), an insight relatable to the recognition in *Hinkemann* of a residuum of unavoidable suffering.

Through the swallows Toller learns to cultivate a joy of the spirit that will make his imprisonment more endurable and to rejoice in the phenomenal world, seeing it with the eyes of the fledgling making its first flight. "Über sich die leuchtende,/ Warmende Sonne, unter sich die blühende atmende Erde" (Over him the light-giving, warmth-giving sun: under him the blossoming breathing earth) (p. 43). Lastly, the way in which the swallows face unavoidable tragedy is both an implicit criticism of the way human beings behave under such circumstances and an example; the loving care with which the parent birds sustain each other after frost has killed off their second brood is that which men should display but do not:

> Anders trauert Ihr, meine Schwalben, als Menschen trauern.
> Eure Klage: ein frierendes Erschauern vor dem Hauche der
> Unendlichkeit. (p. 50)

(My swallows, you mourn differently from the way men mourn. Your lament: a freezing shudder at the breath of eternity.)

CHAPTER 9

Toller's Prose

THOUGH Toller wrote a considerable number of articles for various periodicals, he published only four volumes of prose: *Justiz (Justice)*, a detailed and well-researched attack, based partly on personal experience, on the Bavarian treatment of left-wing political prisoners; *Quer durch (Right Across)*, an account of his travels in Russia and America; a volume of letters written while he was in prison in Bavaria *(Briefe aus dem Gefängnis) (Letters from Prison)*, and what some critics regard as his finest work, his autobiography up to 1924, *Eine Jugend in Deutschland (Growing up in Germany)*. Except for *Justiz*, which is too technical to be treated at all, I will have something to say about all of them.

I Quer Durch *(Right Across)*

Quer durch, Toller's travel book about his visits to Russia (1926) and the U.S.A. (1929), is a good piece of journalism. It is lively, makes its points without belaboring them, and yet, in brief compass, conveys a great deal of information about each country. The anecdotes are interesting in themselves and yet illustrate some point in a telling manner: the descriptions are vivid and purposeful and never merely objective or picturesque: they are strengthened not only by factual details, but, where necessary, by statistics.

Quer durch is, however, more than journalism: it has a serious theme, which is suggested not so much by its German title, but by *Which World, Which Way?*[1] the title of the English version. Two societies, one capitalist, the other socialist, are diagnosed and contrasted. Not that the book is wholly successful: the second part dealing with Russia, and fascinating as journalism, is inferior to the first, which has the U.S.A. as its subject and in which journalism becomes art. The inferiority of the second part results from its not

162

having been initially written for publication (and Toller was hesitant about publishing it), and from the fact that, though making penetrating incidental criticisms of the Bolshevik regime, Toller was, in essentials, reflecting to the outside world the regime's own view of itself. Since, therefore, only the first part can claim to be art, I am limiting myself to a consideration of that part only.

It is a work of art not because it is a critique of advanced capitalist society about to slide into a slump, but because of the manner in which the critique is made. Toller rarely emphasizes his points. Indeed, his reports on various aspects of American society often appear casual and fragmentary, mere *Reisebilder* (travel pictures) as he called them; but by juxtaposition and implied accretional thematic development (helped by some cleverly chosen photographs) a unified interpretation emerges. Toller might have made a good producer of television documentaries. There is no vituperation, no flight of rhetoric, just a report of what he has seen or heard or has discovered from reliable sources. Only in the treatment of Aimee Sempel McPherson does he use slight, apparently indulgent, but really telling irony which contrasts favorably with Evelyn Waugh's heavy-handed satire of her in *Vile Bodies* as Mrs. Ape.

The theme is stated in the opening sentence: " 'You have the freedom, we have the statue' is a saying in the revue Fifty Million Frenchmen, which is being played in New York. Of this saying only the second part is true" (p. 9). Immediately Toller develops one aspect of that theme: he narrates how he was held incommunicado by the immigration authorities, not being allowed to leave the ship but having to spend a further night on board ("I was once again a prisoner"—p. 11) before being taken to Ellis Island for screening. The motif that capitalism involves overt injustice and repression is, of course, to be heard again. But a more subtle facet of the theme receives its first treatment in the exchange between Toller and a reporter who was questioning him:

"What is Gerhart Hauptmann worth?" As I was saying a few words about Hauptmann's works, he interrupted me: "No, I mean what he is really worth, what he earns." (p. 11)

Capitalism has gone so far that the creative works of a major artist like Gerhart Hauptmann can be regarded merely as salable commodities. It is significant that this should involve a special use of "wert." Such a society cannot be truly free.

Toller does full justice to the prosperity of the workers, the comfort in which many of them live—I am drawing out explicitly much that Toller left implicit. He can see that, subjectively, many of them share bourgeois values, a process that has been encouraged by certain companies, where twenty-five percent of the share capital is in the hands of the workers. This prosperity, which was about to give way to depression (it was 1929), had been caused by the expansion of U.S. capitalism. The First World War had enabled it to capture markets hitherto dominated by European countries. But this prosperity had led to a weakening of what political consciousness there had previously been: socialism was in retreat and the International Workers of the World was no more. The unions' view of their present role was essentially bourgeois; they charged exorbitant membership dues and excluded negroes from membership.

But, objectively speaking, even the most prosperous of the workers—and prosperity was very patchy—were an oppressed proletariat. They could, for example, be fired at a moment's notice, something that even in Germany could not happen. Moreover, if a worker was ill or injured, there were no adequate safeguards to prevent his sinking into extreme poverty. Carrying his critique further, Toller implies that the workers have bought their prosperity and their subjective feeling that they are middle class by, objectively speaking, allowing themselves to be enslaved by the power of capital. No German industrialist, however much he would like to, would dare to treat his workers as they were treated at Ford's in 1929. There they were not allowed to speak to one another, were not allowed a decent lunch break, had nowhere to sit down in comfort, were charged outrageous fines for being late, and were in the power of the plant's police, who could, and did, beat them up and in one case were said to have actually shot a man. The role of the plant police represents a development of Toller's first motif.

The oppression is exacerbated by the mass production conveyor belt system, which has carried the division of labor to an ultimate. By means of typographical arrangement, Toller clearly conveys its dehumanizing, deadening monotony:

Each man performs one operation, for eight hours, countless times, one and the same operation:
    one and the same operation
    This one fixes a screw

This one a piece of tubular casing
This one hangs crankshafts on overhead moving brackets
This one attaches a piece of the suspension
This one strikes two blows with the hammer
This one bores with an automatic drill
This one puts a strip of brass in the engine
This one piles up the stamped tinplate
Always the same operation. (p. 20)

Such mechanization is inevitable under any system, as he came reluctantly to realize when he saw the workers being trained in Moscow at Zit; but in a capitalist context, where the worker is alienated from the end product of his labor, and where he is oppressed, as at Ford's, it can become a hell on earth. And Toller quotes one of the nicknames given to the factory by the workers: Ford's Hell.

His visit to Armour's slaughterhouse, the animals' hell as he called it, implicitly underscores the significance of a conveyor belt system for the mass production of meat. The suffering of the animals, when the system failed to work, he describes graphically. But, of course, the full significance of his viewpoint here can be grasped only if one knows *Das Schwalbenbuch*.

In the section on San Quentin prison, the critique is both extended and sophisticated. In Germany, Toller had been active in a campaign for the release of Max Hölz, whom he regarded as a political prisoner wrongly incarcerated on a murder charge. But Tom Mooney's was an even clearer case then that of Max Hölz. There was no doubt that he was framed, and even the judge who had sentenced him no longer believed in his guilt and had sought to secure his release. But the government of California had insisted on keeping him in prison. The political motivation was obvious: Tom Mooney was a socialist, and before his arrest the authorities had been trying to nail him for a number of years.

And now Toller's critique becomes more sophisticated: he begins to analyze the superstructure corresponding to the capitalist base. It is a superstructure that, characteristically, involves a major contradiction: an alienation from the human which manifests itself in an apparent affirmation of it. That Americans should have no concept of the social causes of crime but should regard criminals merely as "bad people" is a manifestation of this, for it leads to oppression.

The sentences are long and, in some cases, indeterminate; there is overcrowding, so that a prisoner is never left alone but has to share his cell with another prisoner; and the cells are illuminated day and night. Nobody seems aware that such conditions are dehumanizing; the authorities can even believe, for example, that the prisoners are treated well. When Toller visited the condemned men's cells he found potted plants outside them—and a warder, whom he quotes, illustrates his point beautifully:

"Sometimes the prisoners want to be hanged to music. Oh they're well treated" continued the warder. "They get what they want. One wanted jazz music, so the prison band played jazz dances for him. They get better food than we warders do, even chicken for dinner." (p. 38)

As Toller dryly comments later:

Potted plants, chicken for dinner, gallows with music: that's civilization. (loc. cit.)

Before developing his analysis of the superstructure further, Toller backs up the point, made through his visit to Tom Mooney, that the law is used for political repression, by quoting, with a minimum of comment, brief factual reports of the arrests of socialists all over the United States merely for distributing leaflets. And then he apparently abruptly moves on to a full description of the religious activities and shady personal history of Aimee Sempel McPherson. But he is by no means going off at a tangent. Without ever saying so in so many words, he demonstrates how Aimee's appeal is compounded of spiritual (and probably more material) fraud, the extraordinary clever exploitation of theatrical effects, and the most banal appeals to the chauvinism and the gullibility of the American public. While apparently appealing to genuine religious conceptions, she empties them of real content and thus manifests the contradiction in the superstructure of American society which I mentioned earlier. He draws attention to the significance of the relationship between the name of Aimee's church and American mortuary customs:

She is the founder and prophetess of a large church which (what else could a church be called in a country in which the dead are made up: keep smiling in death as well) is called the church of the Smiling Light and has many thousand members. (pp. 44–45)

Toller, who had read Schopenhauer's "Über den Tod" (On Death) when in prison, and who had praised Henri Barbusse for the profundity of his understanding of the nature of death,[2] knew, as did Evelyn Waugh, writing from a Catholic standpoint in *The Loved One*, that such an attitude toward death was the symptom of a profound alienation from life.

In case the essential point had not emerged from an examination of Aimee herself, in the next chapter, by merely transcribing newspaper advertisements of evangelical meetings, Toller demonstrates that Aimee was not a unique phenomenon: she was merely more successful than her competitors. And Toller makes one of his few explicit points to illuminate the relation between base and superstructure:

Everywhere rich people underwrite these sects. Each church has its little Rockefellers as its holy protectors. A good method against discontent, despair and rebellious stirrings. (p. 54)

And, by a vivid description of a service at a Negro church in New York, Toller takes his analysis further. Through religion the thwarted aspirations of the Negroes are expressed in a form which itself represents, through a reflex assertion of worth—that they are God's chosen people—their consciousness of their own subjection. In their case it is understandable because they are without any power base in the community at all. He quotes from the sermon he heard:

"Now the negroes are the chosen people. To them, first of all, will Christ come. To a few he has come today, already. The people have seen it. Yes, he has come, he has come, he has come." (pp. 56–57)

As a result of this, there is a vitality, a spontaneity about the Negroes' services which make them quite different from the results of the calculated theatricality of an Aimee Sempel McPherson. The orgiastic abandon of the dancing in the service that Toller attended, and that he found infectious, is a manifestation of a thwarted and distorted but nonetheless powerful human creativity. This creativity he emphasizes in another context in his description of King Vidor's film *Hallelujah*:

But those noble, black actors. Those faces! Those movements! Those songs! Those dances! Those choirs! Splendid in their wildness, their untameability, their animal grief. (p. 60)

Indeed, in his section on the films (the talkies had recently been introduced) Toller shows that they have a significant part to play in reinforcing the alienated consciousness reflected in the superstructure: "By lies they turn social discords and spiritual conflicts into harmonies. They conceal from themselves the inescapability of cosmic fate, of death." (p. 59)

In making this last point, Toller is enabled to establish a clear connection between the current role of the cinema in American society and that of commercialized religion by again referring to American mortuary customs—this time more fully:

Isn't it strange that in America each corpse is embalmed, that pads of cotton wool are put in the corpse's mouth when he is in his coffin in order to plump up his sunken cheeks, that they are made up. (p. 59)

But Toller is able to perceive the untapped potentialities of the talking film and already understands its artistic requirements. Further, he maintains that the documentary possibilities of the film could help establish a common global consciousness:

If you read over morning coffee that, to recall a saying of Goethe's, away down there in Turkey people are killing each other, scarcely anybody is concerned about it, for most people lack the power of imagination. However, if the news becomes pictures, noise and words, he has a vision which compels him to participate in the fate of men who work and suffer in the farthest corner of the earth. (p. 61)

Toller's examination of the situation of the film (and the theater as well) is, of course, implicitly integrated into his general critique. The function of art is to develop awareness and to change consciousness: it is that part of the superstructure which is dynamic. But in the U.S.A. the dynamic potentialities of the two most powerful, because most popular, media are unrealized because of their relationship to the capitalist base.

Toller now examines certain aspects of the criminal underworld to show here, too, the complexity of the relationship with capitalism. Prohibition brings out corruption in the police. Since the sale of alcoholic beverages is illegal and the police is the only agency that can enforce the law, it is in an excellent position not only to obtain protection money from bootleggers, but to enter the illegal business on its own account. The police is so involved with the capitalist order that it protects, that it not only fails to repress dissent, but is capable of putting private profit before the laws it is supposed to uphold—a contradiction well suggested by a telling detail that Toller includes: the police, when engaged in their illegal marketing activities, used police cars with police sirens.

Prostitution, though illegal, was widespread and organized in various ways which corresponded to the social class of the client. In its lowest stratum, with a clientele largely drawn from the proletariat, its organization was analogous to that of capitalist industrial production:

Even the call: who is going to bed? was an exaggeration. For there was no time to go to bed since the sexual act lasted for from perhaps three to five minutes. I had the impression that the girls had to urge on their customers just as the foremen at Ford's did the workers. The girls, young and old, pretty and ravaged, serve six to ten men an hour when business is good. (p. 68)

The fact that prostitution was widespread was apparently at odds with an ideology of sexual purity expressed in laws protecting American women from exploitation. But this contradiction was only apparent; virginity itself was regarded as capital to invest in such a manner as to get the best material rewards: "Only at the age of marriage does virginity become capital again and the courage to surrender it, folly" (p. 72).

Further, and in an essentially similar way, less scrupulous women exploit the law to make small fortunes for themselves, on the frequently flimsy grounds that they were the victims of improper advances.

Naturally and inevitably, Toller ends this tightly organized critique with an examination of the plight of the American Negro, particularly in the Southern states. It is the finale in which his major themes are restated fortissimo. The Negro was deprived of elementary political rights, being excluded from voting: he was, as Toller has already indicated, oppressed by the white proletariat, not being able to join a union. The Negro was not protected by the law and was frequently framed and lynched (Toller cites several recent instances of each). He was not really regarded as a human being at all. Toller quotes an unfeeling report of a lynching from the *Los Angeles Times*, developing the significance of what he had said in the previous section.

And how very well off the white girls in the Southern States are. If they find themselves pregnant, they have always an excuse ready: some black or other has raped them. They keep their honor and Judge Lynch punishes the negro for his lack of honor. For what does the oath of a negro count? (p. 76)

And yet it was from this, the most oppressed class of all, that Toller saw major changes coming: "Today a band of black pioneers are fighting: tomorrow a self-confident army of millions will be fighting for human rights" (p. 78).

II   Eine Jugend in Deutschland
Growing up in Germany

Many think Toller's autobiography, *Eine Jugend in Deutschland*, his finest work. In February, 1933, Toller had narrowly escaped arrest, in May his books, along with those of many other writers, had been banned and burned, and in August of the same year, he had become officially stateless. During the early months of exile Toller, who was not yet caught up in the whirl of speaking and campaigning to which he was to devote the greater part of his remaining energies, had sufficient leisure to bestow considerable care on the composition of his autobiography, parts of which had been written some time before. It was published and went into a second edition before 1933 was out.

The aim of *Eine Jugend*, which covers the years from boyhood in East Prussia to his release from Niederschönenfeld in July, 1924, was to show that German fascism was a foreseeable development from Germany's recent past. Toller felt, not without reason, that his own experiences had been representative of those of his generation, as is suggested by the deliberately generalizing title: *Eine Jugend in Deutschland* (Growing Up in Germany lit: Youth in Germany). As he says: "Not only my youth is shown here, but the youth of a generation and a piece of contemporary history as well" (p. 27).

But there was another reason why Toller was in a good position to write such a book. His political judgment had always been remarkably sound, and, unlike the K.P.D., he had never made the mistake of underestimating Hitler. Toller, however, must have been aware that, in the circumstances, *Eine Jugend* would be lost on his fellow countrymen. They were not in a position to read a work published in Holland by a stateless, Jewish, socialist refugee whose works had been banned. From his preface it would appear that his real audience were his fellow Europeans, whom he wanted to understand what had been happening in Germany, how serious its probable consequences were likely to be, and yet to prevent their making the mistake of identifying all Germans with the supporters of Hitler's regime. There was another Germany, and he wanted to believe, and others to believe, that eventually it would triumph. The second edition of *Eine Jugend in Deutschland* was dedicated to "The Germany of tomorrow." The real Germans, the inheritors of the spirit of Karl Liebknecht and of the spirit of the German revolution, were not even exiles like himself but those who, defiant and unbroken, held out in Hitler's concentration camps. He pays tribute to them:

Wo seid Ihr, meine Kamraden?

Ich sehe euch nicht, und doch weiss ich, Ihr lebt . . . .

Ihr habt die Furcht überwunden, die den Menschen demütigt und erniedert. In stiller unermüdlicher Arbeit achtet Ihr nicht Verfolgung und Misshandlung, Gefängnis und Tod. (p. 30)

(Where are you, my comrades? I don't see you, and yet I know you live. You have overcome fear which humiliates and debases human beings. In still tireless work you don't care about persecution and ill-treatment, imprisonment and death.)

Although, as a convinced socialist, he sees the German revolution as the moment of opportunity which was thrown away because of the strength of the forces of reaction and the absence of a fundamental commitment in the revolutionaries, the positive values behind *Eine Jugend in Deutschland* are deliberately nonpartisan and such as could obtain the widest measure of support. One may characterize them as the need for reason, self-responsibility, sympathy, imagination, and genuine internationalism. He sees Hitler's success as being grounded in a distrust of reason which is unreasonable:

For the people are tired of reason, tired of consideration and reconsidera-
tion. What, pray, they have asked, has reason done in recent years, what
help to us were insights and facts? And they believe in the condemners of
the spirit, who teach that reason cripples the will, erodes the roots of the
spirit, destroys the foundation of society, that all need, social and private is
its work.

As if reason had ever reigned. (p. 28)

And this distrust of reason is associated with the people's desire to
rid themselves of responsibility for their own lives by throwing it on
an external savior: "The people expect salvation from false saviors,
not from their own knowledge, own work and own responsibility"
(p. 28).

It is characteristic of Toller's capacity for detachment that he had
been disturbed by the Lenin cult, which he had observed in Russia
in 1926.

For a cult always cripples self-responsibility, the development of one's own
possibilities and gives to the devotees of the cult the belief that what must
be known and done, has already been known and done by the idol.
(*Quer durch*, p. 107)

He was still, of course, a socialist, but now with a greater emphasis on the need for political freedom, which made him more
critical than ever of Marxist doctrine on this point:

Some socialists deride the idea of freedom as a bourgeois illusion: they don't
distinguish between freedom as a feeling that pervades life, as consciousness, which gives dignity and self-respect to people, and freedom as the
framework of living. (p. 170)

This was to lead to a modification of the view of the United States
that he had implicitly put forward in *Quer durch:* "They mistake
skyscrapers for Heaven and the Stock Exchange for Jacob's ladder.
But they don't let anybody gag their mouths. That's the most important thing, isn't it?"[3]—a remark of von Grotjahn in *Pastor Hall* that
clearly reflects Toller's own belief.

In *Eine Jugend,* too, Toller affirms his belief in the essential
goodness of man, seeing evil as a result of a failure of imagination, a
view again which differs from that of orthodox Marxism: "I don't
believe in the 'evil' nature of man, I believe that he does the most

dreadful things from a lack of imagination, from sluggishness of heart" (p. 169 f.).

And he sees the functions of education as the overcoming of this sluggishness in the young. For, of course, it was to the young he looked and had, for some time, looked with hope: "The most pressing task of schools in the future is to develop the human imagination of the child, his capacity for feeling: to fight against, and to overcome, the sluggishness of his heart" (p. 170).

Finally, he puts himself on the side of a genuine internationalism, one which does not rule out patriotism. Nationalism and internationalism cannot be opposed in that simple way: "Do not I belong to the people, which have been persecuted, harassed, martyred, murdered for millenia, that people, whose prophets shout the demand for justice on earth" (p. 178).

These explanations illuminate the fine statement in which he defines his position, and, by echoing a pseudo-Virgilian epitaph, lends even greater resonance to it: "eine jüdische Mutter hat mich geboren. Deutschland hat mich genährt, Europa mich gebildet, meine Heimat ist die Erde, die Welt mein Vaterland" (p. 179). (A Jewish mother has borne me. Germany has nourished me. Europe has formed me. My home is the earth: the world my Fatherland.)

Despite what the preface might lead us to expect, Toller does not in *Eine Jugend* adopt a moralizing and didactic attitude. Particularly in the early section what he does is to present, with little or no comment, a series of scenes that embody some significant aspect of his experience, or that develop leitmotifs whose significance can only be appreciated by the interconnections which become apparent when the whole work is read. At times the method approximates the narrative equivalent of film technique. Toller believed that the concrete particulars of experience were more pregnant with meaning than generalizing exposition.[4] The scenes, too, are narrated succinctly and with the maximum use of recollected dialogue.

Such a method is admirably suited to an autobiography that is not confessional but "delineates the man in his public action" (p. 27). For that it should be such an autobiography was implicit in Toller's intention to emphasize the typicality and socially revelatory character of his experiences. But, at the same time, because his narrative method develops a multiplicity of meanings, the significance of his most intimate experiences does emerge.

As an illustration of his method, let me take the scene where his
father dies:

My father is dying. In the hour of death I am alone with him. His hands
grope questioningly over the counterpane: his eyes burn unseeing: his
breath is drawn with difficulty: he wants to get up. I press him back into
bed.
    "You are guilty" he groans, "you are guilty."
    "Father!" I cry horrified.
    Mother runs into the room.
    "Get the doctor" she cries.
    Father begins to breathe stertorously; I rush out. When I come back
mother is wringing her hands uncontrollably and sobbing without tears:
    "Children, your father" she says and is still. She takes a cloth, binds it
round the chin and head of the dead man, closes his eyes, places herself
near his bed, and as she looks at him intently, she begins at last to cry.
    I lie in my bed and shiver. Frost creeps up my legs. I can't forget the
words which Father called out at the last, I will never forget them, although
I know that it was fever that spoke. I would like Father to hear me once
again. I would like to say to him that in fact I bear no blame, it is cancer that
is to blame. Father will never answer any more, he grows cold, his nose
sharpens. Soon I will see him no more: that is death. (p. 40)

This is typically spare and restrained in tone, with concentric
circles of meaning. It is an adolescent's first encounter with death
and bereavement, and in the details there is a fitting emphasis on
features that are common to many deaths: ". . . his eyes burn
unseeing; his breath is drawn with difficulty . . . Father begins to
breathe stertorously . . . She takes a cloth, . . . binds it round the
chin and head of the dead man." The last of these details is the
description of a customary act, which is an indication of a society in
some sense ordered and settled. Mrs. Toller, despite her grief,
knows exactly what to do and does it. Her strength of character,
which we have evidence of elsewhere, is not only emphasized here
but she merges into the archetypal figure of the wife, the mother.
Some details are clearly suppressed; "Children, your father" supposes that at least one brother or sister is present. But it is part of
Toller's method to leave the other children out of account, not only
here but in the autobiography as a whole; for to delineate their
several fortunes would distract attention from his present purpose
which is, when writing about his childhood, to show his own relation
to the traditions from which he sprang.

And yet, of course, here is something that is not all typical: his father's accusation and its effect on him. It is an experience that in relation to *Eine Jugend* as a whole, has a deep resonance.

Did the small child see something horrid in the woodshed/
Long ago?

wrote W. H. Auden in his *In Memory of Ernst Toller*.[5] If Freud's peculiar trinity of father, superego, and God is well founded, we can say that Toller did, for the scene resonates with others: one in which, as a child, Toller prayed to an icon of Christ to forgive him for belonging to the race that crucified Him, and another in which in order to get rid of a sense of guilt for some childish peccadillo, he destroyed a glass tube which a gentile housemaid had assured him was the abode of the Jewish God. In "killing" his God, he was "killing" his father. But the need to kill his God and his father arose from the guilt he had been made to feel by society for being a Jew. This, in its turn, prepared the way for the subsequent transfer of the superego to a father substitue, the Fatherland, and the attempt to assuage the double guilt by identification with it.

But then there follows another transference: in turning against the war, he did what so many of his contemporaries did, too. Fatherland and Father are now identified with betrayal: "The fathers have betrayed us" (p. 79), which means that, in one sense, the superego is destroyed, but since, after all, this is not psychologically possible, it becomes further transferred to an idea, that of socialist internationalism: "die Welt mein Vaterland."[6] Though Toller's was an individual variation of it, there is much evidence to show that this development was widespread and accounts for many features of content, theme, and dramatic mode in Expressionist drama, including the frequent partial identification of their protagonists with Christ.

When Toller wrote *Die Wandlung,* the identification of Friedrich-Toller with Christ was naive. But by the time of writing *Eine Jugend,* when history had gone on and Toller had come to terms with his own development, this identification was ironically placed. Wolfgang Frühwald, a modern German critic, has pointed out that Toller's description of his capture in 1918 echoes that of Christ.[7] There is the same dignified acceptance: "You are looking for Toller: I am he" (p. 140); there is a Judas, and the Pharisees are represented by a woman who, about to enter church for morning mass, gloats over his arrest and shouts "Totschlagen!" (Kill him). But a controlled irony surrounds this identification: Toller's apparently dignified attestation to his identity is an aid to self-preservation merely: to prevent his being shot on the pretext of resisting arrest or trying to escape: "Yes, I am Toller. I will not flee. If I am now to be shot, I don't want to be shot while attempting to escape" (p. 140).

And he was, after all, discovered in his hiding place clad only in his shirt and with dyed hair.

It is here that the meaning of this complex development relates to the failures of the revolution, the need for heroism now, for the qualities which he celebrates in his preface and for which he admired Mühsam—the qualities which are to guarantee the "Deutschland am Morgen," the true Fatherland. For he knows he does not possess them. It is an implied self-criticism. On two occasions in his life—both related in this book—he told lies to escape from the consequences of his revolutionary activities, even in a society which was not lost, as was Hitler's Germany, to all sense of justice. He had done so in 1918, when he had denied the authorship of a strike leaflet; he was to do so again, in 1919, when he denied his responsibility before the court for his signature on a military order:

> From a sudden feeling of fear I lie: I persuade myself that if I am now caught in a lie, the sentence must be stiffer; courage deserts me: my speech becomes confused: I would like to be strong and I am weak. While I am speaking I recollect that I have been as weak once before, when I would not admit to having written the strike leaflet. I want the judges not to believe me, but the judges do believe me: the gathering of proof is over. (p. 151)

The passage further activates the latent meaning of an incident in his youth in which he manifested the first awakening of social conscience. A Samotschin pauper, subject to epileptic fits, was deliberately intoxicated by peasants. This precipitated a fatal fit, and the man was callously left to die, even the authorities providing themselves with a bureaucratic excuse not to help. Toller sent a protesting account of the incident to a Samotschin newspaper, which published it anonymously. But when a rather jumpy mayor insitituted proceedings against the anonymous correspondent, Toller hid behind the editor, and his father, who had guessed its authorship, used his influence as a town councillor with the mayor to get the action dropped. It was a piece of cowardice, understandable in a youth, but nonetheless significant.

Toller was aware too—again it comes through the details that he chooses to present—that he had been let off comparatively lightly by the court at Munich because he had stressed his acceptability to the very world against which he had rebelled by calling on witnesses as solidly respectable as Thomas Mann and Max Weber, and obtaining testimony to his qualities as a soldier. Erich Mühsam, who had been arrested so early that he had no opportunity to have anything to do with the Communist Räterepublik or get involved in fighting, got a ten-year sentence, Toller only five. Tankred Dorst, in his play, evokes effectively the significance of his compromise by having Toller sentenced to his five years imprisonment for treason with honorable motives while, outside, the workers who took part are executed.[8]

Toller allows his awareness of his weaknesses to emerge in *Eine Jugend,* but one regrets to say that they also come out in ways of which he does not allow us to become aware. On occasion we can check Toller's account of an incident against that of a reliable independent witness or a less guarded account he himself gives elsewhere.

The most serious case is that of his misrepresenting his own relationship to Dr. Lipp, the foreign minister of the first Räterepublik, who had to be removed from office because he appeared to spend all his time dispatching eccentric messages. One of these addressed to Lenin complained that when Hoffmann, the Bavarian Prime Minister, had left the Wittelsbach Palace he had taken the key of the ministry toilet with him. We have it on Niekisch's authority that it was Toller himself who had proposed the unknown (and still mysterious) Dr. Lipp for this office though no one who had read only *Eine Jugend in Deutschland* would ever dream it. Here is Niekisch's account:

Now Toller plucked up courage: he acknowledged that the Independent Social Democrats did not see in Mühsam a suitable man for the Commissariat of Foreign Affairs, and Toller proposed a certain Dr. Lipp. He had moreover brought him along. Lipp was praised, he had been diplomatically active during the war; he was known as a writer on foreign affairs, and had all the qualities which are needed for the foreign service. Nobody knew Dr.

Lipp, nobody had heard of him, but since there were no other candidates they swallowed him.[9]

There is no reason to suppose that Niekisch had any interest in distorting the truth; but that account exposes Toller's mendacity when he says: "Dr. Lipp was proposed as Head of the People's Commissariat for Foreign Affairs. Nobody is acquainted with his abilities. He has no face, only a full beard; he wears no suit, only a frock coat: these two appurtenances seem to be the basis of his suitability" (p. 108).

In what might be interpreted as the result of a transferred rage against himself for his folly Toller further compounds his deception by endeavoring to make Lipp not merely eccentric but crazy. He maliciously pretends that the telegram containing the reference to the missing lavatory key was not sent to Lenin, as was actually the case, but to the Pope. As a message to Lenin it was, of course, eccentric, but not ridiculous. Historians have corrected the facts but Toller has made Lipp into a permanent joke. It is perhaps significant, for example, that Tankred Dorst, in his play, deliberately repeats the misattribution of the telegram.[10]

The other major case involves a more subtle misrepresentation. In *Eine Jugend*, one appreciates that Toller could not be altogether frank about the sexual strains of prison life and, in fact, he does little more than hint at the situation which he explains in detail in his introduction to Joseph Fishman's *Sex Life In Prison*. But it involves him in the romanticization of an incident in which a female prisoner uncovered herself in the prison yard, while her "lover" watched from his window. She was discovered by a warder and lost her remission—for she was a convict—because of it.

Then in a moment of overwhelming feeling she springs back from the window, fiddles at her coarse gray linen garment, unbuttons it, shows her body, her firm little breasts, her compact well shaped legs: she cries and laughs for joy: at last she can do some good for him, show him how she loves him: oh she would do everything for him, he must realize it, because she does this. (p. 116)

But, according to his other account, it was not like that at all. She exposed herself regularly and premeditatedly: her "lover" used to masturbate—and so did the other men.[11] That doesn't rob it of a positive human meaning, but Toller has sentimentalized it. He was clearly looking on, too; he didn't just happen to see the woman. Perhaps our questions should stop there.

Misrepresentations of this kind must undermine confidence in *Eine Jugend*. One wonders, indeed, whether the very artistry of its method has not involved distortion; the recollected dialogue, for example, is always vivid, but how many people can reproduce dialogue verbatim ten minutes let alone many years after it has been spoken? Toller may, after all, have sacrificed something to the development of a clear thematic line.

III   Briefe aus dem Gefängnis
(Letters from Prison)

Briefe aus dem Gefängnis consists of a series of letters that Toller wrote when he was imprisoned for high treason. It was compiled in 1934–35 with the help of Hermann Kesten, with whom Toller shared a house in Highgate, London, from personal papers which had been smuggled out of the country by Dora Fabian. It was published in Holland in 1935. An English translation was published in the United Kingdom in 1936 as *Letters from Prison,* and in the U.S.A. in 1937 under a different title: *Look Through the Bars.* Close comparison of the text of the English language version with that of the original, however, indicates that the translation could not have been directly made from it, but that an intermediate version must have been used, as there are a considerable number of discrepancies between the two, some letters or parts of letters being unique to the original and the English-language version, respectively.

There is some doubt as to whether *Briefe aus dem Gefängnis* should be considered merely as an interesting biographical document or whether its pretensions are more exalted. Frühwald has argued that it is meant to be a second volume of autobiography, and a conscious contribution to a politico-literary tradition of prison letters, with Rosa Luxemburg's identically titled *Briefe aus dem Gefängnis* as its immediate model, and that the order of the letters is subordinated to the development of a theme.[12] In support of Frühwald's view, it must be admitted that in his preface Toller does see the volume as having some unity and as illustrating the same kinds of themes as *Eine Jugend in Deutschland;* and it is, like that volume, dedicated to "Deutschland am Morgen" (the Germany of Tomorrow).

But Frühwald's argument is not altogether convincing. The letters are arranged in chronological order, and Toller had, in fact, already covered his years in prison in *Eine Jugend in Deutschland*, using material that is repeated here. Rather, I think, the letters are to be seen as confirming the relevant parts of the narrative in *Eine Jugend*, and showing that its implicit interpretations were not the easy products of hindsight but were actually made at the time. As a result, it has an immediacy that *Eine Jugend in Deutschland* lacks. Toller wants to show, too, that though the seeds of Nazi Germany were implicit in his experience, there were differences. Harshness, injustice, suffering, waste, and strain existed but so did the workings of some kind of order and rule, however capricious and repressive, which were not present in the concentration camps. When Toller was released from prison in July, 1924, he was, for instance, given a military escort as the prison authorities claimed that they wanted to foil a plot to attack him. And yet, by showing the great effort it took to endure in prison, he can bring out the much greater heroism needed in the concentration camps. Toller realizes the limitations imposed on the letters by the circumstances under which they were written. He had always to be careful what he said. Letters to and from the prison were subject to censorship and were confiscated if they complained about specific experiences in prison, or made too direct a reflection on political events. However, this was to some extent overcome by the return to him, after he left prison, of all confiscated letters. Many of those he reproduces were never, in fact, forwarded.

Certain important emphases do, as I say, emerge in the prison letters, and although most of them are to be found in the relevant sections of *Eine Jugend in Deutschland* I did not deal with them when considering that volume so I will do so here. There is the emphasis on class "justice"; for though Toller and his fellow prisoners were confined in a fortress, they were, in fact, allowed scarcely any of the privileges that went with this "honorable" form of imprisonment. Graf Arco-Valley, the murderer of Eisner, on the other hand, was given full privileges, and not only did not serve his full sentence but received a kind of civic reception on his release. And the treatment of prisoners was capriciously varied according to changes in the political situation. The Kapp putsch of 1920 and Hitler's abortive putsch of 1923 were used as excuses to make the treatment of prisoners harsher; and since no reasons were given to the prisoners as to why there was a change of treatment, it appeared as if the prison authorities were acting from pure caprice.

Further, Toller and his comrades were the victims of tensions between the Bavarian Landtag and the Reichstag, which revealed only too clearly that the revolution in Bavaria had led to the triumph of reaction, and thus made Bavaria the cradle of Nazism. In 1922 the prisoners at Niederschönenfeld, where Toller served most of his sentence, were elated to hear of an amnesty which was to be extended by the Reichstag to all political prisoners. The inmates of Niederschönenfeld were overjoyed, but nothing happened and, as they subsequently discovered, the Bavarian government had explicitly refused to be bound by the Reichstag decision. In 1920 there was another example of the Bavarian authorities playing politics with their prisoners, which was to be an earnest of the arbitrariness of the Third Reich. One morning, without notice or explanation, they were got out of bed, moved to other cells, and locked in (cells were not usually locked before 9 p.m.), forbidden to exercise in the yard, or to receive newspapers. Later, again without explanation, certain of the prisoners, though not Toller, were put on remand (which meant they lost what privileges they had) and were detailed to appear before a court in Neuberg. They went on hunger strike, and a civilian doctor who had been called in refused to answer for their lives. Then suddenly, and again without explanation, conditions were restored to normal and the prisoners returned to their accustomed cells. Toller only found out what it was supposed to have been about when he discovered from a French periodical that the Bavarian government was claiming that he and Mühsam had allegedly planned a putsch, involving the disarming of the guards, the use of life preservers, and having as its objective the reestablishment of the Räterepublik. The story was absurd, and Toller was probably right in seeing it as an attempt to call off pressure from France for the release of German political prisoners by conjuring up the bogey of German Bolshevism.

Throughout his imprisonment Toller shows himself aware of the steady rise of Hitler to power. He could see that the threat he posed was not taken seriously. Hitler had been granted a generous remission of his sentence for his part in an affray of 1921, and when arrested as a result of his abortive putsch of 1923, he was not only granted further remission but his previous offense was not taken into account. It was a toleration arising from connivance (pp. 235

ff.). Moreover, Nazi attitudes were reflected in the warders, and Toller once complained to the governor about the defacing of the outer walls of the prison with chalked swastikas and circles with medial dots (p. 151) (a Nazi symbol meaning "Jews live here").

Toller also shows himself aware of just how much the "order" in Bavaria was based on cruelty and violence. When he had been on remand at Eichstädt prison, he could see the wall against which sixty-three of his comrades had been executed. It was riddled with bullet holes, splattered with fragments of hair, flesh, and brain, and the earth fronting it was stained with blood. Some of his comrades had, before execution, been abused and tormented by drunken Württemberg soldiers, who made a practice of shooting first at the legs and hips of their victims. In prison Toller took down careful accounts of the experiences of his fellow prisoners; one man who emerged deaf and dumb could only write his. This man had survived execution by a firing squad, survived another shot in his head when it was realized that he was not dead; and after all that, he had been sentenced by a Bavarian court to several years imprisonment (p. 15).

And there was one point at which the relation of the repressive bureaucratic order of the Bavarian prisons and the anarchic brutality of Nazism became more clearly visible. This was the treatment of August Hagemeister, one of the ministers of the first Räterepublik, who was serving a ten-year sentence. He was allowed to die of a heart condition, the prison doctor trying to maintain first that he was malingering and then that he had a different and much less serious complaint. Hagemeister, who knew he was dying, smuggled a letter out of prison to his wife asking her to intercede with the Bavarian authorities so that he could be transferred to a hospital. Mrs. Hagemeister tried her best, but her efforts were completely fruitless. When Hagemeister died, the governor, fearing a mutiny, installed a machine gun on the roof (p. 185ff.). Toller tried to initiate a legal action against the prison doctor, Dr. Steindl, for neglect, but he did not get anywhere, and Steindl was actually promoted.

It was in prison, too, that Toller lost his idealistic view of the proletariat and learned exactly why the German revolution had failed. Again and again he found that the socialist beliefs of his comrades were a veneer over quite opposed beliefs. A peasant comrade, for example, after boasting of a speech he had made about the inhumanity of war at an antiwar meeting, soon afterwards, and with no sense of inconsistency, revelled in the recollection of bayonetting French soldiers in the stomach. Certain prisoners revealed them-selves as opportunists: as soon as they were released they joined Nazi or proto-Nazi groups (p. 168). And yet, in prison, nothing had been revolutionary enough for them. It was an ominous portent. The political infighting among the prisoners, and the formation of splinter groups (p. 67; 119), the members of which would not talk to the members of other groups, by the very grotesque futility with which it reflected the world outside, made Toller more aware of the significance of the fragmentation of the Left that was taking place in the Weimar republic. That he was aware, too, that the political "disagreements" in prison were a rationalization of prison psychosis must have contributed to an awareness of the irrational basis of much political controversy. That Toller came to the conclusion that nothing was to be hoped for from his own generation is not surpris-ing.

Toller's own inner development in prison is sufficiently clear from his plays, without stressing it again here as it appears in the letters. What the letters do reveal is his political good sense and the flexible and pragmatic nature of his socialism. He came to the conclusion that the collapse of capitalism was not imminent because he could see that it had another phase to go through: internationalization. And so he believed that the putschism which the K.P.D. indulged in until 1923 was misguided and futile (p. 82). He also deplored Lenin's twenty-one points as a condition for socialist parties joining the Third International (p. 69), which led to a split in the U.S.P.D. And yet, for the same kind of pragmatic reason, he praised the thinking behind Lenin's New Economic Plan (p. 107).

Lastly, his letters reveal that Toller was in fact a deeply religious man: his favorite reading in prison was Rilke's *Das Stundenbuch: (The Book of Hours)* The New Testament, Lao Tse, and the Up-anishads. And, as we might expect, he shows himself to have had a deeply reverent and creative response to the world of birds, beasts, and flowers.[13]

CHAPTER 10

Conclusion

WHEN I began to be drawn to Toller, to see a peculiar and enduring significance in his life and work, I was not unaware that at almost exactly the same time there was an upsurge of interest in him in the U.S.A., East and West Germany, and Britain. Others more competent than I were seeing his significance in very similar terms to my own. While I was writing this book, moreover, Tankred Dorst even made Toller the eponymous hero of a play, in which he presented his dilemma in a way I had already formulated in the opening chapter and in the chapter on *Masse-Mensch*. There is now a consensus that Toller is, indeed, a figure of permanent importance. Perhaps a realization of this fact could only become possible after the Second World War had receded into history.

To Germany Toller's peculiar importance is that he belongs to both East and West and is a challenge to both. Despite all its harsh criticisms the Communist East cannot disown him because he was, after all, on their side of the barricades at Munich and was, in practical terms, Hitler's leading opponent in exile. And so they can still express a sense of indebtedness: "Wir schulden ihm Dank"[1] (we owe him thanks), as Bruno Kaiser says. But the West cannot disown him because his socialism is based ultimately on an intense humanism, which in Britain, for example, is the major socialist tradition, and which in West Germany appears in the work of Günter Grass and Heinrich Böll. Neither Germany can say that the "Deutschland am Morgen" in which Toller believed and for which he worked has arrived. The East Germans, of course, claim that it has and that they are it, but a regime that guns down would-be refugees cannot approximate Toller's ideal. Nor can the West Germans lay claim to his inheritance in a country where German socialism as a mass movement is dead and the Communist Party, outlawed for so long, is still discriminated against. It is perhaps not without interest that Kurt Hiller has implied that Toller might have become a significant figure in postwar Germany had he lived.[2] Such speculation is profitless, but that Hiller has made it shows his awareness of the significance of Toller's inheritance.

But it is not in Germany alone that he is with us still. His work and life are a perpetual challenge to many fashionable ideas and dubiously valid formulations which still dominate literary discussion both in Britain and the U.S.A. The old sterile disputes over the relation between literature and commitment, which usually seek to divide the two, have to face the fact that Toller is himself a refutation of such a solution and that his actual practice could affect the way his work was received. A performance of *Die Wandlung*, for example, was capable of becoming a different sort of experience when it was realized that the author was in prison for trying to live its meanings through. For a writer to divide himself into a private self, who means what he says, and a public figure, who does not, is to trivialize literature and compartmentalize people. That Gerhart Hauptmann, for example, could make his peace with Hitler's Germany—for which he earned Thomas Mann's contempt—must say something not only about Hauptmann as a person but Hauptmann as a writer. When it came down to it he did not believe what he had said.

The dichotomy of literature and commitment is only a special version of another and wider one between the impractical emotional idealist (the heart) and the levelheaded practical man of affairs (the head). Isaac Deutscher recounts how a Polish man of affairs, who knew Lenin before the First World War, was astonished and disoriented to find that the man he had written off, in implicit contrast to himself, as an "impractical man," "a quixotic visionary," was actually in power in Russia.[3] And the same kind of thinking had, until recently, become so automatic in Toller's case that it constituted a presupposition almost impossible to shake by obvious evidence to the contrary. John M. Spalek has brought out very well the sheer levelheaded practicality of Toller's work in the 1930s both for his fellow refugees and for relief in Spain.[4] But the main facts were there before. One has only to read the proposals Toller made to the French government with the object of ameliorating the lot of his fellow exiles to realize that he was very much a man of affairs: they are all reasonable and workable. And even in Munich in 1919, young and inexperienced as he was, he did not lose sight of realities, but tried to get his fellow revolutionaries to accept them. And what politician or official showed the political insight in the twenties that Toller did? And yet his political insight was not divided from the feeling and imagination that produced *Hinkemann,* in which his all-too-justified tragic vision of the immediate future is embodied for the first time.

Again, because Toller, like other German writers, has had to face and make sense of the most extreme situations ever experienced in a Western European country or the Western world as a whole, some of the major emphases in British and American literature become more open to criticism and can be seen as the product of a sheltered experience. What about, for example, the conscious celebration of the virtues of ironic balance as a guarantee of maturity and insight? Toller enables us to see that it too often can be a form of self-protection, a failure of responsibility and vulnerability. What, too, of the dichotomy, which is in some ways the obverse of this, between spontaneity and calculation, which goes back to William Blake and comes through Dickens to D. H. Lawrence, where it ends in a celebration, as in *The Plumed Serpent,* of proto-fascistic unreason? Toller's tragic "als ob Vernunft je regiert hätte" (as if reason had ever ruled) comes from a different and more real world. And what has Blake's "Damn braces bless relaxes" to say to Erich Mühsam in the concentration camp where he so heroically endured and died?

Toller was not a great writer like Brecht; but he keeps alive issues that Brecht tried to close both in his dramatic theory and practice. Brecht was, I think, right and Toller wrong in believing that an audience is fundamentally affected by an appeal to feeling: it merely consumes it. But Brecht's methods were in fundamentals already anticipated at his best by Bernard Shaw, and that Shaw seems very dated to some of us may help us to understand Brecht's limitations. It is not without significance that Brecht is at his best not when dealing with contemporary society but when embodying a preformulated interpretation in a version of history, in fable, or in a bizarre Britain and U.S.A. which never existed like that at all. Brecht's plays no longer challenge in the way Toller's still obstinately do. Partly, it is because Toller, unlike Brecht, did not see man as the product of social conditions and therefore infinitely changeable. The best thing that socialism could do was to give the old Adam a chance, as he puts it. Brecht never faces the problem that Toller examines in *Hinkemann.* For Toller, unlike Brecht, knew that some problems would be insoluble in any form of society whatsoever.

Finally, Toller was, for all his weaknesses and faults, something that has fallen out of fashion—a good man. There are not so many of them that we can afford not to be grateful that they have existed. And so I close with Hermann Kesten's tribute:

Er war kein Heiliger. Aber wenn es fühlende Menschen auf Erden gibt, die das Gute wollen so war er einer. Wenn es Menschen gibt, die nicht schweigen können, wenn sie ein Unrecht sehen, so war er einer. Wenn es Menschen gibt, die das Leben auch für andere lebenswert machen, so war er ein solcher Mensch. Er war oft schwach, nie böse, er war ein guter Mensch.[5]

(He was no saint. But if there are feeling men on earth who desire the good, he was one of them. If there are men who cannot be silent when they see a wrong, he was one of them. If there are men who make life worth living for others as well, he was such a man. He was often weak, never bad: he was a good man.)

Notes and References

Preface

1. See Ernst Toller, *Prosa Briefe Dramen Gedichte*, ed. with a preface by Kurt Hiller, Reinbek bei Hamburg, 1961, p. 10.
2. Hermann Kesten, "Ernst Toller," *Meine Freunde die Poeten*. Vienna and Munich, 1959, p. 262, 255–268.
3. *Quer durch*, Reisebilder und Reden, Berlin, 1930, pp. 97 ff.
4. See Martin Reso, "Die Novemberrevolution und Ernst Toller," *Weimarer Beiträge*, v. No. 3, 1959, 387–409.
5. Ibid, passim: Ernst Schumacher, *Die dramatischen Versuche Bertolt Brechts 1918–1933*, Berlin 1955, pp. 18, 23.

Chapter One

1. *Die Wandlung* was finished in March 1918, and when staged on October 30th, 1919, was already out of date. Consequently the producer altered the order of the scenes and having placed the call to revolution earlier in the play made it end with the holding up of the newborn baby to symbolize the future (Bild 9).
2. "Bemerkungen zu meinem Drama *Die Wandlung*," reprinted in Paul Pörtner, *Literatur-Revolution 1910–1925*, 2 vols., Mainz, 1960, vol. 1, p. 361.
3. *Hoppla, wir leben!* Potsdam, 1927, pp. 132–133.
4. Potsdam, 1923.
5. See *Nationalsozialismus, Eine Diskussion über den Kulturbankrott des Bürgertums: zwischen Ernst Toller und Alfred Mühr, Redakteur der Deutschen Zeitung*, Berlin 1930, particularly pp. 26, 32.
6. "Heimarbeit," *Die Weltbühne*, vol. xxiii, pt. 1, No. 26 June 1927, 969–970, esp. p. 970.
7. *Briefe aus dem Gefängnis*, Amsterdam, 1935, p. 205.
8. *No More Peace*, trans. Edward Crankshaw, lyrics adapted by W. H. Auden, London, 1937, p. 97.
9. *Seven Plays* by Ernst Toller together with *Mary Baker Eddy*, by the Author and Hermann Kesten, London 1935, p. X.

10. *Briefe aus dem Gefängnis*, p. 85.

11. P. 118. The second paragraph had already appeared in "Deutsche Revolution", *Quer durch*, p. 232. In "A great Landscape," a review of *Three Cities*, by Sholem Asch, *Time and Tide*, Dec. 16, 1933, p. 1544, Toller repeats it almost verbatim for a third time.

12. *Quer durch*, p. 98. This occurs in the section dealing with Russia, which was written in 1926.

13. In 1929 Toller joined the Gruppe Revolutionärer Pazifisten (Group of Revolutionary Pacifists). See Kurt Hiller, *Köpfe und Tröpfe*, Hamburg and Stuttgart, 1956, p. 296.

14. See "Des Versagen des Pazifismus in Deutschland," printed for the first time in John M. Spalek and Wolfgang Frühwald: "Ernst Tollers Amerikanische Vortragsreise," 1936–37, *Literaturwissenschaftliches Jahrbuch der Görresgesellschaft*, VI (1965), 267–311, 305 ff.

15. Quoted from an unpublished MS "Man and the Masses, the Problem of Peace," in John M. Spalek, *Ernst Tollers Vortragstätigkeit und seine Hilfsaktionen im Exil*, in *Exil und innere Emigration* l. herausgegeben von Peter Uwe Hohendahl und Egon Schwarz, Frankfurt am Main, 1973, 85–100, esp. p. 100.

16. J. Nehru, *A Bunch of Old Letters*, New York, 1960, p. 205 (in a letter dated July 21, 1936).

17. *Sind wir verantwortlich für unsere Zeit?* printed for the first time in Spalek and Frühwald, *Ernst Tollers Amerikanische Vortragsreise*, p. 286.

18. Ibid., p. 286.

19. Address at Conference of the Internationale Schriftstellervereinigung zur Verteidigung der Kultur, *Das Wort*, 1937, Vol. 3, 46–53, p. 51.

20. *A Bunch of Old Letters*, p. 230 (letter dated March 30, 1937).

21. See Spalek and Frühwald, *Ernst Tollers Amerikanische Vortragsreise* 1936–37, p. 304.

22. See Felix Emmel, *Das ekstatische Theater*, Prien, 1924, p. 294, "No dramatist, but a lyricist of pregnant symbols." Bodo Uhse, Vorwort, *Toller: Ausgewählte Schriften*, 2nd ed., Berlin, 1961, p. viii "Toller is too much of a lyricist to subject himself to the laws of drama."

23. Richard Samuel and R. Hinton Thomas, *Expressionism in German Life, Literature and Theatre*, Cambridge, England, 1939, p. 45.

24. See for example Julius Bab, *Das Theater der Gegenwart*, Berlin, 1929, p. 170. "Fehling created a mise en scène of thrilling power from the very feeble text of Toller's *Masse-Mensch*."

25. Herbert Jhering, *Von Reinhardt bis Brecht*, 3 vols., Berlin, 1961, vol. 1, pp. 356 ff.

26. *Briefe aus dem Gefängnis*, p. 76.

27. Ibid., p. 214. "I am not responsible for the disfigurements, the

melodramatic sweetnesses, production cuts, and, as long as I remain here in prison I have no influence over the mode of production."

28. *Prosa* . . . , p. 293.

29. See his lecture on "The German Drama Today" at Manchester University, reported in *The Manchester Guardian*, February 16, 1934, p. 16.

30. Thus he directed a production with Robin Robert of *Hinkemann* at Frankfurt in 1924 in which all realism was avoided, and was again a co-producer of the same play in 1927 (with Ernst Lenner) at Berlin. On February 11, 1935, he was likewise co-producer with Dominic Roche of *Feuer aus den Kesseln!* (in English) at the Opera House, Manchester.

31. *Quer durch*, pp. 167–168. He claimed to have been the first writer in Germany to make use of the *Sprechchor* form.

32. "Art and Life," *The London Mercury*, vol. xxii, no. 191, Sept. 1935, 459–461, esp. p. 459.

33. *Quer durch*, pp. 278–279.

34. Quoted by Ernst Schumacher, p. 532. See note 5.

35. "The German Drama Today." "This was the school to which he adhered, loath as he was to be attached to any slogan."

36. *Quer durch*, p. 280.

37. Lest this be thought at variance with some of the ideas expressed above, Toller says (*Briefe aus dem Gefängnis*, p. 153), "The perennial human problems as the proletariat experiences them—only that can be the content of proletarian art."

38. Julius Bab, *Das Theater der Gegenwart*, p. 227.

39. *Nationalsozialismus*, p. 23.

40. "Une Leçon de Litterature sur Moi-même," *Revue d'Allemagne*, Jan.–April, 1929, 217–222, esp. p. 222.

41. *Quer durch*, p. 288.

42. *Prosa* . . . , p. 294.

43. Ibid.

Chapter Two

1. *Quer durch*, p. 282.

2. *Briefe aus dem Gefängnis*, p. 43.

3. *Prosa* . . . , p. 176.

4. *Quer durch*, p. 190.

5. The use of a Death's head is found in Station 1, Bild 2, Station 3, Bild 6, Station 5, Bild 8, and Bild 9.

6. In this connection one may notice the contradiction between the fact that Friedrich addresses certain passages in his speech to the soldiers and the rich (Ich weiss) "um dich, du Reicher/ Und du Soldat" (p. 284) as if they were among the crowd, while later he tells the crowd "Geht hin zu den

Soldaten," "Geht hin zu den Reichen" (p. 285) as if soldiers and the rich were somewhere else.

7. The idea of crucifixion is present right from the grave crosses of the Prologue through the false values represented by the red cross, the iron cross which Friedrich receives as a decoration, and the misused Christian cross of the Parson in the hospital scene.

Chapter Three

1. Potsdam 1920, 2nd ed., 1922, subtitled *Ein Stück aus der Sozialen Revolution des 20. Jahrhunderts*. First produced Nuremberg Nov. 15, 1920, but closed by the Bavarian authorities after 4 performances. Produced at Chemnitz, Feb. 27, 1921. Fehling's production at the Volksbühne, Sept. 29, 1921, which ran for 70 performances, is described in Kenneth McGowan and Robert Edmond Jones, *Continental Stagecraft*, London, 1923, 144–155. It is interesting to note that at the end of Bild 5 Fehling substituted the singing of the "Marseillaise" for that of the "Internationale."

2. *Prosa* . . . , p. 175.

3. Ibid., p. 294.

4. Ibid., pp. 83–84. The name of the woman, Sonja Lerch, has likewise been adapted and disguised by Toller.

5. Ibid., p. 175.

6. *Masses and Man*, trans. V. Mendel, London, 1923, with "Note on the production of Masses & Man" by Jürgen Fehling, p. 55.

7. *Briefe aus dem Gefängnis*, p. 45.

8. Ibid., p. 44.

9. Ibid., pp. 133–134.

10. Ibid., p. 43.

11. Ibid., p. 236.

12. The play is divided into seven Bilder. Of these Nos. 1, 3, 5, 7 are *realen Bilder*, Nos. 2, 4, 6 *Traumbilder*.

13. Sonja appears in Bilder 2, 4, 6: in Bild 2 (p. 304) she has no doppelgänger appearing in propria persona: in Bild 4 (p. 312) she is merely "das Weib," while in Bild 6 (p. 320) "eine Gefesselte" (a prisoner in shackles). But then the real Sonja is in prison at this time.

14. The relation of the Begleiter to Sonja is shown in Bild 2, p. 304. In Bild 4, p. 312, the Begleiter is in "the form of a policeman" and in Bild 6 (p. 320) in "the form of the warder."

15. A doppelgänger of the husband appears in Bild 4, p. 313. "*A guard leads in the prisoner with the husband's features.*" Later, p. 314, "*The face of the prisoner is transformed into that of a sentry.*"

16. This, of course, strongly resembles those passages in *Die Wandlung* that I had associated with weaknesses in the play. The objection I made to

this feature of *Die Wandlung* is not applicable here precisely because the tragic deadlock is recognized.

17. There is contradiction between the lines quoted above, "Der Mensch wie Baum und Pflanze etc.," and those quoted here, the first seeming to imply that struggle is a continuing process, the second that it is not. There is undoubtedly ambiguity here which weakens the play.

18. This is based on Toller's own experience: "Indeed when in Stadelheim prison an opportunity was offered me to escape, I turned down the plan of escape because it would have cost the life of a warder," *Prosa . . . ,* p. 175.

Chapter Four

1. First ed. Leipzig, 1922: 2nd rev. ed. Leipzig, 1922. The revised edition is used as the basis of this chapter, and all page references are to it. Unfortunately *Ausgewählte Schriften* and *Prosa . . .* reprint the first.

2. It is first mentioned in a letter of December 9, 1920: by January 23, 1921 Toller had already completed the first draft. See *Briefe aus dem Gefängnis,* p. 75.

3. First produced June 30, 1922 (director Klaus Pringsheim) in the Grosse Schauspielhaus, Berlin.

4. The Engineer's lines were reassigned from the first edition, where they were given to Albert, one of the workers. This might be an appropriate point to note some of the main differences between the two editions. In the later edition John Wible's soliloquy in Act III, Scene 1 (p. 53), has been altered, while the commination litany (pp. 15–16) departs considerably from what it was originally. Act III, Scene III, which shows John Wible undermining Jimmy's position with one of the workers, has now been moved forward to Act V, Scene I.

Other changes are of interest because they reveal a change of emphasis. Besides the reassignment mentioned above (which involved some alterations) the Beggar's attack on Jimmy in what is now Act V, Scene II, has become more bitter and elaborate: he now mockingly crowns him with straw and hails him as a prophet (p. 97). There have likewise been alterations in the worker's song (pp. 16–17) to make it perhaps more defiant and less hopeful. One last change might be mentioned. In Act IV, Scene I, where two women attack Mary Wible, the first wife is now identified with Margaret Lud.

5. *The actor playing Jimmy might appear in Lord Byron's mask: the actor playing Ure in that of Lord Castlereagh* (p. 5).

6. Both the Beggar's and Old Reaper's language is characterized by biblical diction and imagery. Both have a habit too of talking obscurely or gnomically. The Beggar, in fact, has been directly influenced by the Shakespearean fool.

7. The use of the worker's song is probably modelled on that in Hauptmann's *Die Weber*.

8. In addition to the Vorspiel, verse is used occasionally in Act I, Scene 1; Act II, Scene 2; Act III, Scene 3; Act IV, Scene 1; Act V, Scene 3.

9. See Clare Hayden Bell: "Tollers *Die Maschinenstürmer*," *Monatsheft* vol. xxx, 1938, 59–70. Toller (*Briefe aus dem Gefängnis*, p. 214) repudiates the connection.

10. Thus it is clear from Margret Lud's speech (p. 79) that she has had experience of factory spinning while John Wible says (p. 50) "I worked for twelve years in Mr. Ures' factory."

11. Some of Toller's symbolism is rather crude. One may note, for example, the following:

A *blind man led by a deaf-mute gropes forward.*
Old Reaper: Hey, Comrade Blindman. Tell me, where can
                   I find God?
The Blind Man: I do not hear him. Ask the man who is
                 leading me.
Old Reaper: Hey, Comrade, tell me where can I find God?
The deaf-mute makes a gesture of incomprehension. The blind man laughs.
Old Reaper: What are you laughing at?
The Blind Man: He is deaf and dumb and he doesn't see him.
Old Reaper: The blind man doesn't hear him: the deaf
                   man doesn't see him. I have two good eyes
                   and two good ears: I do not find him. (p. 58)

12. *Quer durch*, p. 286.

13. *Briefe aus dem Gefängnis*, p. 214.

14. Ibid., p. 77. Toller also sent to London for other books. These appear to have included *Erewhon*, and it is clear that it was Chap. XXI-XXIII, *The Book of the Machines*, which he thought might interest him.

15. Ernst Niekisch, *Erinnerungen an Ernst Toller*, *Theater der Welt*, Berlin, 1949, p. 28.

16. Toller, however, had profounder doubts about the nature of mass production in any society than he allows to appear here. See *Quer durch*, pp. 123–124, for his disquiet after visiting the Central Institute of Technology (2, E) in the U.S.S.R. and witnessing what appear to have been early experiments in work study.

17. See E. P. Thompson, *The Making of the English Working Class*, London 1963, chap. 14.

18. The exchanges between Jimmy Cobbett and John Wible are again probably reminiscent of those between Toller and Leviné. Interestingly, however, it is Jimmy in this play who says (to Ure) "Nennen Sie mich 'Namenlos' " (p. 70) (Call me nameless).

19. Since the speech quoted above is addressed ostensibly to En-

glishmen but in actuality to Germans, it would make a covert reference to the proletarian betrayal in the 1914–18 war on both sides highly appropriate.

Chapter Five

1. By August, 1922, *Hinkemann*, which had been completed in the previous June, had already been rejected by the Deutsches Theater, Berlin, and the Berlin Volksbühne. It was first produced at Leipzig on September 19, 1923. Details of the disturbances which accompanied the Dresden and Vienna productions are to be found in *Prosa . . .* , pp. 177–178, and in *Briefe aus dem Gefängnis*, pp. 240 ff.

2. Though Grete Hinkemann commits suicide in all versions of the play, Toller changed his mind as to whether Hinkemann should prepare to do so too. In *Der deutsche Hinkemann*, Potsdam, 1923, the first edition of the play, it is clear that Hinkemann is going to hang himself (p. 61). This was dropped from the second edition in which, besides minor changes in the text, Act 2, pp. 20–21, was moved to Act 4, pp. 40–41. The edition used is the second ed. as reprinted in *Prosa . . .* though, unfortunately, this is not a completely satisfactory text, as it is partly conflated.

3. Toller makes creative use of the convention whereby a fairground showman can make exaggerated claims for his show and promise what, if taken seriously, would be clearly illegal. So his invitation "As an extra attraction come and see how a child is beheaded, a real live child," (p. 406) is a comment on the sadistic fantasies of a sick society.

4. Hinkemann's job is thus described by the *Budenbesitzer:* "Your number: to bite through the throats of a rat and mouse at every performance. To suck a few mouthfuls of blood. Flourish! Off!" (p. 404).

5. See particularly Hinkemann's concluding speeches, pp. 434–435.

6. Rudolph Jentzsch, "Ernst Toller in seinen Dramen," *Zeitschrift für Deutschkunde*, 40, 1926, 813–822, esp. p. 815.

7. See Toller's letter to the Director of the Deutsches Theater, *Briefe aus dem Gefängnis*, p. 204.

8. "Ordinary working men to whom I have read the play have realized the symbolic meaning of the 'embarrassing mutilation' as human need," *Briefe aus dem Gefängnis*, p. 149.

9. Ibid., p. 244.

10. Ibid., p. 244.

11. Grosshahn is a figure analogous to John Wible in *Die Maschinenstürmer* but he does not even have Wible's motives, being neither deformed nor jealous. It is part of the play's pessimism that Paul Grosshahn cannot be dismissed, like John Wible, as the odd bad hat among the workers; his faults, on the contrary, are much more typical though occurring in him in a peculiarly intense form.

12. This is relevant to *Der entfesselte Wotan*.
13. *Quer durch*, p. 283.
14. *Briefe aus dem Gefängnis*, p. 244.

Chapter Six

1. For details see *Das politische Theater*, newly revised by Felix Gasbarra, Hamburg, 1963, pp. 146–147, esp. 149. *Hoppla* opened at the Piscator Bühne, Berlin, on September 3, 1927, though the premiere was on September 1, 1927, in a production by Hans Lotz in Hamburg. Page references in this chapter are to *Hoppla, wir leben!* Potsdam, 1927.

2. *Das politische Theater*, p. 146.

3. See *Quer durch*, pp. 292–294, and C. D. Innes, *Erwin Piscator's Political Theatre*, Cambridge, England, 1972, p. 128.

4. For the preparation of the film, over which Toller appears to have had no control, see *Das politische Theater*, pp. 150–151. From *Hoppla wir leben!* p. 7, it is clear that Toller did not consider the film indispensable.

5. *Quer durch*, p. 294.

6. Herbert Jhering, *Von Reinhardt bis Brecht*, 3 vols, Berlin, 1961, vol. 2, p. 276. W. F. in *Deutsche Rundschau*, vol. 213, Oct.-Dec., 1927, pp. 83–84, even though he did not care for Toller's text, sees Piscator's influence as baneful. Piscator himself was aware of the discrepancy between the style of acting demanded by his scenic apparatus and the kind of acting to which his actors were accustomed. See *Das politische Theater*, pp. 151–152.

7. Jhering, however, criticizes the motivation here not without point (*Von Reinhardt bis Brecht*, vol. 2., p. 275) as "sentimental middle-brow theater."

8. Nor is Pickel a minor character: he is meant to be a comic counterpart of Karl Thomas. (See *Das politische Theater*, p. 152). Not only is Pickel conceived in too simple a comic mode, but some of the would-be comic ideas connected with him lack validity. Pickel's reason for trying to obtain an audience with the Prime Minister is that he objects to a railway which is to be laid through his village. Jhering quite rightly objects that this is "antediluvian humor in an age in which almost every village is near a branch line," p. 275.

9. See for example Felix Hollaender, *Lebendiges Theater*, Berlin, 1932, p. 157.

10. Compare Karl Thomas's speech beginning "Plötzlich, nachts, hörten wir Schreie" (*Hoppla*, pp. 62–63) with the passage in *Eine Jugend in Deutschland*, p. 70, "Eines Nachts hören wir Schreie" etc. Similarly, the Second Worker's speech about the gracious way his sister was treated by her mistress in whose house she worked as a maid (*Hoppla*, p. 77) repro-

duces what one of Toller's fellow revolutionaries had said to him in prison (*Eine Jugend*, p. 164). In both play and autobiography Toller's aim is to provide an example of how revolutionary attitudes were frequently a veneer concealing quite conventional ideas.

11. *Quer durch*, p. 291.

12. A similar point is made in the exchange between Jimmy Cobbett and John Wible in *Die Maschinenstürmer*, Act 3, Scene 3. Significantly Thomas appears to have aligned himself with a version of Wible's point of view.

13. I have had to interpret the play as it stands, but in justice to Toller it should be emphasized that:

(a) The ending which appears in the play is the one that Piscator actually preferred, for to him Thomas's suicide made a clear ideological point.

(b) Toller's original ending involved a far more obvious rejection of Thomas's attitudes and endorsement of the activities of Albert Kroll and Eva Berg. That would have made *Hoppla* a grimly ironical treatment of the transformation theme, with Karl Thomas waking up to the truth at the very time when he is denied any power to act on it.

14. For the response to *Hoppla* by the K.P.D. (German Communist Party), see *Literatur der Arbeiterklasse, Aufsätze über die Herausbildung der deutschen sozialistischen Literatur*, herausgegeben von Der Deutschen Akademie der Künste zu Berlin, Berlin and Weimar, 1971, pp. 469 ff.

Chapter Seven

1. *Der entfesselte Wotan*, Komödie, Berlin, 1924, p. 4.

2. Feb. 23, 1926 at *Die Tribüne* directed by Jürgen Fehling. It was, however, performed in a Russian translation at the Bolshoi Theater, Moscow, on November 16, 1924.

3. In a letter of February 5, 1923 to Kurt Wolff, Toller has this to say: "I would never have believed that I would ever be able to write a comedy. You must be aware of the naive and sophisticated, the foolish and pliant Quixotery of the human heart," Kurt Wolff, *Briefwechsel eines Verlegers*, 1911–1953, Frankfurt am Main, 1960, p. 330.

4. Written in collaboration with Walter Hasenclever and staged in Berlin on February 2, 1929. The play was never printed and the MS is lost. For a summary see Walther Hasenclever, *Gedichte Dramen Prosa, unter Benutzung des Nachlasses*, ed. and introduced by Kurt Pinthus, Reinbek bei Hamburg, 1963, pp. 44–45.

5. For adverse comment see *Die Literatur*, April 1926, p. 417; Felix Hollaender, *Lebendiges Theater*, 96 ff.; Albert Soergel, *Dichtung und Dichter der Zeit*, Leipzig, 1925, p. 772; Herbert Jhering, *Von Reinhardt bis*

Brecht, Vol. 1, pp. 182–184. Jentzsch, *Ernst Toller in seinen Dramen*, pp. 821 ff., even though regarding it as Toller's weakest play, has some good things to say of it.

6. Though the young worker (p. 17) is the only one not to be taken in by Wotan, while the play is dedicated to the Pflüger (to the ploughers).

7. Jentzsch, p. 822.

8. *Briefe aus dem Gefängnis*, p. 206.

9. Ernst Toller, uber sein Stück "Der entfesselte Wotan," *Die Szene*, *Blätter für Bühnenkunst*, xvi, no. 1, Jan. 1926, p. 26–27.

10. Ibid., p. 27.

11. Ibid., p. 27.

12. Ibid., p. 27.

13. On August 31 at the Theater am Schiffbauerdamm by Ernst Josef Aufricht. There were two editions of the play: *Feuer aus den Kesseln mit Anhang: Historische Dokumente*, Berlin, 1930, and *Feuer aus den Kesseln, Bühnenfassung*, Berlin, 1930. The second edition contains many cuts and alterations which may have been the work of the producer rather than of Toller. At any rate, the English translation, *Draw the Fires!* which was supervised by Toller and used as the basis for his production of the play in Manchester in 1935 is clearly from the first edition, though it contains significant departures from it which Edward Crankshaw, the translator, in a private communication to the present writer, is at a loss to explain. In 1938 Toller wrote but did not publish a prologue which warned of Hitler's war-like intentions. All quotations in the text are from the 1st edition as re-printed in *Ausgewählte Schriften*.

14. Toller does, however, allow himself some deliberate liberties, as he says in the note prefacing the play (p. 273).

15. These included Dittman and Louis Zeitz, Independent Socialist Party Deputies in the Reichstag 1917, Beckers and Weber, two of the original mutineers, and Admiral von Scheer. However, Toller changed the name of the Prosecuting Counsel for the Court Martial, who was still alive, from Dobring to Schuler.

16. See *Ausgewählte Schriften*, p. 338.

17. In this connection the following exchange at the beginning of the play may be noted:

President Deputy Moos:	It is not our business to investigate the question as to whether the verdicts were legally justified or not.
Voice from the wings:	But it's ours! (p. 277)

18. See p. 349 for the original letter, p. 325 for Toller's dramatic version. The letter has only been abridged to make it more effective emotionally.

19. The circumstances that lead to the growth of at least a partial revolutionary consciousness among the men are (a) inadequate provision of

soap for the stokers accompanied by punishment if they are not clean (p. 290); (b) Inadequate supplies of poor food while the officers are well fed (pp. 290 ff.); (c) favoritism (pp. 292–293); (d) official inhumanity over compassionate leave (p. 292); (e) constant competition among officers of different ships to see which ship can coal the fastest (p.300). The men are likewise resentful of lying newspaper propaganda about the war (pp. 296–297). The unofficial news that Food Commissions are to be officially established leads the stokers of *Friedrich der Grosse* to forestall their captain by setting up one of their own (p. 298), which becomes a forum for general discontent (p. 300). When deprived of shore leave in order to coal up at the whim of their captain, the men mutiny and go A.W.O.L. (p. 300): and at a meeting at Rüstersiel they express solidarity with the mutineers who have been arbitrarily selected for punishment, and decide to oppose the war and propose action for peace (Scene 5).

20. The further development of this—to define solidarity not in nationalist terms but in terms of identification with the international working class and to come out openly for social revolution—is confined to Köbis. (See pp. 324–325)

21. As Weber says, "What has the food commission to do with coaling?" (p. 300). See also his testimony at the Court Martial, p. 324.

22. In the English translation this is made explicit. See, for example, "The revolution will have to pay for it sooner or later, you'll see" (*Seven Plays*, p. 384). In the German original, in which such passages are absent, Toller is probably relying on his audience's knowledge of history to make the appropriate qualifications.

23. See the activities of Dames who, at the shore meeting at Rüstersiel (p. 301), tries to inflame the sailors to open treason by suggesting that either they fly the white flag and make for England or blow up the ships after hanging the officers (pp. 304 ff.), and who later gives evidence at the trial.

24. It is, however, only Weber who begins to lie and excuse himself under pressure (pp. 323–324).

25. See *Seven Plays*, p. 379.

26. "I don't believe in war any more. I believe in the commandment 'thou shalt not kill' " (p. 323).

27. It must be admitted that in the English version of the play Toller, if, as seems likely, he was responsible for the addition, brings out the gratuitous violence that characterizes revolution by his presentation of the avoidable murder of a naval captain. (See *Seven Plays*, p. 384)

28. First staged at the Mannheim National Theater, Oct. 7, 1931, under the title *Wunder in Amerika*. It was, however, performed on November 6, 1931 at the Kurfürstendammtheater, Berlin, under the title, *Die Heilige aus U.S.A.*

29. *Aufbau* 3–4 (1957), 408–416, esp. p. 416 (Wolf's article was originally published in 1934).

30. See the chapter in *Quer durch* entitled "Aimée oder die mondäne Prophetin" (Aimée or the worldly prophetess).

31. This and subsequent translations are from the mimeographed acting version of the text, Berlin, 1931.

32. First staged at the Raimund Theater, October 31, 1932. The text was published in Berlin, 1933. All quotations are translated from this text.

33. See the exchange on pp. 80–81:

Dr. Färber:	Haven't we bought our freedom dearly enough? Haven't we a right to live without a care in the present? We've suffered enough . . . .
Anna:	We mustn't keep quiet. I know that I no longer have the right to live, as I did earlier, for myself, for you, for what I could save.

34. First produced June 11, 1936 at the Gate Theatre, London, with Christiane Toller in the part of Rachel. The version was by Edward Crankshaw with lyrics adapted by W. H. Auden (London, 1937: New York, Toronto, 1937). The American version is slightly different from the English. Edward Crankshaw states in a private communication "The way Toller produced his manuscript for us to work on was so patchy that I doubt if I ever saw the whole thing in one piece . . . We would all meet at the Gate Theatre, where rehearsals were in progress, and changes would be made by Toller himself in his original German, by me in the translation, by Auden in the verses, while rehearsals were actually in process."

35. First performed at the Deutsches Theater, Berlin, Jan. 24, 1947. It did, however, provide the basis for a British film of the same name released in 1940. The English translation was published after Toller's death (London, 1939: New York, 1939) and this version, for which the original German version is not extant, must be considered the final form of the play since Stephen Spender, the translator, had the assistance of Toller himself. Nonetheless, though naturally taking note of the English version, I have preferred to use what is presumably an earlier German version printed in *Stücke gegen den Faschismus, Deutschsprachige Autoren*, Berlin, 1970, though this version offers many significant discrepancies. All quotations, unless otherwise indicated, are from this text. A still earlier version of the final scene (for its significance see below) was published in *Das Wort*, January, 1939, 42–51.

36. First performed 1928. It is reprinted in Walther Hasenclever, *Gedichte Dramen Prosa*.

37. See *Reichskanzler Hitler. Die Weltbühne*, October, 1932, 537–539.

38. See *Nationalsozialismus: Eine Diskussion über den Kulturbankrott des Bürgertums, zwischen Ernst Toller und Alfred Mühr*, Berlin, 1930, p. 35.

39. There is still a trace of earlier methods, however, in Act II:

Glazed sky. Thin mist. Hot sun. In order to give the realism of this scene the monotony of a beginning with no end, it should be played in a subdued way behind gauze. After the end of the scene the impression must be given that it has lasted months . . . years. (p. 159)

Toller is clearly hoping for too much here. There is no equivalent scene in the Spender translation.

40. See Toller's speech at the meeting of the Internationale Schriftstellervereinigung zur Verteidigung der Kultur, p. 125. Toller paid for this material and was hurt when his informant accused him of plagiarism and threatened him with a law suit. This rather sordid fact is itself a comment on the theme of the play.

41. Kurt Pinthus, "Life and Death of Ernst Toller," *Books Abroad*, vol. 14, 1940, 3–8, esp. p. 6, points out that Toller was under strain and found it difficult to concentrate for longer periods before his suicide. *Pastor Hall* was completed only a few weeks previously. Pinthus also says, p. 8, "he knew that he was no longer able to play the role with which fate had burdened him, and that perhaps he never had been."

42. He often mentioned Mühsam. See for example "Unser Kampf um Deutschland," *Das Wort* Vol. 6, 1937, 46–53, esp. p. 50. He also made an unpublished speech in memory of Mühsam on what would have been his sixtieth birthday, April 6, 1938. He does not appear to have learned about Mühsam's fate until 1936.

43. For details see John M. Spalek, "Ernst Tollers Vortragstätigkeit und seine Hilfsaktionen im Exil," *op. cit.* Chap. 1, fn. 20, p. 86.

44. In *Unser Kampf um Deutschland*, p. 51 he had in contrast said that Hitler only understood the language of "Will und Macht."

45. Kurt Wolff, *Briefwechsel eines Verlegers*, p. 324. That Toller really had a truer sense of the situation than that which he allows himself to reveal in the play is shown in a letter to Nehru dated August 23, 1937 (*A Bunch of Old Letters*, London, 1960, p. 250): "The news which I get from Germany tells me that the anti-Nazi opposition continues its heroic fight but is not strong enough to affect the present regime."

46. See John M. Spalek and Wolfgang Frühwald, "Ernst Tollers Amerikanische Vortragsreise, 1936–37," p. 272.

47. In a newspaper report on February 1, 1937 at a dinner meeting of the Common Sense Club at which Toller spoke.

48. Carl von Stein, *Great Democrats*, ed. A. Barratt Brown, London, 1934, 605–614.

49. It was, in fact, the French branch of the Schutzverband, *Das Wort*, No. 2, Feb. 1939, p. 136.

50. *Pastor Hall*, trans. by Stephen Spender, New York, 1939, p. 56. See "Head of a Leader," *Encounter*, vol. 1, no. 1, 1958, 29–33, esp. p. 31.

51. First published in *Die weissen Blätter*, VII, no. 11, 1920, 489–504.

Published in book form (with revisions of the original text) as *Die Rache des verhöhnten Liebhabers oder Frauenlist und Männerlist . . . ein galantes Puppenspiel in zwei Akten frei nach einer Geschichte des Kardinals Bandello*, Berlin, 1925. There was also a limited luxury edition on linen paper. The premiere was on September 7, 1924, at the Volksbühne am Bülow-Platz.

52. *La Prima Parte*, Novella 3, *Beffa d'una donna ad un gentiluomo ed il cambio che egli le ne rende in doppio*.

53. See Joseph Fishman, *Sex Life in Prison*, with an introductory essay on the Sexual Life of Prisoners by Ernst Toller, London, 1935, VI ff.

54. See "Sachliche Richter," *Die Weltbühne*, August, 1928, 297–298, where, with reference to his own experience, he objects to the practice of probing into a prisoner's sexual life in order to smear him politically.

Chapter Eight

1. Munich, 1921: 2nd ed. Munich, 1923.

2. The original title of the second poem was *Requiem den erschossenen Brüdern*. The text was heavily revised for the third edition, 1925, from which all quotations are cited. *Requiem den gemordeten Brüdern* was also published separately in *Vormorgen*. The premiere of both choral works was at the Proletarische Feierstunde on November 22, 1920.

3. Potsdam, 1924. Second ed. (with epilogue), 1925. Third ed. (revised), 1927. All quotations are from the first edition.

4. Potsdam, 1924.

5. Published in *Die Sammlung*, December 4, 1934, pp. 173–182 and *Internationale Literatur*, vol. 4, No. 4, 1934, 4–8.

6. *Das Wort*, no. 6, 1938, 35–36.

7. There is no evidence that musical accompaniment was intended, though it is difficult to believe it was not.

8. For the elevation of Rosa Luxemburg and Karl Liebknecht into secular saints of the German Communist Party (the K.P.D.), see Pierre Broué, *Révolution en Allemagne, 1917–1923*, Paris, 1971, p. 609. Enormous portraits of them were carried in an annual demonstration where the "Song of the Martyrs" was sung en masse in their honor.

9. See Eugene Lunn, *Prophet of Community, the Romantic Socialism of Gustav Landauer*, Berkeley, Los Angeles, London, 1973, pp. 338–339.

10. All quotations are from the text in *Ausqewählte Schriften*.

11. This is implicit in the title *Gedichte*, later *Lieder*, der Gefangenen: i.e. not *the prisoner's* poems but *the prisoners'*. In the first edition Toller stresses what he feels is his typicality by giving his prison number on the title page: *Ein Sonettenkreis von Ernst Toller*, Nr 44. That Toller was aware of the weaknesses of his prison poems is shown by the heavy revision of *Gedichte der Gefangenen* for inclusion in *Vormorgen*. Toller shortened the

poems and tautened their phraseology and, in doing so, sacrificed their sonnet form.

12. *Das Schwalbenbuch* was the only work of Toller's which the prison authorities would not allow to be published, partly on the grounds that it contained incitement to revolution. Toller, however, managed to smuggle a copy of the text out of prison. For the fullest account of the circumstances see *Justiz, Erlebnisse*, Berlin., 1927, pp. 119 ff.

Chapter Nine

1. Translated, with a new introduction by the author, by Hermon Ould, London, 1931; the *Reden und Aufsätze* section was not translated.

2. *Quer durch*, p. 270.

3. *Pastor Hall* (English version), p. 106.

4. "You know, of course, I prefer meaningful anecdotes to abstract descriptions because they are pregnant" (*Quer durch*, p. 184).

5. *Collected Shorter Poems, 1927–1957*, London, 1966, p. 143.

6. While Toller was in prison his mother had a serious illness which seemed as if it might prove fatal. Toller himself applied to the Bavarian authorities for permission to see her and was prostrated with anxiety while he awaited the outcome of his application. At this time he had a hallucination of someone looking at him while he lay in bed who was both himself and his father. See *Briefe aus dem Gefängnis*, pp. 198 ff.

7. "Exil als Ausbruchsversuch. Ernst Tollers Autobiographie" in *Die deutsche Exilliteratur 1933–1945*, herausgegeben von Manfred Durzak, Stuttgart, 1973, 489–498, esp. p. 492.

8. Tankred Dorst, *Toller*, Frankfurt am Main, 1968, pp. 100 ff.

9. *Revolution und Räterepublik in München 1918/19 in Augenzeugenberichten*, ed. by Gerhard Schmolze mit einem Vorwort von Eberhard Kolb, Düsseldorf, 1969, p. 268.

10. *Toller*, p. 48.

11. *Sex Life in Prison, Introduction*, p. vi.

12. *Exil als Ausbruchversuch*, pp. 491, 493.

13. See, for example, *Briefe aus dem Gefängnis*, p. 25.

Chapter Ten

1. *Ausgewählte Schriften*, p. 356.

2. *Prosa Briefe Dramen Gedichte*, p. 19.

3. Isaac Deutscher, "E. H. Carr as a Historian of the Bolshevik Regime," in *Heretics and Renegades*, London, 1955, p. 98.

4. "Ernst Tollers Vortragstätigkeit und seine Hilfsaktionen im Exil," passim.

5. *Meine Freunde die Poeten*, p. 265.

Selected Bibliography

For a checklist of printed and MS material by or about Toller up to 1968, see John M. Spalek, *Ernst Toller and his Critics*, Charlottesville, 1968.

PRIMARY SOURCES

1. Anthologies

Seven Plays by Ernst Toller, together with *Mary Baker Eddy* by Ernst Toller and Hermann Kesten, with a new introduction by the author. London, 1935.

Ausgewählte Schriften, with commentaries by Bodo Uhse and Bruno Kaiser, ed. by the German Academy of Arts at Berlin. 1st ed., Berlin-Ost, 1959. 2nd ed., 1961.

Prosa Briefe Dramen Gedichte, with a preface by Kurt Hiller, Reinbek bei Hamburg, 1961.

2. Plays

Die Wandlung, Das Ringen eines Menschen. Potsdam, 1919; 2nd ed. revised, Potsdam, 1920. Translated by Edward Crankshaw as *Transfiguration (Seven Plays).*

Masse-Mensch, Ein Stück aus der sozialen Revolution des 20. Jahrhunderts. Potsdam, 1920; 2nd ed., Potsdam, 1922, with a preface by Toller. Translated by Vera Mendel as *Masses and Man.* London, 1923, with "A Note on the Production of Man" by Jürgen Fehling (translation without Fehling's note included in *Seven Plays*).

Die Maschinenstürmer, Ein Drama aus der Zeit der Ludditenbewegung in England. 1st ed., Leipzig-Vienna-Zurich, 1922. 2nd ed., revised, 1922. 2nd ed. translated by Ashley Dukes as *The Machine Wreckers.* London and New York, 1923. This translation included in *Seven Plays.*

Hinkemann, Eine Tragödie in drei Akten, originally published as *Der deutsche Hinkemann.* Potsdam, 1923, but title changed before edition exhausted. 2nd ed., revised, Potsdam, 1924. Translated by Vera Mendel as *Brokenbrow.* London, n.d., with adapted names of dramatis personae. Published in *Seven Plays* with the original names restored.

205

Translated by J. M. Ritchie, in *Vision and Aftermath, Four Expressionist War Plays*. London, 1969.

Der entfesselte Wotan, Komödie. Berlin, 1924. Not translated.

Die Rache des verhöhnten Liebhabers, Galantes Puppenspiel nach einer Geschichte des Kardinals Bandello. Berlin. 1925. Translated by Alexander Henderson as *The Scorned Lover's Revenge*, in *8 New One Act Plays of 1935*, ed. J. Bourne. London, 1936.

Hoppla, wir leben! Ein Vorspiel und fünf Akte. Potsdam, 1927. Translated by Hermon Ould as *Hoppla!* Potsdam, 1927. Later included in *Seven Plays* as *Hoppla! Such is Life!*

Feuer aus den Kesseln! Historisches Schauspiel (mit Anhang; Historische Dokumente). Berlin, 1930. *Bühnenfassung.* Berlin, 1930 (slightly different text). Translated by Edward Crankshaw as *Draw the Fires!* (*Seven Plays*), which, except for the conclusion, follows the original edition.

Wunder in Amerika, Schauspiel, with Hermann Kesten. Berlin, 1931 (mimeographed acting version). Translated by Edward Crankshaw as *Mary Baker Eddy (Seven Plays)*.

Die blinde Göttin, Schauspiel. Berlin, 1931. Translated by Edward Crankshaw as *The Blind Goddess*. London, 1934 (included in *Seven Plays*).

Nie wieder Friede, Komödie. Only Scene 2 (in *Das Wort*, I, No. 2, 2nd Aug., 1936, 32–37) and an early version of Scene 2 (*Das Neue Tagebuch*, II, pt. 2, No. 51, Dec. 22, 1934, 1220–21) published in German in Toller's lifetime. Translated as *No More Peace*, by Edward Crankshaw, with lyrics adapted by W. H. Auden and music by Herbert Murrill. London, 1937; and with slight alterations, New York, Toronto, 1937.

Pastor Hall, Schauspiel. There is no authorized German text of the play. That printed in *Stücke gegen den Faschismus, Deutschsprachige Autoren*, Berlin, 1970, differs considerably from *Pastor Hall*, translated by Stephen Spender with assistance from Hugh Hunt and Ernst Toller. London, 1939; New York, 1939 (the translation of the *Moorsoldatenlied* was by W. H. Auden). An earlier and different version of the final act was published in *Das Wort*, IV, No. 1, 1939, 42–51.

For details of MS versions of *Nie wieder Friede!* and *Pastor Hall* and of an early version of *Die Rache des verhöhnten Liebhabers:* of Toller's unfinished or unpublished plays—*Bourgeois bleibt Bourgeois; Berlin, letzte Ausgabe!; Des Kaisers neuer Rock; Blockade im Scheunenviertel; Bordelle des Krieges;* the outlines of three Massenfestspiele performed in Leipzig, 1922, 1923, 1924 (*Bilder aus der grossen französischen Revolution; Krieg und Frieden; Erwachen!*); and three film scripts (*Der Weg nach Indien; Forget Europe; The Heavenly Sinner*) see *Spalek*, passim.

3. Poetry

Gedichte der Gefangen, eine Sonettenkreis, vom Nr. 44, Munich, 1921, 2nd ed., with additional prefatory poem, *An alle Gefangenen,* Munich, 1923; 3rd ed., completely revised with additional material, *Verse vom Friedhof,* and retitled *Vormorgen,* Potsdam, 1924. English translation of *Vormorgen,* incomplete and with poems rearranged, in *Letters from Prison, including Poems and a new version of the Swallow Book,* translated from the German by R. Ellis Roberts, London, 1936 (American ed. *Look through the Bars,* New York, 1936).

Tag des Proletariats, Requiem den gemordeten Brüdern, 3rd ed., revised, Berlin, 1925 (originally published in earlier form 1920–1921; see *Spalek,* pp. 71–73). Not translated.

Das Schwalbenbuch, 1st ed., Potsdam, 1924; 2nd ed., with epilogue, Potsdam, 1925; 3rd ed., revised, Potsdam, 1927. First ed. translated by Ashley Dukes as *The Swallow Book,* London, 1924; 3rd ed. translated by Ellis Roberts. *Letters from Prison.*

Weltliche Passion. Die Sammlung, 2, No. 4, Dec. 1934, 173–82, and *Internationale Literatur,* 4, No. 4, 1934, 3–8. Not translated.

Die Feuerkantate, Das Wort, III, no. 6, June 1938, 35–36. Not translated.

For uncollected poems, see *Spalek,* pp. 121 ff.

4. Prose

Justiz, Erlebnisse. Berlin, 1927. Not translated.

Quer durch, Reisebilder und Reden. Berlin, 1930. 1st part (Reisebilder) translated by Hermon Ould as *Which World Which Way, Travel Pictures from America and Russia,* with a new introduction by the author. London, 1931.

Nationalsozialismus, Eine Diskussion über den Kulturbankrott des Bürgertums zwischen Ernst Toller und Alfred Mühr, Redakteur der Deutschen Zeitung. Berlin, 1930 (transcript of a broadcast issued as booklet). Not translated.

Eine Jugend in Deutschland. 1st ed., Amsterdam, 1933. 2nd ed., Amsterdam, 1933. Translated by Edward Crankshaw as *I was a German.* London, 1934.

5. Articles, Contributions to Books, Speeches, Etc.

"Bemerkungen zu meinem Drama 'Die Wandlung,' " reprinted in Paul Pörtner, *Literatur-Revolution,* 1910–1925. 2 vols., Mainz, 1960; vol. I, 361–62.

"Arcos Festungshaft," *Die Weltbühne,* xxii, pt. I, No. 3, Jan. 19, 1926, 95.

"Erschiessung auf der Flucht," *Die Weltbühne,* xxii, pt. 2, No. 5, Feb. 2, 1926, 173–75.

"Ernst Toller über sein Stück 'Der entfesselte Wotan,' " *Die Szene, Blätter für Bühnenkunst*, xvi, No. 1, Jan. 1926, 26–27.

"Der Brüsseler Kolonial-Kongress," *Die Weltbühne*, xxiii, pt. 1, No. 9, March 1, 1927, 325–28.

"Imperator Noske," *Die Weltbühne*, xxiii, pt. 1, No. 13, March 29, 1927, 515.

"Die Erschiessung des Gutsbesitzers Hess," *Die Weltbühne*, part 1, No. 18, March 3, 1927, 696–97.

"Gott bei den Beduinen," *Jüdische Rundschau*, Nos. 41–42, May 25, 1927, 297, cols. 1–3.

"Heimarbeit," *Die Weltbühne*, xxiii, pt. 1, No. 26, June 1927, 969–70.

"Sachliche Richter," *Die Weltbühne*, xxiv, pt. 2, No. 34, Aug. 21, 1928, 297–98.

"Der eiserne Gustav," *Die Weltbühne*, xxiv, pt. 2, No. 39, Sept. 25, 1928, 479–82.

"Une Leçon de Littérature sur Moi-même," *Revue d'Allemagne*, III, No. 17, March 1929, 217–22 (in French).

"P.E.N. Kongress in Polen," *Die Weltbühne*, xxvi, pt. 2, No. 28, July 8, 1930, 49–51.

"Reichskanzler Hitler," *Die Weltbühne*, xxvi, pt. 2, No. 41, Oct. 7, 1930, 537–39.

"Menschliche Komödie in Genf," *Die Weltbühne*, xxviii, pt. 1, No. 11, March 15, 1932, 396–99.

"Das neue Spanien," *Die Weltbühne*, xxviii, pt. 1, No. 15, April 12, 1932, 550–54; xxviii, pt. 1, No. 17, April 26, 1932, 622–25; xxviii, pt. 1, No. 18, May 3, 1932, 667–71; xxviii, pt. 1, No. 20, May 17, 1932, 749–51; xxviii, pt. 1, No. 25, June 21, 1932, 929–33.

"Rede in Budapest," *Die Weltbühne*, xxviii, pt. 1, No. 23, June 7, 1932, 853–56.

"Rede auf dem Penklub-Kongress," *Die Weltbühne*, xxix, pt. 2, No. 24, June 15, 1933, 741–44.

"Flamencos," *The Sackbut*, xiv, No. 2, Sept. 1933, 39–40 (in English).

"The Modern Writer and the Future of Europe," *The Bookman*, LXXXV, Jan. 1934, 380–81 (in English).

"The German Theatre Today," report of speech. *Manchester Guardian*, Feb. 17, 1934, 13.

"Promenade in Seville," *New Statesman and Nation*, NS, vii, No. 164, April 14, 1934, 544–45 (in English).

"The Mantilla of Senor Cobos," *Atlantic Monthly*, CLIII, June 1934, 727–29 (in English).

"Carl von Stein" in *Great Democrats*, ed., Alfred Barratt Brown, London, 1934, 605–14 (in English).

"Stalin and Wells: A comment by Ernst Toller," *New Statesman and Nation*, NS, vii, No. 193, No. v3, 1934, 614–15 (in English).

"Vom Werk des Dramatikers," reprinted in *Zur Tradition der sozialistis-chen Literatur in Deutschland, Eine Auswahl von Dokumenten,* ed. by the German Academy of Arts in Berlin, Berlin-Ost & Weimar, 1967, 621–24.

"Art and Life. From my Notebook," *London Mercury,* xxii, No. 191, Sept. 1935, 459–61 (in English).

"Grabbed by the Tail," *New Statesman and Nation,* NS, x, No. 234, Aug. 17, 1935, 220–21 (in English).

Joseph Fishman. *Sex Life in Prison, with an introductory essay on "The Sexual Life of Prisoners" by Ernst Toller.* London, 1935.

"Das Versagen des Pazifismus in Deutschland," first published in John M. Spalek and Wolfgang Frühwald, "Ernst Tollers Amerikanische Vor-tragsreise 1936–1937," *Literaturwissenschaftliches Jahrbuch der Gör-resgesellschaft,* N.F., xi, 1965, 267–311.

"The Refugee Problem," *Political Quarterly,* vi, No. 3, July-Sept. 1935, 386–89 (in English).

"The Word. Opening Speech on the International Writers' Conference, June 19, 1936," *Life and Letters Today,* XV, No. 5, Autumn 1936, 34–36 (in English).

"Sind wir verantwortlich für unsere Zeit?," first published in "Ernst Tollers Amerikanische Vortragsreïse" (see above).

"A British Free People's Theatre," *New Statesman and Nation,* NS, xii, No. 290, Sept. 12, 1936, 350–51.

"A Communication: The Meaning of the André Trial," *New Republic,* Jan. 13, 1937, 331–32.

"The Function of Drama," *New York Times,* Jan. 24, 1937, Sect. 10, 1:5–6 and 3:3–5.

"Abschiedsworte von Ernst Toller an Paul Grätz," *Das Wort,* II, No. 6, June 1937, 101–102.

"Unsere Kampf um Deutschland. Ansprache gehalten auf dem Deutschen Tag in New York," *Das Wort,* II, No. 3, March 1937, 46–53.

"Rede auf dem Pariser Kongress der Schriftsteller am 25. Juli, 1938" *Das Wort,* III, No. 10, Oct. 1938, 122–26.

"Madrid-Washington," *New Statesman and Nation,* NS, xvi, No. 398, Oct. 8, 1938, 521–22.

For Toller's speeches when a member of the provisional National Council in Bavaria, and of the Bavarian Workers, Peasants & Soldiers Soviet, see Spalek, pp. 485 ff.

6. Letters

Briefe aus dem Gefängnis; co-editor, Hermann Kesten. Amsterdam, 1935. For the English translation which does not completely correspond with the German text see *Letters from Prison* above.

The following contain letters not published in *Briefe aus dem Gefängnis:*
Wolff, Kurt. *Briefwechsel eines Verlegers. 1911–1953.* Frankfurt am Main,
   1960, 321–331.
Nehru, Jawaharlal. *A Bunch of Old Letters.* London, 1960, 205–206: 226,
   229–30: 250–51.
Kesten, Hermann, ed. *Deutsche Literatur im Exil, Briefe europäischer Autoren, 1933–1949.* Vienna, Munich, Basel, 1964, 46: 53.

SECONDARY SOURCES
(excluding biographical material mentioned by Spalek)

ARNOLD, R. F. "Die blinde Göttin," *Die Literatur,* xxxv, No. 4, Jan. 1933,
   220.
BAB, JULIUS. *Das Theater der Gegenwart.* Leipzig, 1928, passim.
–––––––. *Die Chronik des deutschen Dramas,* Vol. 5: *Deutschlands
dramatische Produktion,* 1919–1926. Berlin, 1929, 39–50.
BAULAND, PETER. *The Hooded Eagle. Modern German Drama on the New
York Stage.* Syracuse, 1968, 78–82: 111–15.
BECKLEY, RICHARD. "Ernst Toller" in *German Men of Letters,* Vol. 3, ed.
   A. Nathan, London, 1968; 85–104.
BELL, C. H. "Tollers 'Die Maschinenstürmer,' " *Monatshefte,* xxx, No. 2,
   Feb. 1938, 59–70.
DROOP, FRITZ. *Ernst Toller und seine Bühnenwerke.* Berlin, 1922.
EMMEL, FELIX. *Das ekstatische Theater.* Prien, 1924, 290–95.
F., W. "Kritik über die Aufführung vom 'Hoppla wir leben!' " *Die deutsche
Rundschau,* ccxiii, Oct. 1927, 83–84.
FRÜHWALD, WOLFGANG. "Exil als Ausbruchsversuch. Ernst Tollers Au-
tobiographie" in *Die deutsche Exilliteratur, 1933–1945,* ed. Manfred
   Durzak. Stuttgart, 1973.
–––––––. "Kunst als Tat und Leben. Sprache und Bekenntnis," *Sonderband
des Literaturwissenschaftlichen Jahrbuchs,* 1971, 363–89.
GARTEN, H. F. *Modern German Drama* 2nd ed., London, 1964, 138–47.
GRUNBERGER, RICHARD. *Red Rising in Bavaria.* London, 1973, passim.
HEILBORN, ERNST. "Echo der Bühnen, Berlin, 'Der entfesselte Wotan,'
   Eine Komödie von Ernst Toller," *Die Literatur,* xxviii, No. 7, April
   1926, 417–18.
–––––––. "Echo der Bühnen, Berlin, 'Hoppla wir leben!' Ein Stück von
Ernst Toller," *Die Literatur,* xxx, No. 1, Oct. 1927, 39–40.
–––––––. " 'Des Kaisers Kulis.' Schauspiel von Theodor Plivier, 'Feuer aus
den Kesseln!' Historisches Schauspiel von Ernst Toller," *Die
Literatur,* xxxiii, No. 1, Oct. 1930, 38.
HERMAND, JOST. " 'Hoppla, wir leben!' " in *Unbequeme Literatur, eine
Beispielreihe.* Heidelberg, 1971, 128–49.
HERN, NICHOLAS. "The Theatre of Ernst Toller," *Theatre Quarterly,* Vol.
   2, No. 3, Jan.-March 1972, 72–92.

HOLLAENDER, FELIX. *Lebendiges Theater*. Berlin, 1932, passim.

JACOBSOHN, SIEGFRIED. "Kaiser und Toller: über Kaiser, 'Die Bürger von Calais' und Toller 'Die Wandlung' " *Die Weltbühne*, xv, pt. 2, No. 42, Oct. 9, 1919, 450–54.

JENTZSCH, RUDOLF. "Ernst Toller in seinen Dramen," *Zeitschrift für Deutschkunde*, XL, No. 12, 1926, 813–22.

JHERING, HERBERT. *Von Reinhardt bis Brecht*, 3 vols. Berlin, 1961. Vols. 1 & 2, passim.

KERR, ALFRED. *Die Welt im Drama*, ed. G. F. Hering. 2nd ed., Cologne and Berlin, 1964, 155–63.

————. *Literatur der Arbeiterklasse. Aufsätze über die Herausbildung der deutschen Sozialistischen Literatur, 1918–1922*, ed. by the German Academy of Arts at Berlin. Berlin-Ost and Weimar, 1971, 469 ff.

McGOWAN, KENNETH, and JONES, ROBERT EDMOND. *Continental Stagecraft*. New York, 1922; London, 1923, 144–55.

MENNEMEIER, K. N. "Das idealistische Proletarierdrama, Ernst Tollers Weg vom Aktionsstück zur Tragödie," *Der Deutschunterricht*, vol. 24, No. 2, 1972, 100–16.

MURET, MAURICE. "M. Ernst Toller et la Révolution Allemande," *Mercure de France*, CCLII, June 15, 1934, 526–41.

PETERSEN, CAROL. "Ernst Toller" in *Expressionismus als Literatur, Gesammelte Studien*, ed. Wolfgang Rothe. Munich, 1969, 572–84.

PINNER, ERNST. "Der Dichter Ernst Toller," *Der Jude*, xiii, 1924, 483–87.

PISCATOR, ERWIN. *Das politische Theater*, revised by Felix Gasbarra. Hamburg, 1963, passim.

RESO, MARTIN. "Die Novemberrevolution und Ernst Toller," *Weimarer Beiträge*, V, No. 3, 1959, 387–409.

————. "Gefängniserlebnis und dichterische Wiederspielgelung in der Lyrik Ernst Tollers," *Weimarer Beiträge*, VII, No. 3, 1961, 520–56.

Revolution und Räterepublik in München, 1918–1919 in Augenzeugenberichten, ed. by Gerhard Schmolze with a preface by Eberhard Kolb. Düsseldorf, 1969, passim.

SCHEIDWEILER, PAULA. "Wunder in Amerika. Schauspiel in fünf Akten," *Die Literatur*, xxxiv, No. 3, Dec. 1931, 161.

SCHUMACHER, ERNST. *Die dramatischen Versuche Bertolt Brechts, 1918–1933*. Berlin, 1955, 22 ff. and passim.

SPALEK, JOHN M., and FRÜHWALD, WOLFGANG. "Ernst Tollers Amerikanische Vortragsreise 1936–37" (already cited).

SPALEK, JOHN M. "Ernst Tollers Vortragstätigkeit und seine Hilfsaktionen im Exil" in *Exil und innere Emigration*, II, ed. by Peter Uwe Hohendahl and Egon Schwarz. Frankfurt am Main, 1973, 85–100.

SIGNER, PAUL. *Ernst Toller*. Berlin, 1924.

SOERGEL, ALBERT. *Dichtung und Dichter der Zeit*. Leipzig, 1926, 762–65.

SOKEL, WALTER. "Ernst Toller" in *Deutsche Literatur im 20. Jahrhundert*,

Strukturen und Gestalten, ed. by Hermann Friedmann and Otto Mann; 5th ed., Munich, 1967, Vol II, 284–301.

————. *The Writer in Extremis.* Stanford, 1959, passim.

————. *Le Théâtre Moderne, Hommes et tendences,* Études réunies et présentées par Jean Jacquet. Paris, 1958, 117–30, 166–74.

TUCHOLSKY, KURT. *Gesammelte Werke,* ed. by Mary Gerald-Tucholsky and Fritz S. Raddatz, 3 vols. Reinbek bei Hamburg, 1960, passim.

VIVIANI, ANNALISA. *Dramaturgische Elemente im expressionistischen Drama.* Bonn, 1970, passim.

————. *Das Drama des Expressionismus.* Munich, 1970, 139–45.

WILLIAMS, RAYMOND. *Drama from Ibsen to Brecht.* London, 1968, 261–66.

WILLIBRAND, W. A. *Ernst Toller and his Ideology.* Iowa City, 1945.

WOLF, FRIEDRICH. "Zehn Jahre, Zehn Dramatiker," *Aufbau,* 3–4, 1957, 408–16 (originally published 1934).

Index